Capitol Investments

ECONOMICS COGNITION AND SOCIETY

This series provides a forum for theoretical and empirical investigations of social phenomena. It promotes works that focus on the interactions among cognitive processes, individual behavior, and social outcomes. It is especially open to interdisciplinary books that are genuinely integrative.

Founding Editor: Timur Kuran
Series Editor: Peter J. Boettke
Editorial Board: Tyler Cowen   Richard Swedberg
Diego Gambetta   Viktor Vanberg
Avner Greif   Paul Zak
Daniel Klerman

Titles in the Series

(continues on last page)

Capitol Investments

The Marketability of Political Skills

Glenn R. Parker

THE UNIVERSITY OF MICHIGAN PRESS • Ann Arbor

2011   2010   2009   2008   4   3   2   1

A CIP catalog record for this book is available from the British Library.

Library of Congress Cataloging-in-Publication Data

Parker, Glenn R., 1946–
    Capitol investments : the marketability of political skills / Glenn
R. Parker.
        p.   cm. — (Economics, cognition, and society)
    Includes bibliographical references and index.
    ISBN-13: 978-0-472-07037-4 (cloth : alk. paper)
    ISBN-10: 0-472-07037-1 (cloth : alk. paper)
    1. Legislators—United States.   2. Politicians—United States.
3. Lobbyists—United States.   4. Occupational training—United States.
5. Career development—United States.   6. Human capital—Political
aspects—United States.   I. Title.
JK1021.P364   2008
650.14024'32873—dc22   2008002886

To Suzie, the best . . . , well, just the *best*.

Contents

Figures

Tables

Acknowledgments

Readers will quickly notice that references to the author throughout the book are written in the plural, although but a single name appears on the title page. My wife, Professor Suzanne L. Parker, played an instrumental role in this inquiry but refused to take any credit whatsoever. Not only did she formulate, administer, and conduct the entire survey on which subsequent analyses are based, but she was a willing listener (sometimes more willing than others) as I rattled on about human capital, Congress, and postelective officeholding; she also advised me about statistical procedures, properties, and potential pitfalls and rendered invaluable assistance when it seemed that statistical packages and I were on different pages. I clearly could not have even started this project, let alone completed it, without her assistance.

I have always felt that such dedicated effort warranted at least half a piece of the prize, so to speak—that is, coauthorship—but Suzie insisted otherwise. To my relief, she assured me that her position had nothing to do with the quality of the work; still, this is slight consolation. No matter how much I tried to convince her of the irrationality of her preferences, she stood steadfast in her position. So, I am left with no other option but to recognize her assistance—but refusal to take any credit for it—by treating her as an unnamed co-conspirator, silent partner, or shadow author through the use of plural personal pronouns throughout the study. This, I believe, is but a small way of acknowledging her pivotal and selfless contribution to this endeavor.

Other people also have helped bring this study to fruition. Ranking at the top of this list are the initial readers of this book, Bert Rockman and Charles Shipan. I have listened carefully to what they have said and have followed their guidance as best I could; I would have been a fool to do otherwise, considering the thoughtfulness of their suggestions. The manuscript has also benefited from the sage advice of David Brady and Michael Munger, who reviewed the entire manuscript. Their suggestions did more than simply lead me to shore up my arguments and fix loose ends; they caused me to revisit central ideas, with profitable results. In total, I cannot envision a better set of scholars to peruse any manuscript; collectively and individually, their intellectual breadth is stunning. I consider myself unusually and extremely fortunate in this regard.

David Mayhew commented on important elements of my argument. His thoughtful remarks and keen insights led me to address holes—possibly sinkholes—in my arguments that heretofore had escaped my notice. He has come to my rescue in this fashion more than once in the past; hence, my thanks to Dave come supersized.

Like most scholars, I am indebted to my diligent research assistants, Terri Towner and Abigaile Van Horn, for their extraordinary efforts in responding to my requests for instant data and analyses; in the process, they too have been transformed into devoted human capitalists. I owe Purdue University special acknowledgment and thanks for assistance to this project in the form of a generous stipend attached to my distinguished professorship; without such support, I doubt that I could have completed this book in a timely fashion, if at all.

Other friends and scholars have made the writing of this book far more enjoyable than I ever would have imagined: William McLauchlan, who refused to let a day pass without cornering me into a discussion of human capital and its implications for his research; graduate students in my course on the economics of political institutions, who served as a polite—though certainly not docile—audience for many of these ideas; and Robert Tollison, who has taught me by example to never sidestep controversy. He no doubt would be proud of this effort, even though our intellectual perspectives seemingly part ways at junctures in this inquiry.

And of course I am indebted to Jim Reische, former editor at the University of Michigan Press, who conjured up images of the book's scholarly reach that greatly expanded my sense of its potential scope. His visions have fueled my own. My debt to all of these individuals should be evident throughout this book; none of them, as one would expect, bears any responsibility for what is contained within the pages of this manuscript—that is my doing alone, for better or for worse. With a bit of luck, *only* the former.

Chapter 1

Introduction

Although important studies of the effects of human capital in the market
sector can be expected, I anticipate that the excitement will be generated by
studies of its effects in the nonmarket sector.
                                            —Gary S. Becker, *Human Capital*

As the subtitle suggests, this book concerns the marketability of political
skills, where *marketability* refers to the speed and ease with which securities
can be sold and *securities* represent instruments indicative of ownership or
rights to ownership. Applied to politics, then, our inquiry deals with how political skills (or securities) acquired through elected office translate into sal-
able commodities after politicians leave office—or, put more simply, the economic value political skill sets (politicians' "human capital") command in the
marketplace. These types of questions do not normally preoccupy political
scientists, although economists, particularly labor economists, are no doubt
quite familiar with such topics. Yet we have fashioned this inquiry to be more
than a first shot at an economic analysis of the labor market for politicians. It
would be more accurate to say that this book concerns the connection of what
politicians do in office to what they do after they leave office and how political institutions operate in this regard. We demonstrate that the acquisition of
marketable human capital through institutional service is relevant if not essential for a broader understanding of politics.

The acquisition of human capital within political institutions provides
more than just another useful perspective from which to view the actions of
politicians while on the job. Of greater significance is the extent to which this
approach yields fresh insights into the operations of institutions and the motivations and behavior of politicians, raising imaginative questions about how
and why elected officeholders acquire political skills, the economic effects of
doing so, and political institutions' role in that endeavor. In the process, we
touch on important issues about Congress and the legislative process, such as
the economic imprint of specialized and general training in congressional
politics, the allure of lobbying, the effects of special interest money in legislatures, and the impact of generational changes in congressional membership.
We hope that readers expecting a simple account of what happens to legislators after they leave Congress will be pleasantly surprised.

Understandably, our analysis supplies different versions of conventional conclusions about politicians, especially legislators; we think of it as only "picking up the other end of the stick" (Kuhn 1996, 85)—that is, expanding the purview of normal or routine inquiry beyond the here and now of politics (for example, elections) to include the postelective careers of officeholders as well. We recognize that theories are merely instruments of inquiry, and other theories may also explain the same set of facts about the postelective employment of legislators. Nonetheless, we are confident that none of these theories can account for the range and diversity of facts, or their interconnectedness, with the degree of simplicity found in applying our set of human capital propositions.

One final point, lest our intentions be misconstrued: we are not attempting to undermine the reelection assumption or any other motivation, for that matter. Nor are we, in the end, hoping to justify the grooming of legislators for lobbying. Ours is merely an earnest desire to better understand why politicians behave in the manner they do and how political institutions shape their actions. We recognize that these are timeless issues in political analysis, but we do not offer our human capital interpretation as the final word on these matters; we expect, however, deservedly or not, that our approach will stir substantial controversy, leading to new questions to explore and revisiting old answers, which is always healthy for inquiry.

Human Capital in Politics

One of the dilemmas tormenting political scientists and economists is trying to explain why candidates literally spend millions of dollars to obtain public offices that provide compensation that amounts to only a fraction of these costs. This paradox has provided fodder for attacks on the blatant corruption of political officials and likewise for assaults on politicians' rationality. The arguments are straightforward: the only reason rational politicians would spend more to obtain public office than they receive in remuneration is either because they collect quasi-legal pay under the table in addition to their salaries, or because they behave less strategically than rationality would dictate. We believe another explanation exists: political office represents investments that are expected to accrue value, like any other security. Whereas doctors and lawyers spend tens of thousands of dollars acquiring postdoctorate degrees and certifications that will more than offset these exorbitant educational expenses, holding office also represents an investment of a sort—specifically, an investment in on-the-job training—that similarly pays off for politicians when they leave office. The postelective employment of former fourteen-term Representative Richard Gephardt, for instance, exemplifies some of the ways in which congressional training can payoff.

> Most people know that life after Congress can be very lucrative. . . . But few people know what that work entails. In Gephardt's case, it involves an astonishing array of projects. He has brokered labor settlements, cleared the way for corporate acquisitions, represented a foreign country and pushed for cutting-edge health programs—only some of which fit the stereotype of lobbying. . . . *Indeed, a lot of what Gephardt does is an extension of what he used to do, especially in Congress.* Only now he has paying clients from the private sector. (Birnbaum 2007, 1)

In short, politicians spend hefty amounts of money to obtain and stay in public office because they expect a good return on their investments.

The Human Capital Premise

The basic premise underlying our study is that politicians invest their time and themselves in acquiring human capital—that is, skills, knowledge, information, expertise, reputation, and the like—that become embedded or embodied within them. They do so in large part to improve their lot in the future; rational politicians think and plan prospectively, not merely for the next campaign but beyond that, too. "The concept of human capital, or 'hard core' of the human-capital research program, is the idea that people spend on themselves in diverse ways, not for the sake of present enjoyments, but for the sake of future pecuniary and non-pecuniary returns" (Blaug 1976, 829). Given this definition, it is easy to see why a leader in human capital research, Ben-Porath (1967, 353), has characterized human capital "as a concept analogous to 'machines' in the case of tangible capital."

We should, however, quickly distinguish human capital from other forms of capital. Human capital is rooted in the investing individual, while nonhuman capital is property income; labor compensation, for example, constitutes the return on investment in human capital, while the return on nonhuman investments, such as research and development, typically occurs in terms of royalties. Nonhuman factors of production include plants and equipment, advanced technological tools, rental space, physical infrastructure, and intangibles such as patents, copyrights, and so forth.

Despite the centrality we attribute to human capital production in politics, we do not feel that this is an all-consuming motivation of politicians, like perhaps reelection (Mayhew 1974); nonetheless, investments in human capital need not directly enter politicians' utility functions to significantly affect their behavior. Skill accumulation only has to profitably increase the marginal productivity of future employee-politicians, and therefore their potential marketability, to shape politicians' behavior in the present. This is not to deny that politicians' behavior reflects manifold considerations, such as electoral contingencies, constituency preferences, and party. We are merely stating the obvious: if politicians act rationally, we can expect their behavior to be geared toward self-interested ends. Consideration of postelective employment obviously is one such end.

Careers in political office are of course not necessarily short-lived, and particularly not with regard to the subset of politicians studied here—specifically, members of Congress. Therefore, a good case could be made that electorally safe politicians, like Becker's (1968) characterization of criminals, do not fear the occupational risks associated with their jobs. Yet even safe politicians realize that the unexpected may occur (for example, adverse national forces), resulting in the loss of office (Mann 1978). Politicians consequently must plan for the future, which often means anticipating their marketability. Thus, the specter of losing office leads rational, risk-averse politicians to plan for the perils and uncertainties of unemployment.

Human Capital and Politicians' Wealth Gains

Characterizing the behavior of politicians in terms of investments in human capital offers an alternative to the rather pervasive "dark" economic treatments of politicians as wealth maximizers—that is, manipulating their offices for economic gain (see, for example, McCormick and Tollison 1981; McChesney 1987; Rose-Ackerman 1999). It is of course hard to ignore the role of politicians and institutions in engineering wealth transfers and the desire of groups and individuals, including politicians, to obtain such transfers. Wealth gains also enter our model, but in a more subtle and less direct way. Simply put, politicians profit as a consequence of accumulating marketable political skills.

In our model, rational politicians obtain material benefits but do not do so through any devious manipulation of policies or office prerogatives, as in private-gain interpretations. Rather, in our thinking, politicians anticipate the returns that can be obtained through on-the-job investments in human capital and accordingly adjust their activities in office. Legislators then seek out experiences, information, and skills in Congress that enhance their attractiveness to future employers. While unmistakably continuing to reap measurable economic benefit from service in Congress, legislators profit from the skills they have acquired, the contacts they have made, and more generally the human capital they have accumulated.

We recognize that ours may be a relatively docile treatment of the wealth gains obtained vis-à-vis public service employment. For instance, we skirt the issue of the value of the economic returns gained through bribery (see, for example, Rose-Ackerman 1999) or the extortion of rents by avaricious officeholders (McChesney 1987; Parker 1996), but we do not do so out of ignorance of these returns; we recognize that these phenomena, too, constitute economic earnings from officeholding. However, it is virtually impossible to collect reliable and systematic information on these sources of monetary benefit aside from the occasional exposé of bribery in office. Therefore, our treatment of the economic boon derived from public office, like most empirical studies of this phenomenon, will necessarily be incomplete to the extent that bribes and rents constitute a normal return of public office, an empirical question not only beyond the confines of the present analysis but also steeped in considerable controversy. As novel as the study of human capital in politics might be in terms of shifting attention to new questions, what riches might it hold for the study of Congress?

Why Study Human Capital and Congressional Behavior?

Rational-behavior models of legislatures frequently focus on the electoral benefits derived from congressional activities (Mayhew 1974; Fiorina 1989), principal-agent issues (Kalt and Zupan 1984; Peltzman 1984; Denzau and Munger 1986; Lott 1987), or the rents obtained through officeholding (Rose-Ackerman 1978; McChesney 1987; Parker 1996). We add to this repertoire by offering the view that legislatures provide opportunities for members to acquire unique political skills, including knowledge of the intricacies of the federal bureaucracy and the lawmaking process, experience in making public policy, and contacts in government. All of these skills are economically valuable to groups doing business with government, a category that includes most groups in society, from universities to large industries.

Economic Effects of Congressional Experiences

Legislators acquire political skills with the expectation that this human capital can subsequently be rented in the labor market after leaving Congress. Rationality leads legislators to consider their lives (and livelihoods) beyond Congress and the attendant prospects of reentering the labor force; accordingly, legislators prepare for this eventuality during their terms in office by acquiring suitable human capital. Legislative activities provide opportunities for members to acquire valuable political skills with potential economic pay-offs. Not surprisingly, most legislators avail themselves of these opportunities. These economic returns, realized after leaving Congress, provide an underappreciated rationale for legislators' activities.

Those possessing these political skills have the wherewithal to manipulate governmental policies to promote group goals, which makes them economically valuable to most societal interests. This statement probably is not much of a revelation to members of Congress, if we are to judge by the length of time legislators spend acquiring human capital and the wages left behind when entering office (table 1.1).[1] Indeed, the effects of training on postelective salaries rival those associated with precongressional salaries (chapter 6)[2]

TABLE 1.1.   Mean Salaries for Former Legislators' Precongressional Vocations

Vocation	Mean Salary ($)	S.D. ($)	Number of Cases
Lobbyist	268,215		1
Nonprofit/Education	159,903	68,499	16
Private sector and financial	307,480	323,247	76
Lawyer	330,420	251,917	73
Public service (government)	168,909	147,324	48

Source: Authors' survey of former members of Congress, 2004.

Note: Salaries have been converted to 2004 dollars. These salary differences are statistically significant in an analysis of variance (ANOVA) test (alpha < .003). See note 1 to this chapter. S.D. = standard deviation.

---

1. The salaries reported in table 1.1 are statistically different as determined through a one-way ANOVA (alpha < .003). Unfortunately, however, the Levene statistic is highly significant, indicating that the variances are not homogeneous, thereby complicating the conclusions drawn from the analysis. Consequently, we applied a conservative one-way ANOVA post-hoc test that uses multiple pairwise comparisons—specifically, Tamhane's T2, which is based on the *t*-test and does not rely on equality of variances as one of its assumptions—to test for occupational differences in the salaries of entering legislators. Pairwise multiple comparisons test the differences between each pair of means in terms of their statistical significance. The patterns embedded in the resulting matrix of salary comparisons indicated significant differences among occupations.

    Regardless of the test (for example, Tamhane's T2, Dunnett's T3 or C, or Games-Howell) every occupational comparison test reveals significant differences (alpha < .05) with two (of the three) other occupational groupings; the smallest and least significant differences occur between those reporting the lowest precongressional salaries—that is, those entering Congress from educational and philanthropic institutions and public or governmental service. With respect to these post-hoc tests, we have removed the single legislator who was a lobbyist before entering Congress from the analysis, since such tests cannot be conducted when (occupational) categories have fewer than two observations.

2. The salaries of former legislators have been converted in all instances to 2004 dollars. The general formula is:

    Real Salary (2004 dollars) = Nominal Salary (year) / [CPI (year) / CPI (2004)].

The consumer price index (CPI) is based on statistics calculated by the U.S. Department of Labor, Bureau of Labor Statistics.

despite the latter's incorporation of economically valuable talents and endowments. Individuals may have a knack for politics, but job training in Congress is a first-rate substitute, especially when looking for a job.

Uniqueness of Work Environment

We believe our findings and conclusions are applicable to politicians by and large, although our empirical analysis is based on the career patterns of a particular group of politicians—former members of the U.S. House of Representatives and Senate. We focus on the behavior of ex-legislators both during and after exiting Congress because our theory emphasizes the effects of job training in political institutions in creating marketable political skills. We feel that among all political structures, Congress provides both unique on-the-job learning experiences and the acquisition of novel political skills.

There are of course plenty of examples of members of the Federal Reserve going to work for investment houses, accounting firms hiring former internal revenue administrators, and Justice Department attorneys joining private law firms, and all no doubt merit human capital analysis. But what makes members of Congress unique is the fact that their training experiences are unrivaled. For example, the legislative know-how derived from trading votes, developing expertise about legislative practices and procedures, and drafting legislation represents a rather arresting array of skills that can be obtained through years of congressional service. Thus, legislatures provide settings whereby politicians acquire untold information, skills, and experiences as by-products of their involvement in lawmaking.

Perhaps what is most intriguing about on-the-job training experiences in Congress is that they are applied to important, real-life problems—that is, significant questions and controversies relating to society and everyday life. Such experiences augment members of Congress's attractiveness to potential employers—whether they are philanthropic foundations, educational institutions, municipalities, or trade organizations—because groups willingly lay these problems at the doorstep of government. Despite—or perhaps because of—the uniqueness of their political skills, legislators face a narrow (that is, specialized) market for their services, primarily lobbying.

Why Study the Postelective Employment of Former Legislators?

Even if we admit that analyses of the accumulation of human capital are worthy of inquiry, the question could still be asked: Why study the postelective careers of legislators in particular? The lack of attention this topic has received might lead to the question of whether it really warrants any study whatsoever. After all, a great deal of scholarly research examines why legislators or politicians retire (see, for example, Hibbing 1982a, 1982b; Hall and Van Houweling 1995; Groseclose and Krehbiel 1994; Coates and Munger 1995; Moore and Hibbing 1998; Theriault 1998; Bernstein and Wolak 2002) or seek higher office (for two early classics on this topic, see Schlesinger 1966; Prewitt 1970). Yet little attention has been dedicated to the postelective careers of politicians as they reenter the workforce (for notable exceptions, see Lott 1990; Parker 1996, 2004; Diermeier, Keane, and Merlo 2005).

Relevance of Information

If, like most employees, rational legislators plan for the future during the present, neglect of postelective concerns seems certain to impoverish our understanding of Congress as well as shortchange our explanations of congressional behavior. We might seek comfort by rationalizing that only a few legislators harbor such postelective designs, but we would be deluding ourselves, since the vast majority of members of Congress do not turn to a life of leisure and relaxation after leaving the institution. Most find other jobs, frequently abandoning their precongressional occupations in the process; as we demonstrate in chapter 5, they can do so because they have accumulated human capital through on-the-job training in congressional politics.

Because many legislators leave Congress to assume income-earning jobs, it stands to reason that they engage in activities to obtain skills increasing the market value of their human capital. As a result, questions naturally emerge about the processes of skill acquisition and the economic value attached to these skills in the marketplace. To address these issues, we are drawn to an examination of the careers of politicians both while in office and after leaving office. Doing so enables us to estimate the effects of different investment strategies on subsequent returns from officeholding, in particular, job mobility and postelective employment earnings. For example, we can link the returns from officeholding to service and experiences in party or committee leadership posts or membership on certain types of committees. Knowledge of the payoffs of various congressional activities helps us better understand the rationale underlying legislators' career choices.

Postelective career considerations may be important for another reason: legislators may currently prepare for their postelective careers not merely by acquiring skills but also by some form of job signaling. Because economic and political employment loom large in postelective planning, accounting for about 20 percent of the reasons offered by those who acknowledged thinking about what they would do after leaving Congress (table 1.2),[3] we might imagine legislators as emitting job signals—for example, by casting votes or transferring to clientele-servicing committees. Such information would be invaluable to potential employers, who, wary of the asymmetries in information and moral hazards that inevitably plague politics (see, for example, Crain, Leavens, and Tollison 1986; Weingast and Marshall 1988), are desperate for reliable evidence of future behavior before making hiring decisions. Legislators' postelective employment choices could provide an opportunity to intercept, isolate, and trace these signals back to in-office actions.

Finally, analyses of the postelective careers of legislators can best address the question of why the latter so readily become lobbyists, as the literature suggests, after leaving office. That is, what types of congressional investments and experiences lead to postelective employment as lobbyists? We might say,

TABLE 1.2. "Was There Anything in Particular That Made You Think about What You Would Do when You Left Congress?"

Reason	Frequency	%
Electoral threat hastened planning	9	3.9
Economic opportunities	16	7.0
Political opportunities	9	3.9
Noneconomic interests	21	9.2
Prior experience and background	24	10.5
Nothing (stated as such)	7	3.1
Blank (no reason given)	20	8.7
Always planned on leaving Congress	3	1.3
Wanted to retire	10	4.4
Other	6	2.6
Never thought about it	97	42.4
Refuse to answer (specified)	7	3.1
Total	229	100.0

Source: Authors' survey of former members of Congress, 2004.
Note: Table title is actual wording of survey question.

3. The exact wording of the question was as follows: "Was there ever a time during your congressional career that you anticipated working at the job you held immediately after leaving Congress?" Those who responded "yes" to this query—that they had given thought to what they might do after leaving Congress—were then asked, "Was there anything in particular that made you think about what you would do when you left Congress?" The figures cited in the text exclude refusals and those who never thought about what they would do after leaving Congress. A total of 104 respondents are therefore excluded from the calculation. The large percentage of former legislators who never thought about what they would do after leaving Congress (42.4 percent, table 1.2) is not unexpected, because service in Congress is a career in most respects and because the electoral advantages of incumbency ensure longevity in office.

to paraphrase Becker's (1968) wry description of criminals, politicians are not born to eventually become lobbyists, as seems so common in today's Congress; rather, they just face different costs and returns and invest accordingly by pursuing on-the-job experiences that are pertinent only to a narrow range of occupations—primarily lobbying.

Legislators as Lobbyists

Some scholars might quibble with our perspective on politics by contending that only during the course of officeholding do politicians really influence policy outcomes. Thus, it is rather irrelevant, or perhaps even foolish, to study politicians' postelective careers, since their out-of-government employment pushes their behavior beyond the threshold of interest for students of politics. We feel that such arguments severely limit our understanding of political decision making by diverting attention away from ways in which politicians influence policy-making after they leave office—for example, through the skillful use of their knowledge and contacts to lobby former colleagues. By characterizing politicians as merely executing the responsibilities of their office (such as casting votes and formulating legislation) or even using their positions for expressing their own opinions (that is, shirking), we give short shrift to another important asset at their disposal in shaping policy—namely, their hands-on experience in government—that makes them effective lobbyists.

Lobbyists are frequently characterized as the handmaidens of special interests. Indeed, if one resilient black mark has stained American democracy, it is the perceived diabolical influence of special interests in politics. They are ubiquitous, frequently lampooned in cartoons, and, with rare exception, vilified in journalistic treatments, but only a fool would doubt lobbyists' effectiveness. We have long recognized that their reach goes well beyond working their will at election time and supplying campaign monies (see, for example, Dahl 1956, 130–33). We now suspect that lobbyists are not above enticing politicians with the prospects of future employment as a means of obtaining benefits in the present (see, for example, Eckert 1981). The rather sordid implication is that politicians who do favors for special interests are rewarded with postelective employment.

Reformers and media investigators have been among the first and loudest to bemoan politicians' willingness to accept postelective employment with the same interests they were responsible for overseeing or regulating while in office. And this argument is echoed throughout the rent-seeking literature. Still, the evidence supporting a postelective employment "bonus" for loyal in-office service to special interests is mostly anecdotal. Without explicit knowledge of how the postelective careers of ex-legislators unfold, it is difficult to assess the validity of this claim or even to challenge it.

Here we offer a contrasting perspective: politicians receive postelective employment through the auspices of special interests, at least partially as a result of the skills they have acquired in politics, which makes them valuable employees. In short, postelective jobs, even as lobbyists, go to the well-trained and not to the useless or the incompetent, no matter the legislative favors supplied to special interests while in office. As we explore the postelective careers of former legislators, we weigh the evidence surrounding two contrasting interpretations of postelective employment: Does postelective employment represent an ex post facto payoff for services rendered to special interests while in office, or does it reflect demand for the skills and knowledge accumulated through training in congressional politics? The study of the postelective employment of legislators deals with another equally important issue: the relative economic value of the acquisition of general or specialized political skills.

Specialized and General Training

Scholars long seem to have ignored the obvious fact that Congress couples training in legislative politics with the making of laws; in so doing, we have overlooked the role of political institutions in the production of human capital. Consequently, we have minimized the importance of these structures for enhancing skills relevant to postelective vocations. The significance of congressional structures such as committees and processes such as logrolling is not merely that they determine how policies are enacted; they also equip legislators with the necessary human capital to make something of themselves after leaving Congress.

We are not the least bit surprised by Frisch and Kelly's (2006, 94) well-documented conclusions about congressional committee assignments: "Members are motivated by policy concerns and the desire to accrue political power as much or more than they are concerned about reelection or the need for their committee assignment to reflect some major interest in their district." Frisch and Kelly demonstrate that politicians harbor motivations that stretch beyond those commonly associated with constituency interests and elections; however, the authors failed to notice that such motivations (that is, policy and power) may represent more than just another set of Fenno-like member goals (Fenno 1973). These motivations also underlie the acquisition of specific and general human capital in congressional politics.

Just as the general practitioner still has a role to play in medicine and the treatment of patients despite vast specialization in medical careers, so, too, the generalist has a role to play in politics, especially congressional politics. Both specialized and general training in congressional politics are important, and both are prized inside and outside of Congress. The arguments about training's effects on the internal workings of Congress are quite familiar: specialists help Congress counter the expertise of the executive branch, while generalists ensure that the specialized operation of the institution does not lose sight of the broader picture—the forest rather than individual trees, so to speak.

But more importantly from our perspective, each constellation of skills produces different types of economic returns. Specialization pays off not merely in lubricating the passage of laws by ensuring expertise, reciprocity, and deference, for example, but also in equipping legislators with skill packages that ensure a degree of job mobility. Those receiving a general education in legislative politics, conversely, receive the largest postelective salaries because their inclusive skill packages provide greater employment options, thereby enabling them to maximize their wages.

The value of specialization has universal appeal within political science as well as economics, especially with respect to the study of Congress, an institution that seems to epitomize specialization and its benefits. We have no quarrel with this conventional interpretation or the reverence generally accorded specialization. However, we feel that general training in congressional politics—that is, the acquisition of broad and inclusive sets of legislative skills—has been underappreciated and therefore undervalued almost everywhere except in the marketplace. The economic trade-offs between specialization and a more general training in congressional politics are best judged by analyzing the returns to these investment decisions; this process leads to an examination of legislators' postelective salaries and to the tracking of their postelective careers.

Structure of the Inquiry

Our analysis is based largely on a mail survey of 229 former members of Congress—214 former members of the House of Representatives and 15 ex-senators—conducted from September through December 2004. Three waves of mailings were employed in obtaining these interviews. Although survey researchers quibble to some extent about what constitutes an acceptable return rate for mail surveys, our rate of return (45 percent) would be considered acceptable according to the standards promulgated by most survey practitioners.

Survey

Our survey respondents were drawn from an original list of 513 (living) former U.S. senators and representatives who were members of a nonprofit organization, the U.S. Association of Former Members of Congress, as of January 2004. In chapter 3, we assess the representativeness of our sample and the membership list from which it was drawn relative to a variety of characteristics possessed by living ex-members of Congress.

The survey probed such issues as salaries before and after entering Congress, types and number of jobs held before and after leaving Congress, skills acquired while in Congress and how they benefited postelective employment, and legislator satisfaction with postelective employment opportunities. These data permit us to develop a panel of legislators and to track their postelective employment histories for a considerable period after they exited the institution. When these survey data are matched with publicly available data about the same legislators, we can tie the postelective careers of representatives and senators to their behavior while serving in Washington, such as their committee assignments.

While our study addresses conventional issues about Congress that others have studied, our analysis is unique in addressing broader issues about the marketability and economic value of elective office. In this regard, we examine three important economic effects of politicians' investments in human capital: (1) the range of skills acquired through on-the-job training opportunities; (2) the mobility in postelective employment resulting from human capital production; and (3) the expected earnings returned by investments in human capital. Each economic effect forms the focus of one of the three substantive chapters (chapters 4–6).

Chapter Outline

Before exploring the effects of legislators' investment decisions in chapters 4–6, we develop a theory that translates the behavior of politicians and the role of political institutions into terms consistent with Becker's (1993) framework for the study of human capital. Chapter 2 explains the concepts, assumptions, and hypotheses in our theory of politicians' investments in acquiring political skills and knowledge. Following the presentation of the theoretical framework, chapter 3 describes the methods underlying the inquiry, addressing issues of sample representativeness and bias, introducing the statistical model, and briefly describing the accompanying independent and dependent variables.

The substantive analysis begins with chapter 4, where we describe the human capital acquired in and marketed after leaving Congress. In addition, we analyze legislators' investments in on-the-job training and how they relate to the breadth of skills acquired through congressional service. Chapter 5 examines how specialized training in congressional politics promotes career mobility. We analyze ex-legislators' precongressional occupations and postcongressional employment and the factors underlying career changes. Here we also examine the pull or attraction of lobbying—the "lobbying trap"—and assess the possibility that lobbying by ex-legislators may be naturally constrained by something akin to a life cycle. Chapter 6 deals with a fundamental question in this inquiry: What is the economic value of congressional service? In particular, how does on-the-job training in congressional politics affect subsequent postelection salaries? This chapter also addresses the extent to which specialized legislator training is subsidized by groups, while those opting for more general training experiences pay most of the campaign bill themselves.

Chapter 7 summarizes the central findings and draws on these results to discuss possible implications for the study of politics in general and of Congress in particular. Some of our most important findings address issues surrounding the postelective employment of ex-legislators as lobbyists. For this reason, we have devoted a section of the final chapter to summarizing our findings about legislator-lobbyists, describing how they refute seamy characterizations of lobbying jobs, assessing the value of reforms on postelective lobbying by ex-legislators, and discussing the extent to which legislators' investments in lobbying skill sets cost society dearly.

Summary and Discussion

The study of the acquisition and marketability of political skills has immense potential to enhance our understanding of the organization and operation of political institutions, the influences injected into policy-making, and legislators' preferences and choices. Investments in human capital seem to be neglected factors in most explanations of congressional behavior, although few observers would deny that congressional activities incur opportunity costs; hence, their incidence is balanced against gains in utility. Accordingly, most legislator decisions (for example, choices regarding committee assignments) are conditioned by expected returns, whether those gains occur in the near term (for instance, electoral safety) or in the distant future (for example, postelective salary or employment). Investments of time and other resources—that is, human capital—are weighed against these expected returns. Where media attention reduces legislator decisions to immediate, spot-market, quid pro quo transactions, we envision greater complexity induced by considerations of future gain that go beyond the congressional career. Indeed, the study of human capital in politics draws attention away from exclusive focus on how institutions serve in-office purposes in favor of their relevance for acquiring skills and knowledge with economic returns to politicians in the future as well.

Human capital production and the expected returns from it also offer an alternative to conventional explanations for why certain policies seem to dominate the legislative process. Earmarked legislative appropriations and bureaucratic regulations, for example, represent opportunities for legislators to develop as well as to demonstrate their political skills. Such policies have obvious economic implications, and those skilled in manipulating public policies in this fashion are likely to be in demand. But since everyone can claim to have these skills, and moral hazards may cloud evaluation of these assertions, explicit evidence of such effort is necessary; hence, legislators build résumés of their political skills through their daily (policy-related) actions.

Next, our study goes beyond normal treatments of politicians' ability to sell their votes or to extract benefits from groups doing business with government, as the rent-seeking literature implies (see, for example, Parker 1996). We do not contest, however, the arguments that special interests influence politics in such ways. Nonetheless, we believe that the influence of special interests seeps into the political process in additional, perhaps more subtle, ways. Beyond the occupation of lobbyist, the market for legislators' services is rather narrow. Therefore, politicians may adjust their behavior in office through their on-the-job investments in acquiring skills and information about politics in anticipation of the job opportunities that await them, a situation that works to the advantage of special interests, given the limited market for the talents of most ex-legislators.

Since lobbying is where their skills and on-the-job training are most relevant, legislators naturally gravitate to those jobs where their human capital is put to its best use. After all, legislators have already made the necessary investments in acquiring political knowledge and skills. Lobbying thus does not for the most part represent a major occupational transition. We expect, therefore, that legislators will be attracted to lobbying because their skills and training are most appropriate to this vocation and because the market for legislators—if they want to change careers—is somewhat narrow, thereby foreclosing numerous employment options. Just as we have found that going to prison makes criminals more proficient at committing crimes, so too, legislators serving long tenure in Congress are apt to become skilled at lobbying. It is an externality of service in Congress, whether we like it or not.

The objective of this book, however, is not to assail legislators for their appetites for employment as lobbyists; nor is it to characterize them, as some scholars might do, as just waiting for opportunities to prostitute themselves to the first special interest that happens by. Defamation aside, not only are these depictions difficult to substantiate empirically, but they ignore the nature of their human capital. As we have noted, legislators acquire knowledge and skills in using the legislative process, and most corporations, businesses, and nonprofit institutions, like universities, find it necessary to gain access and influence within that process. Even "constituents" such as cities, towns, school districts, transit authorities, and utility agencies find it increasingly necessary to employ individuals (aside from local legislators) who know how to leverage local tax dollars into federal largesse (Rudoren and Pilhofer 2006). Simple legislative skills, acquired through congressional service, seem to be highly valuable to a wide assortment of individuals, groups, and interests. No wonder few ex-legislators stay unemployed for very long (chapter 5).

We conclude by pointing out the obvious: this is not our idea—we have borrowed it from Becker.[4] We have cultivated, nurtured, and expanded the reach of human capital analysis into politics, which is largely virgin territory. The significance of our inquiry is that it responds to Becker's challenge, noted in the epigraph to this chapter, to extend the theory of human capital to nonmarket sectors. We have found this task enjoyable but daunting. We hope we have not done an injustice to his imaginative analysis. We leave it to readers to decide about the persuasiveness of our arguments regarding the role of on-the-job training in Congress, the acquisition of political skills, the job opportunities facing legislators after they leave Congress, the effects of specialized and general training on the postelective earnings of former legislators and their job mobility, and above all the extent to which the study of human capital in politics is worthy of future inquiry.

One final caveat: this is not a book solely about the economics of the political labor force; we hope to show how the study of human capital directly relates to the operations of Congress and the behavior of its members. Ours is not, of course, a complete and exhaustive explanation of these important aspects of congressional politics, but we aspire for far less. We would be quite content if our inquiry provided important clues that engendered a better understanding of the whole story—specifically, why politicians do what they do.

---

4. If we were handing out authorship of ideas, which we are not, the notion of human capital probably predates Becker's work (originally published in 1964), as Becker says (1993, 15). Becker also notes the works of Mincer (1962) and Schultz (1961) as influential in this regard. However, we feel that Becker has done more than anyone else to promote this perspective; hence, we feel that our attribution of credit is warranted. Indeed, *Human Capital* (1993) is considered the locus classicus on the topic.

Chapter 2

Politicians, Institutions, and Human Capital; or, Becker Goes to Washington

It might seem rather pessimistic or perhaps outlandishly cynical to character-ize public officials as consumed with economic self-interest, since they are often depicted in civics texts as just the opposite—that is, as serving broad so-cietal goals rather than merely individual, personal ones. Even when self- in-terest has been assumed, the motive is incorporated into a reelection incentive that binds leaders to followers in a democratic fashion, agent-principal prob-lems notwithstanding (Downs 1957; Mayhew 1974; Fiorina 1989). But if politicians are rational, we might expect them to seek returns that transcend the benefits of reelection in maximizing their "profits" from elected office.

Monetary gain comes easily to mind as a complement or supplement to the desire to be reelected. And, not surprisingly, we all too frequently find ev-idence of politicians taking bribes, manipulating campaign contribution re-ports, and engaging in a wide range of opportunistic acts. It seems that self-interest ensures that politicians (1) pander to voters because they are motivated by the desire to be reelected; (2) seek monetary gain because they can; or (3) engage in opportunistic behavior, such as exploiting coordination and agency problems, because of the near-prohibitive costs associated with policing their behavior (see, for example, Alchian and Demsetz 1972). Self-in-terest enters the calculus of politicians in other less ominous or menacing ways that have equally far-ranging consequences. For instance, rational politi-cians may acquire skill sets designed to augment postelective earnings and in so doing set into motion investment strategies that directly and indirectly shape policy outcomes.

In this initial stage of inquiry, we introduce a theory to explain how and why politicians accumulate human capital through the acquisition of politi-cal skills; propositions drawn from this theory are then explored and tested in chapters 4–6. Conventional and prominent features of the political landscape of legislatures incorporated into our model—in particular, special interests, elections, voters, and party leadership—are discussed next. In elaborating on our theory, we address two supplementary but nonetheless relevant issues—specifically, the acquisition of human capital in politics by public-spirited citizens, and the apparent close connection between our theory and rent-seeking explanations of legislative behavior.

Human Capital Formation in Legislatures

We begin by offering a political variant of Becker's (1993) human capital argument: during officeholding, politicians make investments in human capital—that is, themselves—by undertaking activities in which they obtain skills, knowledge, expertise, experience, and the like. This array of skills, or stock of human capital, increases their marketability by impressing potential employers with their political know-how. Our conjecture parallels Becker's (1993, 120) contention that "persons who invest relatively large amounts in themselves tend to receive relatively high profits and measured earnings after the investment period." Or, to put the matter differently, service in politics and political institutions is a résumé builder in the truest sense of the term; accordingly, those with the best credentials garner the highest postelective salaries and the best jobs. This seems to be the case with labor markets in general, and the market for employee-politicians shares this trait.[1] Our theoretical treatment of politicians' human capital incorporates several interrelated components.

Rational Expectations

Underlying our reasoning is a dose of the logic behind the theory of rational expectations, which has been successfully applied to basic economic questions such as consumption and stabilization. The theory was first proposed by John Muth in the 1960s, but many early economists, including A. C. Pigou and John Keynes, assigned a central role to people's expectations about the future. Economic situations include many examples of rational expectations that lend considerable validity to the notion that anticipation of future conditions influences current behavior. For example, the price of agricultural commodities depends on the number of acres planted, which in turn depends

---

1. While inducements to officeholders, such as bribery, constitute the types of spot-market transactions that are less subject to cheating, they entail greater danger. Quid pro quo transactions between politicians and special interests are the only type of exchanges where corruption—that is, bribery—can be legally claimed. Risk-averse politicians can be expected to avoid such situations; hence, lucrative postelective jobs look like a better way for politicians to cash in on their public service employment.

on the price farmers expect to receive when crops are sold. Similarly, the price of stocks and bonds depends at least partially on what perspective buyers and sellers believe these investments will render in the future.

Applying this logic to politicians leads to the proposition that their behavior depends at least partially on what they expect to happen in the future. More generally, rational expectations implies that legislators' planning and behavior in the present are predicated on their anticipation of prospective gains; future as well as present returns thus enter politicians' calculations. For instance, considerations of prospective employment figure conspicuously in politicians' plans: 56 percent of our sample of former legislators indicated that prior to their departures, there were times during their congressional careers when they "anticipated working at the job [they] held immediately after leaving Congress."[2] Legislators, therefore, definitely think about the future, especially when it comes to employment after congressional service. We suspect that a number of these legislators acted on such expectations when acquiring human capital while in office. For the most part, legislators might be said to be neither ill-prepared nor, as we demonstrate in chapter 4, poorly trained for future postelective employment.

Rational expectations enters our model of politicians' human capital in another, closely related way. The rather specialized job market for the talents of former politicians creates the expectation that variety in postelective employment will be difficult to come by; hence, many legislators anticipate taking jobs that require specialized political skill sets—that is, lobbying. Consequently, legislators often acquire industry-specific assets (for example, skills and knowledge) that will be economically valuable to special interest employers.

Training

The premise of rational expectations is important to this analysis, but the core of the model rests, of course, in Becker's (1993) theory of human capital. Central to both analyses is the notion of training, commonly defined in economics as "investment in acquisition of skill or in improvement of worker productivity" (Mincer 1962, 51). We offer a similar definition: members of Congress build human capital by acquiring highly marketable legislative skills through investments in on-the-job training experiences within the institution. Many ways of accumulating human capital exist in politics, including the development of reputations and service in prior offices, but since political

---

2. The wording of the question is: "Was there ever a time during your congressional career that you anticipated working at the job you held *immediately after leaving* Congress?"

institutions couple training with production, on-the-job-training is one of the most cost-effective means for acquiring such capital.

In a real sense, on-the-job training provides an education in legislative politics, and like education in general, training in politics can be expected to increase postelective returns, such as earnings. Indeed, Becker (1993, 246) equates training with education in terms of its effects on earnings: "Learning on and off the job has the same kind of effects on observed earnings as formal education, training, and other recognized investments in human capital, and can be considered one way to invest human capital." Even university programs, designed to prepare students for careers in politics, emphasize practical, on-the-job experiences, such as internships, and many curricula are taught by present or former politicians, or by those with specialized training in politics, such as campaign consultants and pollsters. A parallel may exist, then, between jobs in politics and learning-by-doing vocations, as in the construction trade—most training remains best given on the job, under the supervision of practitioners. Because training is so basic to our analysis, we will elaborate on this topic later in this chapter.

Subsidized, Specialized Training

Training in politics is neither free nor cheap, if we are to judge by the costs of, for example, congressional or senatorial elections. Rational legislators therefore contrive to obtain subsidies for the costs of their education in politics. This is where special interests enter: they oblige legislators with political action committee (PAC) money, which helps them stave off electoral defeat and encourages them to acquire human capital specialized to the policy concerns of special interests. These funds offset the costs politicians incur in obtaining office and in continuing their specialized training in politics. For this reason, PAC funds can be viewed as subsidizing the tuition and fees associated with obtaining elected office in the same sense that scholarships finance the education of students specializing in certain academic fields.

Groups willingly subsidize the education of legislators, not only because of the benefits derived from hiring well-trained politicians, but also because specialization shapes perspectives on policy issues. Specialized legislators, therefore, see problems and issues from the same vantage points, or "points of advantage," as special interests. Consequently, legislators consciously or unconsciously pursue the interests of groups because their specialized training leads them to internalize the same perceptions of reality; hence, they reach the same conclusions about the substance of public policy as special interests do. These images of reality, or "pictures in their heads," are constantly reinforced because "the more that officials specialize in a particular policy domain, as indicated by the percentage of the time that they devote to that domain, the more contact they have with lobbyists" in that policy area (Heinz et al. 1993, 239). In short, specialization benefits interest groups by equipping prospective legislator-employees with industry-specific assets—an understanding of and expertise in industry issues as well as perceptions of reality that favor the policy positions of special interests.

Groups, Elections, and Party Leaders

No model of politics is worth very much without addressing the roles of the standard actors in American politics—specifically, interest groups, political parties, and elections. What functions do these prominent features of the political landscape play in the production of legislators' human capital? The simple answer is that all of these factors work in concert to encourage the production and accumulation of human capital. We recognize that these political factors have other functions to perform elsewhere in the legislative process, but this does not preclude their involvement in the production of marketable human capital.

Interest Groups

Strong theoretical and empirical reasons exist for the belief that lobbyists provide policymakers with valuable information (see, for example, Austen-Smith and Wright 1992; Ainsworth 1993; Austen-Smith 1993). After all, given the complex, technical nature of many matters of public policy, it would not be too surprising to see legislators turning to lobbyists for information. This is a difficult claim to topple, but it does not threaten our arguments in the least. We need only point out that if lobbyists are rational, they are dedicated to propagandizing, even as they supply truthful information. Thus, lobbyists influence legislators in the same way that Downs's (1957, 83–84) "persuaders" influence voters:

> Persuaders are not interested *per se* in helping people who are uncertain become less so; they want certainty to produce a decision which aids their cause. Therefore they provide only those facts which are favorable to whatever group they are supporting. We have assumed that these "facts" will never be false, but they need not tell the whole truth. And they probably will not, because persuaders are, by definition, propagandists in the original sense of the word—they present correct information organized so as to lead to a specific conclusion.

In sum, there is good reason to suspect that the information reaching legislators from interest group representatives, while factual, is nonetheless one-sided.

Because only a small number of groups operates in any one policy area, as a result of the costs of information and specialization (Downs 1957, 254), it is not difficult for a limited number of special interests to organize, collude (Olson 1968, 1982), or perhaps even logroll their differences (Lowi 1969); hence, information circulated to politicians is filtered to supply a unified version of the "facts." Why should we expect such cooperation among special interests? Becker (1983, 388) provides a good answer: "Cooperation among pressure groups is necessary to prevent wasteful expenditures on political pressure that results from the competition for influence." As a consequence, perspectives on political issues are likely to be shared by lobbyist-persuaders and the politicians they seek to influence—the former are committed to their cause, and the latter either are similarly dedicated or never receive information that would lead them to see things differently.

Our argument about the commingling of policy attitudes and outlooks between legislators and special interests is consistent with many findings about interest groups, lobbying, and campaign contributions. First, lobbyists tend to specialize and interact with similar types of individuals within Congress and the federal bureaucracy (Heinz et al. 1993), and therefore are more likely to associate with legislators who specialize in areas of mutual interest.

Second, lobbyists tend to lobby their "friends" more than their enemies (Bauer, Pool, and Dexter 1963; Milbrath 1963); in addition, "interest groups in the same issue areas tend to have similar policy preferences, and these preferences tend to be similar to the congressional committees that they lobby" (Kollman 1997, 521). Or, as Hall and Wayman (1990, 814) succinctly put it, special interests mobilize "legislators already predisposed to support the group's position." In short, lobbyists and those lobbied are likely to agree about policy issues, solutions, and problems.

Third, legislators support interest group positions whether or not campaign contributions are sizable or even forthcoming. While retiring or exiting legislators are less likely to receive PAC contributions, these politicians nonetheless continue to maintain if not increase their legislative support for special interests (Bronars and Lott 1997). Therefore, politicians' votes are not bought through campaign contributions, since legislators do not alter their support for special interests even after campaign contributions have ceased.

Finally, interest groups target their campaign funds toward legislators sympathetic to group goals and causes (Hall and Wayman 1990; Grier and Munger 1991; Grier, Munger, and Roberts 1991); this ensures the continued specialization of politicians in matters of group interest. We cannot improve too much on Hall and Deardorff's (2006, 75) conclusion about the relationship between lobbyists and legislators:

> In sum, lobbyists freely but selectively provide labor, policy information, and political intelligence to likeminded but resource-constrained legislators. Legislators, in turn, should seek policy-relevant services from like-minded lobbyists. The effect is to expand legislators' effort at making progress toward a policy objective that lobbyists and legislators share.

Taken together, these empirical findings suggest that lobbyists and legislators tend to agree on matters of public policy. We believe they do so because of the specialized training that occurs within political institutions like the U.S. Congress.

Legislator Opportunism

We digress for a moment to discuss a problem that plagues legislator–special interest relationships—specifically, ensuring that legislators live up to their agreements. Asymmetries in information, moral hazards, and unforeseen contingencies afflict contractual matters in politics (see, for example, Weingast and Marshall 1988). More significantly, however, there are no explicit instruments for the enforcement of such bargains. How, then, can special interests prevent postcontractual opportunism on the part of legislators? Or put more simply, how do groups ensure that legislators will keep the promises they make?

Scholars have offered a number of thoughtful solutions to this intriguing question. For example, Snyder (1992) believes that repeat play, trust, and reputations imbue these exchanges with self-enforcing qualities, while Stratmann (1998) places greater faith in near-contemporaneous exchanges. Some observers might conclude from the framework for our analysis that postelective employment opportunities ensure that legislators keep their bargains, since special interests can dangle prospects of generous salaries over the heads of legislators. However, we believe that there is more to postelective employment than reward for faithful in-office service to groups. From our perspective, agreements between legislators and special interests are durable because specialized training creates a relatively frictionless relationship between the two.

Since specialized training equips legislators with views paralleling those of interest groups, politicians and groups behave in concert as a consequence of similar policy views, and no additional policing or prodding is necessary. For legislators, this is a good deal: interest groups pick up the tab for campaign costs, and legislators only have to give expression to their internalized views of policy issues. Groups do not have to worry about legislators keeping their bargains because legislators prefer to do so, strategic behavior and unforeseen contingencies aside.

Another problem associated with the coupling of production and training could lead to legislator opportunism in the eyes of special interests. This problem is common to firms supplying training: trained employees can take their acquired skills to business competitors. Groups underwriting the campaign costs of legislators, like firms providing training, always face the possibility that trained legislators will take their acquired skills elsewhere. So, do special interests need fear that after having made over-time investments, legislators will leave to work for rivals?

Former legislators are not likely to find employment with antagonistic groups, such as business and labor (see, for example, Heinz et al. 1993, 144), and potential employers are not likely to be rivals. First, because specialization equips legislators with particular perspectives on problems that coincide with those of special interests, a new employer runs the risk, or cost, of trying to change these perceptions and beliefs. Thus, distinct disincentives exist for hiring legislators with prior service to adversarial interests. Indeed, why would any rational employer hire legislators who are known to harbor and to have acted on attitudes opposed to those of the employer? Competition for the wares of ex-legislators is therefore unlikely to involve interests antagonistic to one another.

Nor is the rivalry associated with competition among like-minded interests apt to provide conditions for legislators to leverage their training. Legislators normally work for large economic sectors or industries where rivalry is unlikely to transpire because of the collective nature of the policies they seek (Olson 1968), the incentives to logroll intergroup conflicts (Lowi 1969), and the desire to avoid unnecessary expenditures of political influence and resources (Becker 1983).

Elections

Reelection is central to most explanations of legislative behavior, and it plays a role in our theory, too. Like most students of politics, we agree that the desire for reelection motivates political behavior because of the returns it engenders, such as institutional power (Fenno 1973), discretion (Parker 1992), and/or access to wealth-earning opportunities (Krueger 1974; McChesney 1987). Reelection is indeed necessary to pursue member goals, but our theory suggests that scholars have taken too narrow a perspective on these goals, ignoring the fact that reelection provides additional opportunities to acquire marketable human capital.

Reelection is significant in our model because it enables politicians to continue their education in politics, and therefore to increase the accumulation of human capital through on-the-job training. Reelection brings opportunities for politicians to develop new skills, master old ones, and above all repeatedly apply what has been learned to complex, practical problems. These on-the-job training experiences enrich politicians' human capital and their after-office earnings and job mobility; these experiences also provide a security net against unemployment as a result of electoral defeat, retirement, or resignation resulting from office improprieties.

Mayhew (1974, 16) correctly noted that reelection is important because it "must be achieved over and over if *other ends* are to be entertained." Thus, reelection is not intrinsically valuable in and of itself; its value rests in making possible additional terms of officeholding during which politicians achieve other objectives, one of which is the accumulation of human capital through on-the-job training. Reelection also enters our model in another way: the prospect of electoral defeat prompts, or perhaps even accelerates, postelective employment planning.

Threats to reelection lead many legislators to explore intently postelective employment possibilities, thereby fostering considerations of investments in human capital suitable for these employment opportunities (see also table 1.2). Some observers might think that electoral threat would lead legislators only to step up their efforts at electioneering; it probably does, but that does not mean that electorally threatened legislators pay no heed to the consequences of electoral defeat and the resulting unemployment. Not only would that be irrational, it would also be foolish; hence, electoral threat also engenders considerations of postelective employment. Whether as a result of reelection or as a consequence of electoral threat, legislators find training in congressional politics valuable.

Party Leaders

We represent the effects of parties in the production of human capital in terms of the behavior and motivations of their leaders. Party leaders have incentives to clear the market of legislation demanded by groups and legislators since they can extract payments from both for doing so (Parker 1992). Groups want the benefits government provides and offer "favors" (for example, campaign contributions) in return. Similarly, committee members as well as party members fancy the proceeds derived from passing legislation, such as reelection and campaign support, and are willing to compensate leaders for expediting bills. Therefore, the more legislation produced, the greater the returns to party leaders in terms of favors owed them. Some of these returns, or IOUs, are used to pass legislation, promote party goals, reward trustworthy and reliable members for their cooperation (Crain, Leavens, and Tollison 1986), and the like; whatever is left over can be "pocketed" by leaders for their own purposes. Thus, party leaders benefit from a productive legislature. Given that legislatures combine the production of legislation with on-the-job training, party leaders encourage members to further their investments in training, which in turn increases the production of legislation, thereby personally benefiting the leaders themselves. Leaders valuing institutional influence, for whatever reason, realize that a productive legislature creates the currency that earns them power.

Leaders need not worry about voters getting in the way of their plans for party members to spend time accumulating human capital in Washington rather than spending time with constituents in the district. First, rational ignorance on the part of constituents precludes them from keeping tabs on their representatives (Downs 1957; Stigler 1971); moreover, legislators can concoct believable and convenient rationalizations for their actions in Washington (Fenno 1978, 136–70). We recognize that legislators may face conflicting goals in trying to meet the demands of constituents, who prefer unwavering attention to constituency concerns, and the legislators' desire for on-the-job training experiences capable of impressing future employers. Still, voters are less fickle when it comes to electoral support, since they are largely uninformed about what their legislators do in Washington. Legislators are thus less worried that their personal allocations of time and resources will alienate constituents to the point of threatening future reelection. In sum, party leaders view the manufacture of human capital on the part of their members as promoting the production of legislation, thereby yielding returns to them personally.

Theoretical Assumptions

We have now briefly described the major arguments underlying our human capital model and how the theory accounts for the actions of key political actors. In this section, we discuss the application of Becker's theoretical framework to the study of human capital in politics, which requires three explicit assumptions: (1) legislators are rational; (2) legislatures couple training with the production of laws, so all activity in Congress encompasses training of some sort; and (3) legislators base their in-office actions on the expected returns derived from their career investments. The design of these assumptions permits the derivation of testable hypotheses representing arguments tailored for the study of human capital in politics.

We offer one caveat with regard to these assumptions: some colleagues with whom we have discussed our arguments have raised the specter that our inquiry is too critical of politicians. We did not start out with such an objective, although some of our findings obviously might lead to this conclusion. Nevertheless, our conclusions are not a consequence of dispirited assumptions. Indeed, in a number of instances, our findings challenge or rebut sinister indictments of legislator lobbying fostered by conventional wisdom, media exposés, and stylized facts, thereby benefiting politicians. More to the point, the long-standing issue of values entering research aside, the assumptions underlying this study are not tinged with any sort of ideological flavor—they are neutral in every respect. Appearances are not deceiving: the assumptions are innocent of any wrongdoing. We have no corner on immaculate perception; however, we have not begun this study with anything but a sincere and impartial interest in better understanding what politicians do in office and how it affects their livelihoods after they leave. The assumptions are necessary to head us in that direction; the resulting comparative statics are all Nature's doing.

Rationality

As in all studies of economic behavior, politicians are assumed to seek to obtain the most at the least cost: they are rationally self-interested. This assumption is so basic to economic analysis that we dispense with further elaboration. We add only the proviso that this rationality is bounded by the imperfect capacity of individuals to plan and anticipate investment outcomes.

Training

The notion that institutions couple production (for example, laws) with on-the-job training is implicit in our model of human capital formation in politics and leads to our second assumption: all the activities undertaken by politicians contain elements of formal or informal on-the-job training. Production occurs along with training, so activities involved in the former will necessarily incorporate training. For example, legislators gain a mastery of the legislative process as a result of their efforts to navigate through it.[3] Training involves investments of human capital, but politicians differ in how much and in what activities they invest their capital. This implies that politicians make trade-offs in their investments while in office, pursuing some training opportunities more extensively than others and incurring opportunity costs as a result. In doing so, legislators reveal their preferences for certain types of training experiences (that is, specialized or general) and, as we argue, their expectations about prospective postelective returns (that is, occupational mobility or lucrative postelective wages).

With respect to legislatures, then, all activities can be regarded as investments developing or expanding political skills, perfecting those already acquired, and/or gaining knowledge instrumental to legislative business. These actions represent on-the-job training in politics in the same way as schooling occurs in all sorts of vocations. There are other forms of human capital in addition to the skills and knowledge acquired while on the job in public office, such as appearance, personality, and the like; we will, for the most part, limit our discussion to human capital derived from involvement in congressional activities, although we empirically examine the influence of other forms of capital.

Human capital derived from congressional training should be differentiated from private or insider information on which politicians capitalize by virtue of their political positions and contacts. Legislators undoubtedly have access to information, and high-powered experts to interpret it, that are beyond the reach of most citizens. Although access to such information helps politicians financially, legislators market political skill set proficiency to prospective employers. So, for example, while information about the appropriate times to buy and sell real estate or common stock may enrich the personal fortunes, or nonhuman capital, of senators and representatives (Ziobrowski 2002; Ziobrowski and McAlum 2002; Ziobrowski et al. 2004), unless such shrewdness is permanently encased in legislators' skill sets, like congressional know-how and savvy, it is not highly marketable human capital.

Instruction in Favor Trading
Our emphasis on training in politics may seem incapable of accounting for the apparently large amount of favor trading that goes on between legislators

---

3. This means that even shirking (for example, trading work for leisure) requires on-the-job learning (for example, to avoid detection and maximize returns). While some economists (see, for instance, Ben-Porath 1967) exclude shirking from their analyses of human capital, this form of behavior is quite relevant to the study of politicians. We do not see shirking exclusively as a lackadaisical trade-off between work and leisure. That may well be the case in some circumstances, but shirking is also an acquired knack—for example, concealing leisure swaps for work to avoid penalties, such as electoral defeat or admonishment by party leaders.

and special interests. Anecdotal evidence, formal models, and empirical research provide persuasive arguments that politicians perform services for special interests, such as interceding on their behalf with the federal bureaucracy (see, for example, Faith, Leavens, and Tollison 1982; Fiorina 1989) or writing legislation that earns rents for these interests. Our model accounts for such activity, but we view these exchanges in a different light, emphasizing the educational nature of these transactions.

The assumption that all activities in Congress entail on-the-job training means that even doing favors for special interests results in the acquisition of skills or, at the very least, practicing them, perhaps to perfection. Institutions couple training with production, and exchanges of favors are, for better or for worse, part of the business of Congress. Consequently, it is not unreasonable to expect legislators to acquire knowledge about how processes of favor trading work; to develop price schedules for favors (Denzau and Munger 1986); and to devise strategies for enhancing private returns (McChesney 1987, 111). Knowledge of low-cost favor providers, and the going prices for various types of favors, enhances the value of former politicians for the simple reason that, as Becker (1993, 530) observes, "information about the prices charged by different sellers would enable a person to buy from the cheapest, thereby raising his command over resources."

For example, informed lobbyists could easily find the cheapest suppliers of the policies their clients' demand, thereby conserving on search costs and resources and attracting greater business because of their lower supply costs. In the process of doing favors for special interests, therefore, legislators enhance their human capital by acquiring, practicing, and perfecting skills associated with facilitating group objectives—highly marketable and visible talents in a rent-seeking society. While often characterized in unflattering ways, the favor-exchange process provides important educational experiences for legislators.

Returns on Investments

Our final assumption draws on a fundamental tenet in economic analysis: the amount invested is a function of the expected rate of return. In the case of politicians, we need to add some clarification of the term *returns*. First, the nature of the anticipated returns also shapes investment strategies. So, for instance, legislators seeking to change careers after leaving Congress are likely to pursue more specialized legislative training, which funnels them in that direction. Second, returns encompass psychic as well as financial considerations. For some, the intrinsic rewards from officeholding are unimaginable.

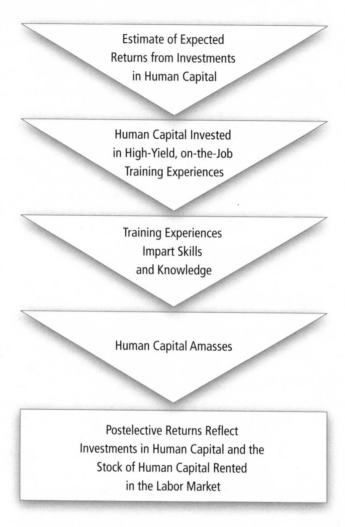

FIG. 2.1. The role of human capital in politics

Finally, not only the returns on investments matter: rational legislators must also weigh the costs of training investments against their benefits in deciding where to invest human capital. Hence, while many legislators might relish a general education in congressional politics, it is rather pricey to acquire. Thus, politicians invest time and energy in activities that they expect will help them efficiently and effectively realize postelective career objectives, whatever they may be.

These relationships are described in figure 2.1. As the figure depicts, legislators estimate the returns they expect to receive from investments in human capital. Some of these returns will be consumed while in office; others will take the form of subsidies for on-the job training; and still others will be in the form of postelective employment and earnings. Based on these estimates, politicians engage in those on-the-job experiences with the greatest returns, acquiring skills, information, knowledge, and opportunities to apply this human capital to practical and complex problems. These on-the-job-training experiences increase a legislator's human capital and subsequent postelective employment earnings and opportunities (that is, career mobility). The assumptions guiding this inquiry seem quite simple, logical, and realistic, which is about all that can be demanded of assumptions; they nonetheless yield some interesting insights into the behavior of politicians in office that we will describe shortly.

Planning and Preparation

Implicit in the notion of training is the idea that legislators follow plans to attain skills relevant for marketing their human capital. This statement implies that legislators have some idea of what they expect to do after they leave Congress. Some observers might resist the notion that planning for postelective employment is a purposive act of legislators. The contention that legislators rationally plan and prepare for their postelective livelihoods is, of course, only an assumption designed to illuminate features of legislative behavior that seem to have escaped notice, and its value is best appraised in exactly these terms—that is, its ability to further inquiry. Still, arguments of this sort go right to the core of this analysis as well as of most rational-choice enterprises.

It would be easy to sidestep this issue by simply asserting that given the assumptions that all congressional activity encompasses training of some sort and that legislators base in-office actions on expected returns, planning for postelective employment is a conscious endeavor inherent in anticipating investment returns and leave the matter at that. However, we believe that this a defensible proposition and that the reader is owed nothing less. Before discussing training in politics, therefore, we address the soundness of characterizing legislators as devoting attention to planning their career investments in anticipation of postelective contingencies in the future. Although we feel that our conceptualization of the production of human capital in politics well matches the realities politicians face, our argument is based on (1) the rationality of planning, (2) the necessity of preparation, and (3) supporting empirical evidence.

Rationality of Planning

Legislators are implicitly assumed to act with purpose, which implies that an element of planning enters into decisions about investments in human capital. For example, a decision about whether to move to a different committee or to stay put in the hopes of obtaining a leadership position on the current committee may depend on the desire to develop a more (or less) specialized skill set. Planning in this sense involves the same type of cost-benefit calculations so common to economics and rational-choice models: weighing the costs and benefits of various investment strategies.

This is not to discount or even diminish the role of opportunity and luck in shaping these investment plans; nonetheless, it is not too much of a stretch in logic or imagination to anticipate that rational legislators will have expectations of how investments in certain legislative experiences will benefit them in the present as well as once they leave Congress, and then plan their activities (that is, investments) accordingly. Nor do we intend to minimize the effects of career longevity and electoral safety. Still, legislators need to consider how their congressional activities relate to the marketability of their human capital. Legislators cannot escape the possibility—indeed, likelihood—that they will eventually leave office alive: only about 2 percent die in office.

While some legislators tire of public service, perhaps as a consequence of the grind of elective office, and seek different vocations, others exit, not voluntarily, but because of voters' decisions. Despite the well-documented longevity of congressional careers, a noticeable upsurge has occurred in the number of House members retiring (Hall and Van Houweling 1995, 132; Ornstein, Mann, and Malbin 1996, 60). A number of interpretations have been offered to explain this change, but the net result is the same—simply put, legislators have found better things to do with their time than serve in Congress. "It is probably fair to say," Fenno (1978, 222) observes, "that at some point most members ask themselves how badly they want to be reelected." Arguably, then, congressional careers are not so inviolable as to render postelective planning obsolete.

And electoral safety also does not negate postelective planning. For example, repeated reelection does not enhance the likelihood of success in the next election (Erikson 1976, 630) and thus does not eliminate thoughts of postelective employment. Furthermore, subjective assessments of electoral safety may be far more relevant to legislators than are objective measures of marginality. "Once having gone through a testing election, early or late, a member will entertain the possibility of its recurrence forever. Even when he is being spared, it will be happening to someone he knows. And he will take it as a warning signal to himself" (Fenno 1978, 13). Electorally safe politicians also know they are never out of harm's way—they may lose office as a result of circumstances beyond their immediate control, something akin to "random terror" (Mann 1978). This threat may not sound substantial, but it is probably treated as such by risk-averse politicians. "Members of Congress feel uncertain and [electorally] vulnerable—if not today than yesterday, if not yesterday then tomorrow" (Fenno 1978, 234).

In either case, rational politicians consider what they would do if they indeed left government employment. Doing so necessitates thinking about the skills and abilities acquired prior to and through officeholding, and how they might contribute to postelective employment and earnings. Accordingly, politicians see officeholding as entailing more than just fulfilling office responsibilities—it also provides opportunities to acquire skills and contacts that are useful in preparing for postelective employment, a haunting prospect hanging over the heads of all elected officials.

Necessity of Preparation

The notion that individuals invest resources and take actions based on expected payoffs is central to many if not most rational theories of economic and political behavior—for example, those encompassing game-theoretic models. Our only modification is to extend this assumption to include postelective payoffs in the calculus. But our emphasis on the postelective returns to officeholding is not intended to ignore the obvious. In particular, investments in training, and the subsequent production of human capital, benefit legislators while they are in office, not merely after they leave. Other future or expected benefits derived from the stock of human capital legislators accumulate while in Congress stop far short of postelection benefits. For instance, the accumulation of a durable set of general skills may pave the way for assignment to powerful committees and clear paths to institutional influence.

Given that the production of human capital (through training) provides returns that can be realized both while in and after leaving Congress, the argument might be advanced that legislators engage in activities that benefit them while they are in Congress; then, as they leave, those activities coincidentally open doors for them in the labor market. Put differently, the search for postelective employment involves no conscious preparation whatsoever. We are certain that legislators wish the situation were that easy; indeed, without any encouragement, a number of respondents wrote on their surveys that preparation for postelective employment was a critical but little appreciated aspect of life transitions for legislators.

It seems highly questionable that, in the absence of any preparation whatsoever, investments made to accomplish in-office goals also increase postelective salaries and pave the way for career changes. Perhaps more to the point, why would rational legislators base the production of human capital on its calculated benefit to their congressional careers, but then leave postelective employment to the vagaries of the labor market, fate, coincidence, and fortune? That argument really does not sound very rational for highly strategic politicians.

We do not want to belabor the point, but some of the postelective opportunities members contemplate, such as career changes, necessitate more than lackadaisical groundwork; the same can be said about the acquisition of broad skill sets. It is quite doubtful that legislators could ever entertain the prospects of these postelective returns—that is, higher wages and career mobility—without preparing for them years in advance. Pursuing training befitting these goals also necessitates strategic thinking and politicking. As we demonstrate in chapter 4, the acquisition of broad skill sets requires a substantial investment in training in congressional politics, which is largely a function of time spent in the institution; similarly, career changes demand years of specialized training. For example, acquiring a broad skill set may involve obtaining a high-profile position in the party's leadership or a position on an elite committee, both of which necessitate considerable groundwork. And although lobbying is not much of an occupational transition for legislators, specialized training (chapter 5) remains essential.

In addition, preparation seems indispensable for employment to which legislators anticipate devoting a large proportion of their remaining earning years. Furthermore, at this point in their lives—most former legislators are well beyond their peak productive years—postelective employment likely represents the last shot most legislators have at high-earning jobs or new careers; hence, given both the significance and inescapability of the outcome (that is, reentering the labor force), we expect legislators to spend time earnestly preparing for this inevitability. Arguably, then, the acquisition of human capital for these purposes entails considerable preparation over a congressional career.

Empirical Evidence

Postelective employment certainly crosses legislators' minds (table 1.2); hence, we suspect that many legislators give thought to what they will do after leaving Congress. Likewise, the systematic relationships among training, skill sets, and postelective employment reported in chapters 4, 5, and 6 belie the notion that pursuing the latter is a willy-nilly enterprise. These empirical findings notwithstanding, we still cannot easily dismiss the notion that some of the human capital produced by legislators is committed to keeping them electorally afloat. It is hard to dispute the claim that human capital stockpiled while in office is perhaps best dedicated to staying in office, since reelection is the only way to accumulate additional terms of officeholding and subsequent opportunities for acquiring further human capital. Many human-capital-producing legislative activities may serve electoral objectives as well, like practices within congressional committees (see, for example, Mayhew 1974; Fiorina 1989).

All the same, it remains far less clear how acquiring general and specialized skill packages serves this electoral imperative, legislators' constituency "explanations of Washington activity" aside (Fenno 1978). Indeed, despite a relatively close-fitting prediction model ($R = .51$), none of the training variables in our analysis (for example, *general training, broad skill set, investments in training, years of committee service*) are significantly related to legislators' average margin of electoral victory during the course of their congressional careers. The acquisition of general and specialized skill sets apparently serves postelective objectives to a greater degree than electoral ones. That is, human capital produced with postelective designs in mind, like general and specialized training, may in fact serve these purposes and few others.

Training in Congressional Politics[4]

Training in politics is important to the study of political institutions, especially Congress, because institutions couple production with on-the-job

---

4. It might be suggested that we exaggerate the significance of training, at least with respect to Congress, since postelective employment is little more than another form of group gratuity for services rendered while in office; hence, training is of marginal consequence to legislators. Legislators undoubtedly would prefer to obtain high-paying jobs without any training or skills, but it is unlikely that their employers feel the same way about the matter. We cannot imagine rational special interests distributing the vast majority of their high-paying jobs, hand over fist, to politicians who are not believed to enhance industry profits. Special interests are like all employers—that is, they are reluctant to hire incompetents. As a result, training looms large, whatever the job, and working for interest groups, as many ex-legislators do, has very little effect on the situation.

training; hence, training encompasses most of what politicians do while in office. For this reason, we discuss this topic in depth. We begin by noting that some readers may question our emphasis on congressional training, arguing that we overstate its effects since many legislators have previously served in state legislatures or in other political positions, both appointive and elective. Under such conditions, learning about the legislative process would represent at best a modest addition to existing stores of knowledge and skills. Most legislators, therefore, can be effective without devoting much if any time to training. While this argument is seductive, as we show in chapter 4, those with previous political experience are in fact more likely than others to invest in on-the-job training in Congress. A background in politics may sensitize quasi-experienced legislators to the importance of acquiring training as well as to how and where those opportunities can best be found. No matter what one's previous experience in politics, the U.S. Congress represents a complex and unique environment. Thus, skills and knowledge of congressional politics cannot be, and are not taken, for granted regardless of precongressional experience.

Our conceptualization of on-the-job training is somewhat broader than used in Becker's analysis (1993, 31), which emphasizes the skills acquired while employed: "Many workers increase their productivity by learning new skills and perfecting old ones while on the job." We consider on-the-job training in politics to include the acquisition of contacts, knowledge, and information as well as skills and experience.

Specific and General Training

There are a number of ways to describe training in Congress. First and perhaps foremost would be in terms of formality. Training on the job, "ranges from formally organized activities such as apprenticeships and other training programs to the informal processes of learning from experience" (Mincer 1962, 50). Formal congressional training can occur, for example, through efforts to familiarize new legislators with the mechanics of constituency services (Fiorina 1989, 52), the running of legislative offices, and the use of congressional prerogatives. Informal training frequently arises as fellow legislators share their experiences and knowledge, thereby allowing the less informed to free ride on their information-gathering efforts. In addition, training can involve learning by doing (Killingsworth 1982), which is inherent in all legislative activities. (Indeed, we are hard-pressed to think of any job where learning is absent.) We distinguish neither between formal and informal training nor between these latter forms of training and the lessons gleaned from experience—all are considered elements of on-the-job training. We will differentiate training in congressional politics, however, in terms of its specificity.

On-the-job training can be defined in terms of the specificity of the skills and knowledge acquired through institutional service. Becker (1993, 40) makes just such a distinction, defining on-the-job training as either "specific training," which has no effect on the productivity of trainees useful to other firms, or "general training" which increases the marginal productivity of trainees by exactly the same amount in the firms providing the training as in other firms. Thus, general training is valuable to numerous firms; specific training, in contrast, has a far more limited clientele. For example,

> the military offers some forms of training that are extremely useful in the civilian sector . . . and others that are only of minor use to civilians, i.e., astronauts, fighter pilots, and missile men. Such training falls within the scope of specific training because productivity is raised in the military but not (much) elsewhere. (Becker 1993, 40)

For our purposes, *specific training* refers to investments in on-the-job training resulting in the acquisition of specialized political skills and knowledge that are relevant to a narrow set of occupations or vocations. This type of training often produces skills dedicated to a particular industry, policy area, or sector of the economy. In contrast, *general training* represents investments in job training to acquire more inclusive or broader skill sets relevant to a wider assortment of occupations and less specialized to a particular industry, policy field, or economic sector. Simply put, we equate general training with the acquisition of a larger repertoire of political skills and experiences, a greater breadth of information, and a more inclusive understanding of politics.

We might think of a broadly skilled legislator as having a more extensive understanding of "government"—that is, how the system works and can be worked—as a result of serving on numerous party committees, holding leadership positions, participating in deliberations on an assortment of political issues, learning the intricacies of legislative procedures, interacting with countless federal agencies and officials, developing a diverse portfolio of committee assignments, and the like. Conversely, a specialized legislator could be characterized as having a more restricted understanding of the ins and outs of Washington politics because of a less cosmopolitan congressional education (for example, lack of service on a diverse set of committees, involvement in a narrow range of issues). This conceptualization is not meant to disparage specialization; we refer only to the inclusiveness or breadth of the human capital acquired through investments in on-the-job training.

We dodge the controversy among labor economists as to whether human capital investments are mainly general (Abraham and Farber 1987; Altonji and Shakotko 1987; Marshall and Zarkin 1987; Williams 1991) rather than firm-specific (Topel 1991; Becker 1993) by noting that political institutions offer both. That is, like many firms (see, for example, Acemoglu and Pischke 1999), Congress offers opportunities to develop portfolios of investments that can include specific and general skill sets. Since general and specialized training engender skill substitutes rather than skill complements (see Shaw 1984), legislators' portfolio investments are slanted to emphasize certain skill packages. One final caveat about general training: as we explain in chapter 4, some human capital is indigenous to Congress; hence, few can avoid acquiring a basic level of general training as a mere by-product of their congressional service, even if they take the job only remotely seriously.

Economic Effects

Many congressional scholars will quickly recognize our conceptualization of specific and general job training as harkening back to textbook depictions of legislators as "generalists" and "specialists"—that is, legislators consumed with matters of broad or narrow policy significance, respectively. Although these concepts are rarely used in contemporary studies of politics, we believe that they remain analytically useful in characterizing politicians' investments in human capital. Our use of these terms goes beyond conventional treatments by associating generalists and specialists with different types of training experiences, skill sets, investments in human capital, and postelective returns.

While scholars have emphasized the importance and relevance of legislator specialization, whether in committee assignments or the norms surrounding participation in Congress, the value of generalists seems to have been ignored. It is not that specialization is overrated—hardly. Rather, it is that general training may be highly undervalued relative to its market appraisal. Whereas specialists are undeniably important to the efficient functioning of Congress, generalists have greater economic leverage in postelective employment. In short, salary benefits accrue to ex-legislators with a comprehensive education in congressional politics.

At least two reasons exist for the economic value of broad skill sets and general training in congressional politics. First, by equipping legislators with an extensive bundle of skills, general training increases the number of markets where politicians can rent their human capital, thereby furnishing them with greater employment versatility and options. And the greater the number of suitors, the larger the salaries ex-legislators can command.

Second, the relative scarcity of inclusive skill packages produced through general training, and the paucity of opportunities for acquiring them (for example, through service on important legislative committees), means that a higher price can be charged to rent this human capital. Since specialists dominate Congress's membership, their superior numbers reduce their leverage in wage negotiations while placing a premium on skills acquired through general training. As a consequence, higher wages are paid to those possessing less common political skills. The acquisition of an extensive set of congressional experiences, skills, and knowledge thus augments postelective earnings to a greater degree than does specialized human capital.

Conversely, specialization engenders the expertise necessary for changing careers, as many legislators do after leaving Congress. More often than not, congressional training furnishes the human capital necessary to gain a foothold in another vocation by supplying, for example, the requisite knowledge, contacts, and skills. We cannot ignore the fact that a large number of legislators abandon preelective vocations when leaving Congress. Specialized training provides them with the wherewithal to do so. In sum, specialization pays off in preparing legislators for career changes, while general training enhances postelective salaries.

Investments in Training by Public-Spirited Officeholders

While some scholars, especially economists, are likely to see material gain in elected or appointed office, others, especially political scientists and politicians, view public service as entailing personal sacrifice. Political life weighs heavily on individuals, or so the argument goes: there are the demands of family, constituents, contributors, and voters; there are the trade-offs that force sacrifices in conscience; and there are, of course, the financial losses associated with the comparatively poor salaries public servants receive. All of these factors take their toll on politicians. But why, then, do rational people seek public office if economic gain fails to offset the down side of officeholding?

Setting aside the possibility that public-spiritedness is irrational, one explanation for altruistic officeholders invokes historical images of the citizen-politician who enters public service as an obligation to society. That is, the citizen-politician embraces the principle that all individuals should take a turn in the running of society, no matter the sacrifice. This perception of public service has had a rich tradition in normative political theory, where public service is viewed as a personal virtue; it has also become something of a poster child for citizen movements to limit the terms of politicians such as state legislators.

Thus, contrary to most economic theories of governmental employment, there is a less materially interested breed of politician: individuals who believe that public service does not constitute employment ripe for financial gain but instead calls for personal sacrifice. As one former legislator volunteered, "I take pride in my independent effort at obtaining employment outside of government and not directly in Washington lobbying. Congressional service should not be viewed as a mere stepping stone to a sinecure, influence, tenure, or fortune." Is this to say that public-spirited politicians make no investments at all in acquiring human capital during tenure in office?

Like all politicians, public-spirited ones also make investments, although we expect their investments to differ from those made by politicians who are less publicly oriented;[5] the former make investment decisions emphasizing intrinsic and psychic returns to a greater degree than financial ones, but these are nonetheless human capital investments.[6] "It is the sum of monetary benefits and the monetary equivalent of psychic benefits (which may be negative) from human capital," observes Becker (1993, 116), "not just the former alone, that determines the demand curve for capital investment." So, in contrast to the investments made by economically motivated politicians, altruistic legislators rationally invest in obtaining skills relevant to vocations with greater intrinsic or psychic rewards—for example, employment in nonprofit organizations. We might characterize this behavior as trading salary for prestigious or psychically rewarding jobs.

We would predict, then, that such "public-spirited politicians" would fol-

---

5. This argument should not be construed to mean that people serve in government out of the goodness of their hearts; even if that statement were true, politicians are likely to have an awfully hard time convincing voters that this is the underlying motivation for seeking office. Constituents want their public officials to fight for them. For voters, it is not merely that politicians feel that they should take their turn at governmental employment; they must also feverishly embrace the notion that elected agents are dedicated to getting as much of the federal largesse for the constituency as is humanly possible. Voters thus expect that those elected to office will work for constituents and perhaps engage in "errand-boy" functions (for example, constituency service and visits).

6. Elected office may entail personal sacrifices; nonetheless, it does not completely lack benefits. In addition to the psychic rewards associated with fulfilling obligations associated with public service, certain returns may make public service more palatable. Specifically, public service has intrinsic, on-the-job benefits, such as media and perhaps national recognition, influence over public policy, and the like. These returns may soften the curse of public service and result in personal gains in utility but not in explicit financial benefits.

low a course of postelective employment in educational or nonprofit institutions. Or, if these legislators are intent on prolonging their sacrifice, they might continue the self-flagellation by returning to some form of public service employment. Thus, our theory, unlike most economic treatments of politics, has a place for selfless officeholders. In this sense, our explanation represents a clear departure from conventional economic theories of officeholding.

Rent Seeking as Political Training

The rent-seeking paradigm (see, for instance, Buchanan, Tollison, and Tullock 1980; Tollison 1982) characterizes the political process as central to the allocation of wealth transfers, but more importantly, as the vehicle through which special interests obtain monopoly-like market privileges. In light of the importance of such rents to economic producers and sellers, special interests exercise considerable effort and resources in trying to influence government and the political process. One of the obvious means of doing so is by swaying those who run government. Thus, the rent-seeking paradigm has twofold implications with respect to public officials. First, rent-seeking politicians gravitate to those institutions and positions that play an integral role in dispensing benefits to economic interests, a form of adverse selection (Parker 1996, esp. 65–68); second, politicians interested in the financial rewards of rent seeking acquire those skills and experiences that place them in positions to cash in on the rent-seeking appetites of special interests (Krueger 1974, 293).

Some readers may find our conclusions about politicians reminiscent of rent-seeking arguments in the literature. They are, but our approach on the one hand can be distinguished from conventional rent-seeking models and, on the other, can still account for many of the basic propositions derived from these theories. In short, rent-seeking behavior, while not a focal point of our inquiry, is nevertheless incorporated into our explanation of legislator behavior.

Model Differences

While close similarities exist in the predicted outcomes between common rent-seeking models and our human capital perspective, fundamental differences are also present. Our theory applies to public-spirited officeholders— that is, politicians in office for the intrinsic or psychic benefits of public employment—as well as to those motivated by the economic gain that can be expropriated through political office. In both cases, politicians make investments and obtain returns. However, the rent-seeking literature has concentrated on wealth-motivated politicians, largely ignoring the investments of public-spirited men and women who enter government seeking nonmaterial benefits. Even impressionistic evidence suggests that some politicians enter public life for reasons that cannot simply be subsumed under "monetary gain" or relegated to "error" in econometric models.

Furthermore, most theories of rent seeking imply quid pro quo exchanges between politicians and special interests, where politicians trade influence over policies in return for lucrative jobs after leaving office. This viewpoint makes sense, but it is not the only route to postelective employment: legislators can enhance their attractiveness to potential employers by acquiring marketable skills through on-the-job training. In our human capital schema, then, many former politicians are employed by special interests, not merely as quid pro quo transactions, but as a consequence of specialized skills and expertise that are economically valuable. Such specialized assets make legislators attractive commodities to interest groups, which is why the latter are so willing to supply (or invest) PAC contributions to encourage further specialized training. To paraphrase Becker (1993, 246), since specific capital is invested in legislators while in office, employers have special incentives to retain these legislators on the payroll even after they leave office.

Model Similarities

Despite these significant differences, there are, of course, numerous similarities between our theory of politicians' investments in human capital and theories of rent seeking. Both models agree that politicians engage in behaviors that ultimately earn favor with special interests, with the expectation that such service will be rewarded with campaign funds to keep the legislators in office and with attractive postelective employment. And both perspectives see special interests as having a strong grip on politicians through the supply of campaign (PAC) contributions, but for quite different reasons. Indeed, in some instances, the similarities between the two theories are rather stark. Although both rent-seeking arguments and our human capital perspective come to some of the same conclusions, the interpretations are quite different.

Perhaps most important, rent-seeking deeds, like other legislative activities, can be regarded as acquired political skills and certainly as skills that can be improved with practice or even, we suspect, honed to perfection. As such, rent-seeking actions (for example, learning how to fashion rent-earning laws, disguising earmarked appropriations, and influencing bureaucratic decisions) also serve as on-the-job training experiences (since all congressional activity provides some sort of training). Hence, our theory of human capital should not be viewed as an alternative to rent-seeking explanations of politicians' behavior, but rather as incorporating officeholders' rent-seeking activities into a broader perspective—namely, as representing investments in human capital. That is, rent seeking involves skills that legislators acquire to further their marketability. In fact, we can recast Krueger's (1974) insight that governmental officials acquire the necessary credentials for entering public service to cash in on the distribution of rents by suggesting that legislators invest human capital in rent-seeking activities as a way of dazzling future employers with their adeptness and effectiveness in these activities.

Hypotheses

From this paradigmatic approach, several generic hypotheses can be derived about politicians and politics in general, but we will use legislators as our reference. We state these propositions as affirmative rather than null statements to ease their presentation. The hypotheses empirically examined appear in italics.

1. The experiences associated with *on-the-job training* affect the future returns of legislators in two ways: first, they *increase post-elective employment mobility* by providing opportunities for "retooling" (chapter 5); second, they *promote the acquisition of extensive legislative skills* (chapter 4), which, as highly marketable commodities, enhance postelective wages.

2. *The nature of the skills acquired through congressional training and their occupational transferability make lobbying a likely career transition for exiting legislators;* indeed, we may think of congressional training as "trapping" legislators into becoming lobbyists because of the ease with which legislative skills are transferred and the lack of demand for those skills and training in other areas (chapter 5).

3. *Specialized training in congressional politics supplies* the types of pointed *expertise required for career changes*—that is, the ability to switch vocations (from precongressional occupations) (chapter 5).

4. *Investments in general training and the acquisition of broad legislative skill sets enhance postelective salaries* because of the

scarcity associated with the opportunities for acquiring such capital and the many employment options available to those who possess it (chapter 6).

5. Special interests "pay" legislators for undertaking on-the-job training in policy areas most *relevant* to group interests by subsidizing election campaigns; such groups do so in part because this expertise ultimately enhances former legislators' productivity as employees. In contrast, *legislators pursuing a general training in congressional politics can expect to foot most of the bill for their campaigns themselves* (chapter 6).

6. Since institutions couple production with training in politics, organizational design enhances or facilitates the accumulation of human capital through on-the-job training. For example, increasing the role of smaller units (for instance, congressional subcommittees and committees) and younger politicians in policy-making provides more opportunities for learning about congressional processes, developing skills, and practicing them.

We will elaborate on each of these hypotheses and their connections to our theory as they are introduced into the analysis. All but the final hypothesis are subjected to empirical testing in this study. The last hypothesis, dealing with the organization of Congress, is consistent with our observations, impressions, and readings of anecdotal evidence, but testing its validity remains beyond the confines of this inquiry. Nonetheless, we believe that failure to see congressional change in this light impoverishes our understanding of institutional evolution.

Summary and Discussion

Our analysis examines legislative politics from a unique point of view that in important ways parallels contemporary thinking about political institutions and the behavior of officeholders. We see legislators as engaged in activities that produce the greatest returns, with the consideration of returns cast in largely economic terms—for example, postelective employment and earnings. As legislators invest their time and energies—their human capital—in these activities, they forgo certain opportunities and incur costs for doing so.

Scholars generally acknowledge that legislators develop congressional careers; they also accumulate human capital beneficial to postelective livelihoods. Both endeavors require more than a measure of planning, preparation, and subsequent execution. Planning for a congressional career, for example, involves learning the ropes surrounding legislative politics, while postelective planning entails accumulating marketable political skills. Consequently, legislators give attention to and plan for both while in office. Legislators realize that successful planning for postelective employment is more than just a matter of hanging out a sign or placard. More often than not, training is essential.

One of the major costs associated with training in politics is campaign debt. Special interests subsidize reelection costs through PAC contributions to legislators undertaking training specialized to the needs of these interests; specialization, in turn, leads legislators to view policy issues from the same perspective as the special interests subsidizing their campaigns. The consequence is a legislative system that provides and subsidizes opportunities for members to acquire unique skills and knowledge. This system also shapes members of Congress's penchant for specialization and service to special interests.

The central premise in our model—that the actions of politicians reflect cost-benefit calculations—is not really novel to political inquiry. It would be rather irrational for rational politicians to do otherwise. Our approach is distinctive because we focus on postelective returns from politicians' investments in human capital. For example, many congressional scholars view the selection of committee assignments as reflecting electoral exigencies, a sort of evaluation of the electoral benefits derived from appointment to one committee rather than another. Hence, legislators gravitate to those committees providing the greatest electoral bang. From this angle, the benefits occur only while legislators remain in office; in contrast, we envision the benefits from investments in human capital as realized in the future as well as the present. Therefore, any calculations of the rational actions of politicians need to consider a broader range of payoffs—in particular, postelective benefits as well as those enjoyed while in office.

Chapter 3

Methodology: Data and Variables

In chapter 2, we described the basic elements of our theory and how Becker's (1993) work on human capital can be applied to politics—in particular, legislative politics. When we say that our analysis draws on Becker's theory of human capital, we are referring to the proposition that investments in the production of human capital are made in anticipation of returns (assumption 3) and to three important attendant hypotheses: (1) investments diminish over the life cycle, (2) on-the-job training enhances skills and earnings, and (3) general training is less subsidized by employers. Taken together, these theoretical propositions provide a framework for analyzing the postelective employment of politicians as a function of their behavior in office.

Here we address methodological questions relating to the data collection and the formulation of our variables: in particular, the survey design, the representativeness of our sample, the independent and dependent variables analyzed, and the incorporation of the latter into our model of politicians' human capital. Our discussion of the conceptualization and analytic operationalization of the variables will be brief at this point, but will be more extensive later when the individual variables are subjected to analysis. In this chapter, we only alert the reader about what to expect in terms of the measures used to reflect important concepts within the analysis. At the risk of appearing repetitive, we begin by returning to our discussion of the more important elements of the survey design. We do so because this information is relevant to methodological issues surrounding the representativeness of our pool of former legislators.

Data: Survey of Former Legislators

Our analysis is based on a mail survey of 229 former members of the U.S. Congress between September and December 2004. Three waves of mailings were employed in obtaining these interviews, with a respectable return rate of 45 percent. The return rate appears even higher if we take into account the fact that several respondents currently serve in high-profile political positions, making them predictably reluctant to answer surveys of this nature. Our survey respondents were drawn from an original list of 546 former U.S. senators and representatives who were members of a nonprofit organization, the U.S. Association of Former Members of Congress, as of January 2004. Thirty-three former legislators were expunged from this list due to death. The survey probed such issues as pre- and postcongressional salaries, jobs held after leaving Congress, skills acquired while in Congress, the value of various congressional experiences (for example, committee assignments) in obtaining postelective employment, and legislator satisfaction with postelective employment opportunities. This information provides a rich and multifaceted view of the career decisions of legislators during and after congressional service.

All the same, the significance of our findings depends on the representativeness of our sample; if it is not representative of the broader universe of members of Congress, biases could result in faulty inferences. Then we would be unable to generalize our findings to all former members of Congress. A potentially damaging bias is the possibility that our sample is composed of unduly satisfied legislators. Since the U.S. Association of Former Members of Congress has among its many civic goals the objective of promoting the image of Congress—in one way or another, deservedly or not—sampling such a membership list might produce respondents with unusually positive, retrospective views of how the institution contributed to their postelective office successes; indeed, membership in the association might be construed as revelation of just how valuable those legislative experiences really were to them.

Thus, conclusions about the value of congressional service might be biased because members of the association had positive experiences in launching their postelective careers. Consequently, we need to look for differences between the characteristics of legislators in our sample and the universe of former members of Congress that might produce biased conclusions. Therefore, we assess the extent to which our sample is composed of respondents who might be unduly positive about their congressional service a priori.[1]

---

1. As would be expected, we have eliminated dead ex-legislators from our mail survey; their characteristics, such as years of service, thus do not figure into comparisons of sample parameters. However, we have no cost-effective way of identifying all the legislators who died after leaving office from readily available computerized biographical directories. Therefore, in this case, it is likely that the estimation of this group's parameters will be based on both living and dead former legislators; hence, the comparisons would not be valid.

We have surmised, on the basis of our study, that legislators elected since 1952 have a very good chance of still being alive in the late 1990s. So, to gauge the representativeness of our sample

Assessing Bias

Politicians disclose their preferences for elected office by continuing to run, and those who stay in office do so because of electoral success and desire— both are necessary. It seems reasonable to expect those most satisfied with congressional service to stay as long as they can, accumulating considerable tenure, while the less satisfied leave quickly, either on their own terms or as a consequence of voter rejection. Tenure in Congress, then, reveals a lot about how legislators feel about their years in the institution, especially in terms of retrospective evaluations. We might expect such satisfaction to extend to self-appraisals of the skills acquired during officeholding. With this in mind, we examined the extent to which tenure, or years of service, might differ between members of our sample and the universe of former legislators.

Of course, the desire to return to office must be coupled with the voters' desire to accommodate that wish. Former legislators booted out of office may shelter far more pessimistic views of the benefits of congressional service and skills acquired than those who chose the time and circumstances of their exit. For this reason, we also explored differences in why legislators left office.

Finally, organizations such as the U.S. Association of Former Members of Congress serve as social and business networks. These connections may be advantageous to postelective employment, thereby not only enhancing earnings but also engendering positive views of the skills acquired in Congress. Since those with preelective employment in business are most likely to benefit from such networking practices, we examine the extent to which our sample is skewed because of an undue number of legislators with business backgrounds.

Seniority
Table 3.1 describes the distributions of legislators in terms of total years served between our sample and the broader population of all House members who served in Congress between 1952 and 1996. As we noted, it might be expected that legislators with long tenure in Congress would attribute greater value to their congressional careers and therefore would join organizations

---

relative to the universe of former legislators, we restrict our comparisons to legislators serving in the House between 1952 and 1996 (the last year for which congressional biographical data are available; see Inter-University Consortium and McKibbin 1997); we do so to reduce the likelihood that the comparisons we make are patently invalid because one sample (for instance, our survey of ex-legislators) excludes individuals included in the other—specifically, dead legislators. We recognize that even this method is not, of course, foolproof, but it is the best way to fashion reasonable comparisons.

dedicated to extolling the virtues of service in Congress. Conversely, brief terms of legislative service might generate contrasting perspectives on the value of congressional careers and the skills acquired therein.

Little difference exists between our sample and the universe of ex-House members. For example, 64.8 percent of ex-legislators in our sample served 10 years or less, while 60.2 percent of former legislators in the larger universe served the same number of terms; 7.9 percent of former members of Congress in our analysis served more than ten terms (21 years), and 8.5 percent of all ex-legislators served as long. Other statistics related to these two groups are also quite similar. For instance, in both our survey sample and the larger universe of former legislators, ex-legislators averaged about 10 years (mean = 10.11); the standard deviation for our sample is 7.68 years, while the standard deviation for the broader set of ex-legislators is 7.49 years. In sum, no compelling evidence demonstrates that our survey sample is composed of legislators who have had longer careers in Congress and therefore are more likely to harbor exceedingly positive impressions of how training in Congress has benefited their postelective careers.

Reasons for Leaving Congress
Electoral defeat may jade ex-legislators regarding the value of congressional training and its contribution to their later postelective ventures. Consequently, former legislators repudiated at the polls may be less positive about the benefits of on-the-job training and therefore unlikely to see much payoff to it; they are probably also less likely to join organizations dedicated to promoting the virtues of congressional service. Thus, our survey sample could conceivably have a greater concentration of ex-legislators who left office on their own terms rather than as a consequence of voter revolts.

TABLE 3.1. Years of Tenure among Former Members of Congress (in percentages)

Years of Congressional Service	Population	Sample
Less than 10 years	60.2	64.8
11–20 years	31.4	27.3
21+ years	8.5	7.9
Statistics		
Mean	10.11	10.11
S.D.	7.49	7.68
Number of cases	1,135	165

Source: Inter-University Consortium and McKibbin 1997; authors' survey of former members of Congress, 2004.
Note: S.D. = standard deviation

Table 3.2 compares the reasons for leaving Congress between the respondents in our sample and the universe of ex-House members. On this account, our survey sample is also quite representative of the broader population of former House members. In terms of losing a general election, virtually no difference exists. Similarly, legislators in our sample, and those in the broader universe, differ little in the degree to which they exited because they had tired of the House. For example, 49.7 percent of our sample exited on their own terms—as a result of either "retirement" (27.6 percent) or the opportunity to run for another office (22.1 percent)—while 47.6 percent of all ex-legislators did so.

Business Connections

Given the networklike nature of the U.S. Association of Former Members of Congress, it is conceivable that we have oversampled those with business connections and that our analysis consequently exaggerates the economic gain derived through congressional service. Yet, if we compare the percentage of ex-legislators with precongressional vocations in business (34 percent) with the percentage who have been elected to the House of Representatives between 1953 and 1995 with the same occupational background (33 percent [Ornstein, Mann, and Malbin 1996, 22–23]), it is clear that our analysis is not biased in this manner.

We have reanalyzed these data including all House members born since 1929 and serving until 1996, rather than using service in Congress between 1952 and 1996, as the basis for constructing comparisons. This condition may better ensure that the two samples are composed of individuals with reasonable chances of being alive at the time of our study. These findings are reported in the appendix. While changing the requirement for inclusion in the analysis to birth since 1929 reduces the number of cases in both samples, it does not alter our conclusions in the least. In short, there is no evidence that

TABLE 3.2. Reasons for Leaving Congress
(in percentages)

Reason for Departure	Population	Sample
Lost general election	38.3	39.3
Lost in the primary	8.6	5.5
Retired	32.2	27.6
Sought another office	15.4	22.1
Accepted federal office	2.0	1.2
Resignation	3.5	4.3
Number of cases	1,672	163

Source: Inter-University Consortium and McKibbin 1997; authors' survey of former members of Congress, 2004.

our survey sample is unrepresentative of the broader population of former House members as a result of some unique characteristic of the population from which our sample of former members of Congress has been drawn.

Major Variables

We turn now to a discussion of our explanatory model of human capital formation in legislatures. Here we briefly describe the variables within the model and their role in the theory. Table 3.3 summarizes the conceptualization, interpretation, and measurement of these variables. The individual variables will be discussed further as they are introduced into the empirical analysis in subsequent chapters; at that time, we will also describe in greater detail the construction of the various measures.

On-the-job training is a central variable in our study of the economics of the political labor market because it is a major way of accumulating human capital; however, human capital can assume many forms. Therefore, to identify the effects of on-the-job-training experiences, we need to differentiate them from other sources of human capital. We do so by including measures of these other types of human capital, along with our indicators of on-the-job training, in our explanatory equations. We begin by describing the variables designed to represent on-the-job training experiences and discussing the rationale behind their use in our analysis. Since some of these variables are measured in terms of factor scales composed of several related measures of behavior, we digress, briefly, to describe the general notions behind the formation of these scales.

Scale Construction

Factor analysis, although a technique commonly used in the social sciences, appears infrequently in economic research. (For a comprehensive treatment of factor analysis, see Rummel 1970.) Still, the technique has been applied to substantive questions in leading economics journals to confirm hypotheses about the underlying structure of measures (see, for instance, Gibson 1980, esp. 1073); create reliable measures or scales (see, for example, Cohen 1991; Hennart and Anderson 1993, esp. 297–99); and to reduce a large number of variables to a small set of composite measures (see, for example, Mayers and Smith 1988, esp. 370–77). All three purposes are served here with respect to the composite measures of *breadth of skill set, investments in training, non-training assets,* and *reputational capital* analyzed in this inquiry.

TABLE 3.3. Description of Variables

Variable	Description	Concept
Investments in on-the-job training	The variable is derived from a factor analysis of attributes that were deemed important in obtaining the first job; the attributes represented on this factor pertain to training capital.	Investments in training
Breadth of skill set	The variable results from a factor analysis of the various private and public sector jobs for which training in Congress supplied the necessary skills: high- and midlevel executive, high- and midlevel government official, interest group representative.	Breadth of skills
Decision to switch careers	The variable is coded 1 if the legislator did not return to his or her precongressional vocation within the first three jobs after leaving Congress, and 0 otherwise.	Career mobility
Lobbyist	The variable is coded 1 if the legislator chose to become a lobbyist after leaving Congress, and 0 otherwise.	Immediate lobbyist
Postelective employment	The variable describes the various postelective employment choices of former legislators, classifying them into six categories: lobbying, private sector employment, government, lawyer, nonprofit institutions, and retirement.	Postelective careers
Precongressional employment	The variable describes the various precongressional employment positions of former legislators, classifying them into five categories: lobbying, private sector employment, government, lawyer, and nonprofit institutions.	Precongressional employment
Postelective salaries	The variable is derived from self-reported salaries for the first job after exiting Congress; the salaries are converted into 2004 dollars.	Postelective salaries
PAC subsidies of campaign costs	The variable calculates the percentage of PAC money that accounts for the campaign costs incurred by legislators during the course of their terms in office.	Special interest campaign subsidies
Time spent in postelective jobs	The variable measures the length of time, in months, that legislators spent in their first, second, and third jobs after leaving Congress.	Job commitment
Precongressional salaries	The variable is derived from self-reported salaries for the last job prior to entering Congress.	Precongressional salaries
Prior political office	The variable is coded 1 if the legislator served in a previous political position, and 0 otherwise.	Prior political experience
Interest group committee	The variable is coded in terms of the number of years spent on a clientele committee.	Service on clientele committees
Prestige committee	The variable is coded in terms of the number of years spent on a prestige or elite committee.	Service on prestige committees
Nontraining assets	The variable is derived from a factor analysis of attributes that were deemed important in obtaining the first job after leaving Congress; the attributes represented on this factor pertain to capital not derived from training.	Nontraining capital

TABLE 3.3.—*Continued*

Variable	Description	Concept
Reputational capital	The variable is derived from a factor analysis of the characteristics of trustworthiness, constituency attentiveness, and leadership attributed by voters to their legislator; based on likes/dislikes reported in NES surveys from 1978 to 2000.	Reputational capital
General training	The variable is a second-degree interaction term between broad skill sets and investments in training.	General training
Life cycle investments	The variable is a third-degree interaction term between broad skill sets, investments in training, and tenure.	Life cycle investments in general training
Political party	The variable is coded 1 if the legislator is a Democrat, and 0 otherwise.	Party affiliation
Senator	The variable is coded 1 if the legislator is a senator, and 0 otherwise.	Member of the Senate
Year of entry	The variable simply records the year when the legislator entered Congress.	Indicator of adverse selection
Year of departure	The variable simply records the year when the legislator left Congress.	Indicator of adverse selection
Tenure	The variable measures the length of time (in years) that a legislator has served in Congress.	Congressional seniority/tenure
Lobbyist within first three jobs	The variable is coded 1 if the legislator took a job as a lobbyist within the first three jobs after leaving Congress, and 0 otherwise.	Lobbying job

An offshoot of factor analysis is the derivation of weights assigned to each variable appearing in a factor scale; these weights, or factor loadings, are based on the variation that a variable has in common with a given factor (Rummel 1970, 137–42). Each variable in a scale is weighted proportionally to its involvement in a factor; hence, the more involved a variable is with the factor, the greater the weight assigned. Patterns among factor loadings describe the underlying nature of a factor or dimension, whereas legislators' factor scores serve as a composite statistical measure of the latent variable.

Breadth of Skill Set

The extensiveness and scope of political skills measures the general marketability of the human capital accumulated in office. This variable is a factor scale composed of several indicators of occupational proficiency acquired through congressional service. It characterizes the range of skills acquired through congressional service from narrow to broad. Those with broad skill sets have greater employment possibilities because of their skill versatility.

Investments in Training

The significance of job-training experiences serves as a proxy for legislator investments in training; this measure is causally related to the acquisition of political skill sets. We consider this variable as representing investments in on-the-job training; it is a composite of several sources for investment of legislators' resources (for example, committees, expertise, contacts). Even though related, we distinguish *investments in training* from *breadth of skill set* because they yield different returns. For example, training alone—that is, in the absence of a vast portfolio of political skills and experiences—cannot engender the same competitive salaries as broadly skilled legislators receive; mere investment in training offers no assurance that the training will be sufficiently general in nature to supply these types of skills. Broad skill sets are of little value, however, when changing vocations; here, as in lobbying employment, investments in training suffice.

General Training

Training may enhance postelective salaries, but it does so only in conjunction with the acquisition of an expansive set of political skills (that is, general training). We construct a measure of general training from the interaction between these two variables—that is, *breadth of skill set* and *investments in training*—that represents the acquisition of general human capital through investments in training. This second-degree interaction term is a critical variable in our theory, as it is in most studies of human capital; its importance is reinforced by our empirical analysis.

Tenure

Seniority reflects time spent in on-the-job learning and therefore should enhance skills and knowledge of politics and the legislative process, thereby increasing human capital. Simply put, tenure in Congress should result in the accumulation of marketable human capital. We envision time, or tenure, as increasing the opportunities for on-the-job training but not as a proxy for the experiences, skills, and information derived through training. We measure tenure in terms of the number of years of service in Congress.

Life Cycle Investments

It might be suggested that the age of politicians needs to be considered when estimating the economic payoff of officeholding, since later investments are less profitable than those made earlier in political careers because the present value of the net benefits (from officeholding) is reduced. From this perspective, then, age should reduce the likelihood of investments in human capital during congressional careers. We feel that the dynamics of aging in politics is a more complex phenomenon than can be captured through a simple measure of age. This is especially true when considering the production of human capital.

In lieu of age, we create a measure of the life cycle dynamics associated with accumulating human capital—that is, investments in general training, conditioned by seniority. This variable is computed as a third-degree interaction term combining *general training* with *tenure* (*general training* × *tenure*). The idea is that incentives to expand skill sets through investments in training are likely to diminish with increased tenure. We refer to this variable as *life cycle investments in general training* and describe it in greater detail when we examine career mobility (chapter 5).

Congressional Committees

The income-earning effects of institutional mechanisms for general and specialized training—that is, congressional committees—are captured by differentiating committees into those that are powerful and possess the broadest jurisdictions in Congress (prestige), and those that are narrow in jurisdiction, attractive primarily to clientele or special interests (interest group). Perhaps a crude delineation of congressional committees, it serves our purposes nevertheless. It does so by distinguishing between legislators who have received a more comprehensive or inclusive education in congressional politics as a consequence of their positions on legislative committees possessing broad jurisdictions and executing considerable power, and legislators who are more impoverished in both regards (that is, specialized training). We measure the effects of committees in terms of the number of years ex-legislators spent on these two types of committees. Again, we expect the inclusive education in congressional politics provided by prestige committees to function like general training in enhancing postelective wages; service on clientele committees, in contrast, provides a more specialized education in legislative politics that we expect to facilitate career changes.

These measures of congressional training play distinctive but complementary roles in our analysis. This is, of course, an accounting of only some of the important sources of human capital resulting from on-the-job training in Congress. As we alluded earlier, a large number of important forms of human capital are not derived through congressional service but could nonetheless affect postelective employment and earnings. We now describe some of these variables.

Abilities and Endowments

In estimating postelective earnings, we consider the income-earning effects stemming from differences in ability. How training matches up against ability in augmenting income is a major issue in human capital research—a sort of economic twist on the nature-versus-nurture argument. We address this question by comparing the income-earning effects of congressional training with the wage gains engendered by economic and political talent.

In our analysis, *precongressional salary* and prior officeholding (that is, immediately before entering Congress) serve as proxies for economic and political abilities, respectively. Ex-legislators with the highest precongressional salaries are viewed as possessing greater economic talent; those with political experience prior to entering Congress are considered to have a greater aptitude for politics. Prior officeholding is an indicator of talent in the political sphere since it usually incorporates a knack for fund-raising, public speaking, leadership, nurturing contacts, and the like. Aside from reflecting political adroitness, previous officeholding supplies relevant political skills that may supplement training experiences offered in Congress. We recognize that precongressional wages—and prior political officeholding, for that matter—depend on a number of factors, including nepotism and luck; nonetheless, to a significant extent, ability is involved. In short, prior political officeholding and precongressional salary represent talents, and these abilities can be expected to increase the postelective returns of ex-legislators ipso facto.

Even though precongressional salary reflects more than just ability, this is a benefit rather than a drawback to our analysis because we can use it to represent the market value of the human capital with which legislators entered Congress. To shape postelective wages, then, congressional training must overcome the effects of not only political and economic talents, but all factors and endowments incorporated into human capital and capitalized into precongressional salaries. Sharing the same equation with *precongressional salary* is therefore a stern test for the effects of training: they must appreciably increase the market value of human capital beyond precongressional levels.

The inclusion of precongressional salary is more than merely beneficial to our analysis; it is essential to the study of postelective wages. In estimating the earnings resulting from on-the-job training in Congress, we need to consider the stock of human capital already accumulated through prior acquisition of skills and experiences. Some of the human capital that legislators take with them when they leave Washington is an upshot of the buildup of experiences and skills acquired prior to entering Congress. Put another way, if we seek to measure the effects of training, we must take account of the value of human capital accumulated prior to engaging in congressional training; to do otherwise mixes the two and confounds the measurement of the effects of precongressional capital with training in Congress.

We measure *precongressional salary* as midpoints of the following salary categories: less than $40,000, $40,000–60,000, $61,000–80,000, $81,000– 100,000, $101,000–150,000, $151,000–200,000, $201,000–250,000, and more than $250,000 (assumed to be $300,000). These salary midpoints are converted to 2004 dollars.

Reputational Capital

No one needs to be reminded that lobbying is regarded as a rather distasteful vocation. Given the lucrative salaries awaiting those joining the trade, losing reputational capital by becoming a lobbyist may not seem like much of a gamble. But for many legislators, it is reason enough to look for employment elsewhere. Bluntly put, someone who is worried about his or her reputation probably should not choose lobbying as a career. Thus, politicians who have amassed high levels of reputational capital—such as reputations for trustworthiness—are likely to steer clear of this occupation.

Some journalists link reputational capital to the organization employing the lobbyist: lobbyists for the "good guys" (for example, environmental lobbyists) are well received, but those working for the "evil empire" (for instance, oil lobbyists) are despised. We doubt that citizens, who disseminate reputational information (Parker 2004), have the same view since they really do not have much of an informational basis for making such distinctions. Therefore, lobbying is frequently viewed as operating against the interests of society as well as insinuating corruption into the political process, and those carrying the label *lobbyist* are probably lumped together. Thus, we include a measure of legislators' reputations for trustworthiness, leadership, and constituency service as a potential influence on postelective employment.

These assets are far less salvageable than, for example, the skills and knowledge acquired about congressional politics, but threats to reputational capital nonetheless are taken seriously (Parker 2004).[2] Our measure of reputational capital is quite gross; however, to exclude an indicator of why legisla-

---

2. The variables comprising our measure of reputational capital were derived from pooled National Election Surveys (NES) from 1978 to 2000, and in particular, from the candidate "likes and dislikes" asked of respondents in the districts of these legislators. We tabulated the number of voters characterizing their legislator as possessing the qualities of leadership, demonstrating concern for constituents, and inspiring trust or confidence, and then calculated the percentage of each district's voters (in the pooled sample) who saw their legislator in these terms. Voters' responses were categorized in the following manner:

tors might be resistant to entering lobbying—employment that makes the most profitable use of legislative training—seems even more disastrous. Consequently, we expect reputational capital to restrain ex-legislators from entering the financially enticing, but reputably risky, profession of lobbying.

Political Party

This variable may also carry some income-earning potential, assuming that the association of business interests with the Republican Party enables former GOP legislators to obtain higher-paying jobs in the private sector. In addition, we might expect some repercussions on postelective employment and wages resulting from former majority leader Tom DeLay's directive that firms expecting to be effective in lobbying the then-Republican Congress employ Republicans. Thus, we include a measure of party identification, with Democrats coded as 1 and Republicans coded as 0.

Dependent Variables

We examine six dependent variables in gauging the economic effects of investments in training on the postelective employment of members of Congress: *breadth of skill set acquired through congressional training* (chapter 4), *investments in training* (chapter 4), *career mobility* (chapter 5), *decisions to be-*

Leadership: qualified for office and informed about the job; person you can follow; communicates well with people and knows how to deal with them.

Constituency Service: helps people in the district; keeps people informed about government and what it is doing; listens to what people have to say; watches out for district interests.

Trustworthiness: fulfills promises; not politically motivated; represents well the views of the district; honest; has high principles; takes the job seriously; does not exploit public office for personal benefit.

Each of the "likes/dislikes" responses (NES) was evaluated by three informed political scientists and was then placed in one of these categories; only responses on which all three judges agreed are used to compile the categories of relevant responses. These three variables were subsequently factor analyzed, and a single component emerged; this component represents the reputational capital of legislators among their constituents.

Readers may rightly be skeptical about the value of this variable, given the small number of cases in which an adequate sample of observations were actually obtained (≥ 30 respondents) and the consequent fact that the vast majority of former legislators are positioned at the mean. We are not ignorant of these limitations; we ask only that readers withhold their misgivings until the analysis unfolds because the variable fits very nicely within the pattern of the reported findings and the hypothesized relationships. Indeed, the statistical significance of reputational capital among the number of other relevant human capital variables included in our equations makes us confident that a relationship worth exploring exists here. Still, the use of this variable should be considered exploratory.

come lobbyists after leaving Congress (chapter 5), *postelective salaries* (chapter 6), and *training subsidies offered by special interests in the form of campaign contributions* (chapter 6). We discuss each of these variables as they are introduced into the analysis in subsequent chapters. At this point, we note only that each conveys information about the economic effects of on-the-job training in politics in general and Congress in particular. Because there are numerous ways to characterize the economic effects related to training, we will limit our discussion to just a few of the most salient effects.

Postelective Wages and Employment

First and foremost, congressional training should affect postelective salaries and employment. An inclusive skill package provides legislators with more employment areas in which to rent their human capital; since scarcity affects price, the dearth of these skills and the time it takes to accumulate them make such human capital financially rewarding. Legislators who have acquired broad skill packages thus stand the best chance for lucrative postelective salaries, and those who specialize suffer in this regard.

Campaign Subsidies

Legislator investments in general training influence the extent to which special interests subsidize campaign costs. Groups prefer to restrict campaign assistance to those willing to specialize in policy areas important to group interests. Consequently, generalists pick up the tab for their campaign costs, while specialists have their expenses subsidized through political action committee campaign contributions.

Career Mobility

In addition to larger campaign subsidies, specialization yields greater returns for legislators anticipating future career changes. We expect that specialized training in congressional politics—for example, within the confines of a clientele-serving committee—will ease legislators' career transitions after leaving Congress. Legislators with specialized training are in a better position to acquire the in-depth expertise necessary to move into different occupations, though the specialized nature of their human capital may reduce their initial (postelective) earnings—that is, the shadow price associated with career changes. Thus, we expect the acquisition of specialized human capital to enhance legislators' ability to change occupations after exiting Congress to a greater degree than broad political skills.

Lobbying

All of these relationships between career mobility and postelective salary are related in one way or another to training in congressional politics. But congressional training also equips legislators all too well for lobbying. Job training, after all, provides opportunities for acquiring the skills, information, and experiences—that is, human capital—that special interests find so appealing. Thus, skills acquired through congressional service are easily transferable to jobs as lobbyists, and we expect to find legislators abandoning their precongressional vocations and gravitating to lobbying since they are well-equipped skillwise to make that career transition.

The Politicians' Human Capital Model

The general model for explaining the returns to legislators from investments in human capital can be conceptualized as follows:

$$R = f(H, T, N, S).$$

Here R represents the returns on legislator investments in human capital, H is the (value of the) human capital that legislators possess prior to entering Congress (which includes abilities and endowments), T signifies the on-the-job training amassed in congressional politics, N represents the accumulation of human capital that is not (or only remotely) related to legislative training, and S stands for the breadth of skill sets.

The basic statistical model is as follows:

$$Y = f(X_1, \ldots X_{10}),$$

where Y represents postelective returns (for example, salary, job change), and

    Ability and endowments:
        X_1 = precongressional salary
        X_2 = prior political office
    Nontraining capital:
        X_3 = nontraining assets
        X_4 = reputational capital
    On-the-job-training in Congress:

X_5 = years of service on interest group committees
X_6 = years of service on prestige committees
X_7 = investments in on-the-job training
Breadth of skills:
X_8 = skill acquisition, or breadth of skills acquired
X_9 = general training (breadth of skills acquired × investments in on-the-job training)
X_{10} = life cycle investments in general training (breadth of skills acquired × investments in on-the-job training × tenure)

The measurement of these variables is described in table 3.3, and the appendix illustrates some of the basic statistical properties of these variables.[3] We elaborate further on these issues, and discuss the theoretical and substantive importance of the variables in greater detail, in each of the subsequent chapters. We add additional variables to our analysis as necessary in the case of particular equations. For now, we will refer to this equation simply as the *politicians' human capital model.*[4]

Summary and Discussion

In the preceding paragraphs, we have briefly sketched the conceptual and theoretical relevance of the variables used in our study. The independent variables form the politicians' human capital model, to which we will refer in subsequent chapters. The model incorporates (1) indicators of on-the-job training experiences in Congress, (2) measures of human capital accumulated during the congressional career, (3) estimates of the capital amassed prior to

---

3. We have examined some of the extreme outliers associated with various variables in the analysis and have found no reason to believe that these data points are inconsistent with the underlying dynamics of the variables. For example, two of the legislators scoring the highest in terms of life cycle effects were in Congress a total of sixty-eight years; the lowest score for general training went to a one-term legislator; two of the three legislators with the highest precongressional salaries were lawyers who graduated from prestigious law schools and who were employed in private practice, the highest-earning occupation for legislators; the lowest salary was paid to a legislator without a college education; the two highest postcongressional salaries went to a legislator in private law practice with former service as a judge and to a distinguished politician who served at all levels of government for about thirty years.
4. As a rule in testing propositions drawn from this model, we will normally consider variables with a .05 or higher level of significance (in two-tailed tests of significance) as exhibiting reliable relationships. In interpreting our results, however, we will not neglect variables approaching this level of statistical significance.

entering Congress through abilities and endowments, and (4) estimates of the breadth of the skills acquired through congressional service. We use this basic model or variants of it to assess the economic effects of on-the-job training in congressional politics. We believe that it captures the basic sources of human capital in politics and permits a reasonable assessment of the economic returns to congressional service.

We have explored the possibility that our sample of ex-legislators might be biased in some manner, thereby confounding our generalizations, but have found no evidence of such a problem. Ex-legislators in our sample were no more likely to experience long terms of congressional service, and therefore harbor more positive feelings toward their congressional experiences, than were legislators serving in the House between 1952 and 1996. Respondents in our sample also were no more likely to have exited the House on their own terms through either retirement or running for higher office. In addition, no evidence indicates a bias resulting from an oversampling of those with ties to business. In sum, our sample arguably is representative of legislators serving in Congress for the past half century.

Chapter 4

Congress as Workplace: The Production of Marketable Human Capital

In analyzing the organization of legislatures, scholars have highlighted a number of important characteristics, including susceptibility to decentralization (Weingast 1979), accent on retention (Mayhew 1974; Fiorina 1989; Parker 1992), and capacity to constrain opportunistic behavior (Shepsle and Weingast 1987; Weingast and Marshall 1988). But lost in these illuminating, firmlike comparisons is the fact that legislatures, like firms, supply training in conjunction with the production of goods, such as laws. And the experiences that go hand in hand with lawmaking are matchless: trading votes, becoming informed about legislative practices and procedures (for example, legislative earmarks, killer amendments, logrolling), gaining expertise in policy matters, developing personal relationships with high-ranking government officials, and deriving firsthand knowledge from hands-on opportunities to formulate legislation (for example, committee markups, pork barreling), to name a few. Given the panoply of skills acquired through legislative service, Congress is, among other things, a workplace for the production of human capital.

Legislatures, then, provide settings whereby politicians acquire esoteric information, skills, and experiences as by-products of their involvement in lawmaking. As one ex-legislator, reflecting on his training in Congress, wrote at the end of his survey: "10 years in Congress was a Ph.D. in people, issues, and management. It was the big leagues—if you didn't like the sight of blood, especially your own, you couldn't compete." Although many scholars see legislative activities as exclusively serving electoral goals, dedicated to promoting collective goods, or focused on internal career ambitions, we believe that there is more to congressional service than that. Specifically, the experiential learning that goes on in Congress also incorporates the formation of profitable human capital. By coupling training with lawmaking, then, Congress ensures that legislators derive marketable human capital from their everyday legislative experiences. This is a latent function of many political institutions.

In this chapter, we examine on-the-job training in Congress and the skills it imparts. We start by briefly identifying some categories of marketable human capital. We then describe the legislative activities that impart this capital—in particular, the general training that occurs through service in Congress. Next, we discuss how congressional committees supplement this human capital with specialized and general training. Such information is part and parcel of the capital legislators derive from training in congressional politics. In the final sections, our attention shifts to the forces that influence legislator investments in on-the-job training and affect the breadth of political skills acquired during congressional tenure.

Legislators' Marketable Capital

While legislators might merchandise a number of aspects of their congressional training, such as their familiarity with policy issues and bureaucratic agencies, the human capital commonly marketed by legislators falls into three broad categories: contacts inside Congress and the bureaucracy, knowledge of policy questions and the political process, and legislative skills exhibiting political know-how and savvy. We frequently think of legislators obtaining these skills as part of the job, and this may well be true; however, some legislators invest greater amounts of time and effort in acquiring and strengthening their grip on these facets of marketable human capital. We suspect that they do so because they anticipate reaping rewards a cut above those making smaller investments in these same congressional activities.

Contacts

Investments of human capital in nurturing and cultivating government contacts would seem to be particularly valuable, since legislators can exploit their network of personal friendships—for example, in the federal bureaucracy—to help both constituents and clients. Or they can draw on long-standing personal relationships with other legislators to pave the way for incorporating special interest benefits within legislation. We have assumed that contacts, knowledge, and political skills are equally worthwhile investments, but some observers may disagree. With respect to legislator contacts, for instance, Milbrath (1963) reported that the lobbyists he interviewed were convinced that knowledge of political issues and policy-making processes were more valuable than their governmental contacts. In a similar vein, Heinz and his colleagues (1993, 123) found that lobbyists felt that their experiences in Congress were key to understanding issues and decision-making processes.

We wholeheartedly agree about the significance of knowledge, but we urge caution before disregarding the relevance of contacts to congressional training, since some of the human capital marketed to special interests incorporates contacts made during officeholding. Such human capital can be effectively marketed to groups for good reason: contacts supply special interests with bureaucratic and legislative benefits dispensed only to those with personal connections. We might say that affable relationships provide personal incentives for bureaucrats to assist legislators in whatever way they can. For example, legislators' ability to benefit special interests by intervening within the bureaucracy, or expediting bureaucratic red tape that hinders special interests, is predicated on strong personal relationships with agency officials (Downs 1967, 69–70; Fiorina 1989, 41).

Knowledge

Knowledge comes in many different forms—information about issues, congressional practices, and legislative procedures are just a few of the ways knowledge is packaged. Issue-related knowledge is clearly important for obtaining congressional expertise; it also facilitates the switch to a different occupation when legislators leave Congress. Some legislators may translate their knowledge of specific legislation into postelective employment with groups affected by the legislation or regulated by agencies implementing that legislation. For example, legislators interested in taking jobs in the Defense Department when they leave Congress benefit from service on the House or Senate Armed Services Committees.

Information about congressional politics and contacts, however, have an edge over issue substance as sources of investment because issue familiarity fades with time, while knowledge of political processes and contacts in government remain intact far longer (Heinz et al. 1993, 125–27). This is one reason why information about congressional processes is so important—its durability through time makes such knowledge a worthwhile investment of human capital. Whereas issues and solutions to them may change (though this is certainly not a sure thing, as Kingdon [1984] notes), congressional procedures and practices exhibit far greater stability. Because of the half-life of such knowledge and its low rate of decay, information regarding legislative practices and procedures is especially invaluable to any group or industry doing business in Washington on a regular basis. This lesson does not escape the notice of politicians, legislators, or people who work the K Street corridor.

Skills

Aside from the obvious value derived from bureaucratic contacts and knowledge of congressional politics, legislators' investments also include highly marketable political skills. Even if only to enter lobbying, former legislators who decide to leave their precongressional vocations in favor of something different realize that they will need the appropriate skill sets. And since the jobs ex-legislators are best qualified to handle involve dealing with government, they, like the special interests employing them, place a premium on political skills acquired in Congress.

Political skills with commercial value as a rule incorporate adroitness in bargaining, brokering agreements, persuading adversaries, and shepherding legislation through the legislative process. For the most part, these skills equip legislators with the necessary political acumen and know-how to effectively advance group interests in Washington and engineer favorable policy outcomes. Legislators display their proficiency at these skills in their daily actions, well aware that repetition aids groups in evaluating the worth of this human capital.

Human Capital Formation through Legislative Service

We noted in chapter 3 that although specialized and general training were substitutes for one another, in the sense of generating different skill packages and returns, most legislators intentionally or unintentionally acquired doses of general training as by-products of their service in Congress. This human capital represents the general side of a legislator's investment portfolio, and all legislators acquire this asset to a degree. Indeed, it is hard to serve in Congress and do otherwise. Although marketable human capital can be derived from congressional experiences, and legislators are exposed to most of these experiences, legislators still make decisions regarding how much of this human capital to acquire.

It would be shortsighted to construe these congressional experiences as operating like a pinball machine, bouncing legislators from one educational experience into another with little rhyme or reason. The congressional process may seem to work in such a fashion, but legislators pick and choose the depth of their investments in these common (general) legislative experiences. Some legislators, therefore, devote greater amounts of time to—that is, invest larger amounts of human capital in—mastering the general information, skills, and knowledge acquired through service in Congress; conversely, others acquire little more than a superficial general education in these matters. Legislators, then, can be differentiated in terms of the extent to which they invest time in acquiring this general capital. For example, some legislators will be far better versed on matters of parliamentary procedure because they have invested greater amounts of time learning its intricacies, or more knowledgeable about legislative strategy because they have dedicated more time to ferreting out such information. Legislator decisions regarding the depth of general training to acquire vis-à-vis daily service in Congress are conditioned by preferences for specialized or general skill packages and the returns they yield.

This general education includes many of the lessons necessary to make legislators effective and skilled at their jobs, such as experiences dealing with the bureaucracy, navigating the congressional process, and fashioning legislative strategy. To some, this curriculum may seem little more than an elementary education in congressional politics, ignoring the institutional richness and nuances that make Congress so distinctive. However, general training furnishes more than just basic lessons about the legislative process and explanations of congressional lingo; it also instills a broader, integrated understanding of congressional politics that improves the marketability of human capital. We now turn to a discussion of the basic but informative lessons legislators derive from their everyday experiences in Congress.

Congressional Norms

A number of congressional norms provide valuable information about the nature of politics and the legislative process. Legislative norms go by a variety of names, including "folkways" and "rules of the game," and prescribe certain kinds of behavior or practices within particular situations and contexts. Norms are important because they place effective, informal limits on legislators' behavior, often operating where rules are absent, uncertainty flourishes, and custom and convention are accepted ways of proceeding. Legislators confront many of these conditions on a daily basis in Congress.

Even though legislators frequently disagree about the validity of particular norms and express less than undying devotion to most of them, norms still regulate significant areas of legislative behavior. Legislatively effective members require a good understanding of the nature of norms and how they constrain some behaviors while facilitating other kinds of actions. For this reason, knowledge of norms enhances legislators' human capital and therefore their value to employers.

Types of Norms

Matthews (1960) was one of the first scholars to catalog the norms underlying senators' behavior, identifying six "folkways." According to Matthews, senators were expected to (1) serve an "apprenticeship" period before actively engaging in Senate business; (2) give full attention to "legislative work"; (3) concentrate their legislative efforts in limited areas of "specialization"; (4) temper interlegislator conflicts with respect and "courtesy"; (5) pursue "reciprocity," as in the exchange of legislative votes; and (6) display institutional patriotism toward Congress in general and the Senate in particular. A similar set of norms appears to operate in the House, where members, too, are expected to serve an apprenticeship period, specialize through their committee assignments, avoid criticism of colleagues, and practice vote trading (Asher 1973).

To this list of cooperation-inducing norms, we might add universalism— that is, the notion that every legislator should find the particularistic benefits doled out by Congress equally available. Thus, near-unanimous passage of distributive programs, through the inclusion of pork barrel projects for all who desire them, is an example of how this norm is put into practice. This institutional norm is not only highly desirable but also quite rational. Since the delivery of particularized benefits is central to the reelection efforts of all incumbents, they have incentives to design rules ensuring that no one is forgotten when the pork is doled out. "On legislation supplying particularized benefits two points can be reasonably made. The first is that it is vital for members to win victories; a dam is no good unless it is authorized and built. The second is that winning victories can be quite easy; the best way for members to handle the particular is to establish inclusive universalistic standards" (Mayhew 1974, 114).

In recent years, a number of these Senate folkways have faded in importance, and this loose network of norms has come unraveled from time to time. For instance, new senators are not the least bit reluctant to participate actively in many aspects of the Senate's deliberations, thereby casting doubt on the efficacy of the apprenticeship norm. But then again, the notion of apprenticeship as a means of on-the-job training has just about disappeared from the face of the labor market, too (Schultz 1961, 10). Even specialization, while still common, is not as rigid as Matthews initially portrayed it.

Nonetheless, many of these norms survive; in particular, reciprocity and civility are not dead, although time and again the latter has been pronounced so. The persistence of these two norms may result from the fact that they ease legislative exchange, which is essential to the realization of important legislator goals such as reelection. Indeed, in eras of strong partisanship, reciprocity and civility are essential if the divergent interests of members are to be reconciled—for example, to pass pork-barrel legislation (Wilson 1986).

Benefits of Norms
These norms are frequently justified on the grounds of their relationship to the smooth running of Congress, or members' need to gain power, claim credit, advertise, or take positions on issues to impress constituents. In this vein, Weingast (1979, 259) writes,

> The informal rules of the legislature further collective goals and individual members' goals. Consider the dual norms of specialization and reciprocity which support the committee system. These norms foster the development of legislative expertise in a specific area so that complex proposals on diverse subjects can be considered simultaneously. Consequently the Congress as a whole need not consider each bill and individual representatives need not study and research the details of all legislation. The reciprocity rule provides the incentives to specialize by delegating the decision power of the legislature in a particular area to a specific committee. Individual members thereby gain greater influence in a particular area.

These norms unquestionably function in this way, but our argument pivots on a different point. Aside from its obvious functional utility, learning about norms is important because it magnifies legislators' skill in maneuvering legislation through Congress and in manufacturing bargains, compromises, and logrolls. The acquisition of such information, in turn, increases a legislator's human capital.

For example, effective legislators grasp the nuances and ins and outs of the reciprocity norm, which underlie the basic power of the ex post veto—the institutional power granting committees near-monopoly influence over legislation falling within their jurisdiction. To be ignorant of these matters is to risk influence over policies that fall outside one's own committee assignments (Shepsle and Weingast 1987). This knowledge pays dividends when employers are looking for legislator-employees who are skilled and knowledgeable at steering congressional outcomes toward group-preferred directions. The literature on socialization in Congress (see, for example, Asher 1973, 1975) correctly contends that norms affect legislative behavior but errs in ignoring the fact that this informal training involves the acquisition of valuable human capital.

Bureaucratic Regulations and Intercessions

Stigler (1971, 3) was one of the earliest scholars to call attention to the significance of regulations in earning profits for special interests: "Regulation is acquired by the industry and is designed and operated for its benefit." Before continuing, we should make two points clear: first, we recognize that regulations can in fact work for and in the public interest; second, some regulations can be particularly onerous to an industry and erode profits (McChesney 1987). Neither of these facts can be ignored, yet the same can be said about the considerable effort special interests exert to influence the substance, interpretation, and execution of federal regulations.

Members of Congress have access to a litany of powers and prerogatives for exercising control over the federal bureaucracy. For example, legislative hearings and investigations, congressional vetoes, mandatory reports, appropriations, and monitoring by inspectors attached to nearly every government agency serve this purpose. But legislators do not employ these measures simply to better supervise the operations of these vast bureaucracies. Their interest also stems from the desire to learn the ins and outs of the bureaucracy to better understand how to maneuver and navigate within the morass of red tape and hierarchical organization that represents bureaucratic decision making.

This knowledge is invaluable to groups seeking economic gain by using governmental regulations to get a leg up on the competition. Fifty-three percent of legislators responding to a 1993 congressional survey indicated that they would prefer to spend more time learning (that is, overseeing) how agencies are carrying out policies and programs. Of the twelve activities surveyed, only the personally labor-intensive activities of attending floor debate (59 percent) and studying pending legislation (78 percent) were in greater demand (Davidson and Oleszek 2002, 135). Mastery in bureaucratic dealings apparently constitutes a skill that both special interests and legislators treasure.

Of particular significance to special interests, no doubt, is knowledge of how to sidetrack government investigations, or the imposition of sanctions on industries, by regulatory agencies. A case in point is the Federal Trade Commission, which is responsible for acting against the noncompetitive and deceptive practices of businesses—acting in the public interest, so to speak. Despite its mission to safeguard consumers against corrupt or quasi-legal business customs, agency efforts can be derailed by legislator intervention: members of congressional committees and subcommittees with oversight and budgetary power over the Federal Trade Commission seem able to deflect these decisions in favor of firms and industries in their constituencies (Faith,

Leavens, and Tollison 1982). It is easy to understand why special interests might value such skills.

It is not just knowledge of the operations of the federal bureaucracy and how to manipulate it that is so valuable; contacts and personal friendships with those inside the bureaucracy also pay off. With such skills in hand, legislators are in a position to help potential employers obtain favorable regulations and agency decisions, and to expedite bureaucratic actions. Bureaucratic regulations are a good place for interest groups to enhance profits, and groups are willing to pay generously for those who have well-honed skills at bureaucratic intercessions. Not surprisingly, many legislators can legitimately boast of having major-league talent in this area.

The assistance rendered to groups falls well within the prescribed guidelines of both the House and the Senate. The House Committee on Standards of Official Conduct issued "Advisory Opinion No. 1" (1970, 1077), which provides legislators with considerable justification for interceding in agency business on behalf of groups:

> A Member of the House of Representatives, either on his own initiative or at the request of a petitioner, may properly communicate with an Executive or Independent Agency on any matter to request information or a status report; urge prompt consideration; arrange for interviews or appointments; express judgment; call for reconsideration of an administrative response which he believes is not supported by established law; federal regulation or legislative intent; or perform any other service of a similar nature in this area compatible with the criteria hereinafter expressed in this Advisory Opinion.

In July 1992, the Senate passed Senate Resolution 273, which established a new rule pertaining to representation of petitioners before federal agencies, largely propelled by the investigation of five senators who intervened on behalf of Lincoln Savings and Loan Association—the infamous "Keating Five." The inventory of actions senators may properly take on behalf of constituents in dealing with federal agencies resembles the list compiled by the House Committee on Standards. In short, legislators' bureaucratic interventions are backed by more than practice and precedent—Congress sanctions these efforts.

Bargaining Skills

The variety of political skills acquired through congressional service is rather mind-boggling, both in terms of breadth and uniqueness. There is naturally widespread recognition of the nuances of legislative bargaining, vote trading, coalition building, and the like. As Lindblom (1965, 70–71) characterized the machinations involved in bargaining,

> Partisan discussion . . . is limited to reassessing the gains and losses attached to various possible settlements; in an exchange of threats and promises the gains and losses are themselves deliberately altered by participants in order to influence other participants. . . . Certainly many manipulations of one decision maker by another work almost exclusively on perceptions and evaluations rather than on manipulations of the things perceived and evaluated.

Even learning the ins and outs of compromising requires skill—for example, in identifying and cultivating "focal points" of agreement and developing strategies, such as "commitment," to gain a comparative advantage in negotiations (Schelling 1960).

Nonetheless, the mere acquisition of these skills is not what sets Congress apart from other vocations, political and nonpolitical alike. Legislative skills are unique because legislators "practice" on "real" and often immensely complex problems in government, business, and society. As a result, legislators possess practical experience dealing with problems confronting economic sectors and industries. These learning experiences, derived from the realities that employers face, undoubtedly impress those employers. Thus, Congress provides a context for the development of problem-solving skills, seasoned in contemporary issues and controversies.[1]

And for the most part, dealing with such problems is not a one-shot experience (Lindblom 1965, 147). Legislators have numerous opportunities to practice these skills, which help in perfecting their application and use; indeed, we wonder whether a mastery of these skills could ever be attained without considerable repetition. As the allegoric New York cabbie told the out-of-towners inquiring about how to get to Carnegie Hall, "practice, practice, practice." The same advice could be extended to legislators seeking to become skillful at congressional politics.

Congressional Procedures and Processes

During their tenure, members of Congress gain knowledge about a variety of facets of congressional business such as logrolling and pork barreling. They

---

1. We add to this list the "consumer-service" skills acquired through constituency service, and legislators' ability to develop and practice these skills on a full-time basis—that is, at and between elections. Both business and politics involve consumer satisfaction, and most legislators excel at this dimension of their job (Parker and Davidson 1979).

quickly learn the value of taking cues from trusted colleagues on matters outside their specific areas of expertise. "There are too many decisions to be made across too wide a span of subjects; the issues involved are too complex for quick decision, and there is little time for anything else" (Matthews and Stimson 1975, 25). They find that the ability to wedge themselves into logrolls requires interpersonal skills, and perhaps some kissing up to leaders or at least finding a way to secure their good graces. In sum, legislators become savvy about legislative politics.

This knowledge pays off because there are few institutions as structurally complicated and procedurally intricate as the U.S. Congress. Moreover, the standard procedures that so marked the legislative process in the past have been changed so that less predictability pervades. "Variety, not uniformity," writes Sinclair (1997, 217), "characterizes the contemporary legislative process." It seems obvious that the uncertainties inherent in contemporary congressional procedures place a premium on those conversant with the intricacies of the legislative process as well as of congressional politics.

Perhaps equally important, information of this nature requires years to acquire. Since special interests want legislators who are both skilled in and informed about congressional politics, knowledge of legislative procedures yields potentially valuable income-earning knowledge. As Becker (1993, 53) prophetically speculates, "information about the political or social system—the effect of different parties or social arrangements—could also significantly raise real incomes."

Legislative Strategy

Information about the congressional process also includes awareness of procedural strategies. Not only must legislators skillfully fashion proposals incorporating various sweeteners, such as pork barrel provisions, but they must also be adept at reshaping unpalatable measures into more attractive ones. Along these lines, legislators master the nuances of "saving" amendments (compromise amendments that when adopted enhance the prospects for a bill's enactment), and "killer" amendments (which deliberately strengthen bills to the point that they alienate a majority of legislators, who subsequently vote against the measure). Failure to recognize such distinctions in parliamentary strategy obviously could have dramatic consequences for the odyssey of legislative measures.

For example, the passage of the controversial Iraq War funding bill in May 2007 pitted a Republican president against a newly elected Democratic Congress, conditions ripe for stalemate, conflict, and division. After weeks of haggling, the final agreement resembled a pork barrel measure more than a war spending bill. Snuggled within reasonable war expenditures, such as provisions for land-mine-resistant vehicles ($3 billion), homeland security ($1.1 billion), aid to Iraq ($1.6 billion), and the general conduct of the wars in Iraq and Afghanistan ($94.5 billion), were expenditures with little relationship to the war, like disaster farm aid ($3 billion), fighting wildfires ($465 million), assistance to rural schools ($425 million), and hurricane relief along the Gulf Coast ($6.4 billion).

Equally important is knowledge of how to fashion earmarks—home-district projects funded through narrowly written language in appropriations that avoid statutory or administrative, formula-driven standards. Earmarks are an increasingly important source of interest group income. In 1995, appropriations bills contained 1,439 earmarks, but this figure rose to 13,997 in 2005; likewise, earmarks in highway reauthorization bills amounted to a mere 10 in 1982 but climbed to 6,371 by 2005 (Utt 2006). In the past decade or so, earmarks have tripled in volume, to the tune of some $64 billion per year. Legislators rarely challenge earmarks in House debate out of a fear that their pet projects might come under scrutiny, a self-preserving twist on the reciprocity norm. Earmarks, then, are valuable assets that have universal appeal for those doing business with government or hoping to benefit through the distribution of federal monies; however, the talent for producing earmarks has come under increased scrutiny.

One result of the investigations of the corruption scandal triggered by former lobbyist Jack Abramoff was awareness of legislators' adeptness at securing earmarks on behalf of special interests. Consequently, the House rules adopted in January 2007 specifically targeted earmarks. The efforts of legislators sponsoring earmarks have become more transparent since they are required to publicly disclose the names of the recipients of the benefits; specify the purposes of the earmarks, taxes, or tariffs; and guarantee that they have no personal or spousal financial interest in the special benefit. Additionally, the chair of the House Appropriations Committee, David Obey (D-Wis.), indicated that all earmarks, as well as their sponsors, would be listed in the *Congressional Record* a month before final committee approval (Palank 2007, A21), thereby ensuring ample time for publicizing and criticizing such allotments.

These rule changes came about not merely because of the Democratic takeover of the Congress in 2007, but also in response to alleged past shenanigans in the House of Representatives. For example, former speaker J. Dennis Hastert (R-Ill.) and Representatives Ken Calvert (R-Calif.) and Gary Miller (R-Calif.) personally profited from the sale of land, the value of which allegedly increased as a result of earmarked funding decisions; however, the legislators claim that they were only securing badly needed funds for their districts (Weisman 2006). Whether or not these charges are legitimate, they underscore the visibility of earmarks; hence, legislators develop strategies for concealing them from public view, or at the very least for providing a justification that satisfies voters. Here, Fenno's (1978, 136–70) description of legislators' "explanations of Washington activity" probably comes into play. Thus, more than just deftness at drawing up earmarks adds appreciably to legislators' skill sets; they benefit from the ability to avoid appearing to enhance their own wealth or that of some special interest.

Public Relations

Legislators also gain valuable lessons in public relations and dealing with the mass media, essential training for those seeking high-profile jobs. Top officials in government and business often find themselves in front of cameras, interviewed by reporters, and answering queries from annoyed investors, suspicious stockholders, skeptical voters, snooping congressional committees, and so on. Since legislators are incessantly politicking—that is, of course, what a lot of lawmaking involves (for example, impromptu news conferences, floor speeches)—numerous opportunities exist to develop and sharpen effective public relations skills. Congressional service tests interpersonal communication skills.

Sometimes, however, no matter how hard legislators try, dealing with the media seems to be a losing proposition. Maintaining equanimity in the face of media attack is a trying if not brutal education for many members. One of our respondents recounted an episode in which he was speaking before a group of elderly citizens about the solvency of the social security system. He noted that with advancements in life-prolonging treatments, such as cancer drugs, the social security fund might be threatened even further as longevity increased. While this may seem a defensible if not a reasonable argument, the district press saw the matter differently, with headlines reading, "Local Congressman Believes Cancer Cures Are Bad Ideas." Whether or not experiences dealing with the mass media are pleasant, the wisdom derived from these encounters engenders skills valued outside Congress.

Electioneering and Constituency Service

It might seem odd that in discussing the basics of a general education in congressional politics, we have left until the end reelection and constituency service, even though legislators devote a large amount of their time toward those ends (Mayhew 1974), which seem to be interrelated (Parker 1986, 120–50; Fiorina 1989). We believe that learning about electioneering and constituency service is peculiar to members, so that training is likely to be highly specialized, even bordering by design on individualized instruction. For practical purposes, then, the human capital acquired through legislator experiences in electioneering and constituent service places these topics beyond the training designed to pass on a general sense of congressional politics.

To most members of Congress, elections and constituency service are primarily local matters, and it is difficult to persuade legislators otherwise. After a few elections, many legislators realize that whatever national forces arise do so rather infrequently, and then can normally be neutralized by a good local political base; hence, training tailored to the electoral needs of individual members provides the most appropriate instruction. And after legislators have established successful "home styles"—even though they may have no idea of the exact elements producing electoral victories—they simply continue the same behaviors as in the past (Fenno 1978, 189). Sure, campaign strategies concocted in Washington might fit some districts and states, such as partisan-swing districts. However, when all is said and done, most legislators feel greater comfort in falling back on their own political instincts, given that their livelihoods and congressional careers are at stake. In essence, they prefer to be masters of their own fates. Constituency service, too, must be fashioned to meet voter demands and district pressures, especially since many legislators view their constituencies in rather assorted terms—"kaleidoscopic," to use Fenno's characterization (1978, 1–30).

This is not to ignore the fact that political parties may instruct legislators on the mechanics of constituency service and the use of congressional perquisites for electoral ends, but when put into practice, where on-the-job training occurs, these lessons are ultimately personalized to members' needs. Whereas training in these matters is universal, in the sense that these activities constitute learning experiences for most members, the lessons gleaned are far from uniform. Unlike the general lessons about Congress we have described, campaign and constituency service experiences engender distinctive, personalized training; most of the experiential learning is highly individualized.

Even though the resulting capital is highly specialized, it can nonetheless be marketed for jobs chiefly within the constituency or in politics. This is not to ignore the possibility that these experiences might produce proficiency in other, more general, legislator skills such as public relations talents or a knack for legislative strategy. But such general training skills can also be acquired, perhaps more efficiently, through legislative experiences more general in nature.

Committees: Institutional Settings for General and Specialized Training

The preceding discussion has focused on the skills and information acquired through on-the-job experiences in Congress that generate marketable human capital. This capital is supplemented with additional general or specialized training, primarily occurring within the confines of congressional committees and subcommittees, where most of the real heavy lifting of legislative training occurs.

In the past, we have viewed committee service rather narrowly. At the same time that we acknowledge committees' capacity to help legislators get reelected, promote policy issues, and gain institutional influence (Fenno 1973), we brush aside the job training and the marketability of skills that also come from working in committees. For rational legislators, these considerations, too, come into play when deciding on committee assignments, especially given the economic benefits derived from committee service.

Committee Investments

Serving on certain committees may be a good way to earn electoral credit with the folks back home—position-taking, credit-claiming, and advertising, in Mayhew's (1974) classic vernacular—or even to satisfy the appetites of special interests for monopoly-like benefits. Equally important is the fact that such assignments provide on-the-job training experiences in substantive matters of public policy, contacts with governmental agencies and officials, and first-hand experiences in the formulation of public policy. From our standpoint, then, taking assignments on particular congressional committees requires investments of legislator time and resources, which are expected to pay off in the acquisition of skills and knowledge that enhance human capital and ultimately postelective employment opportunities.

Because committees are such good places to gain skills and to practice what has been learned, members of Congress not surprisingly invest considerable time and energy in their committee work. Davidson and Oleszek (2002, 135), for example, report that 48 percent of the legislators surveyed in 1993 indicated that they spent "a great deal of time" attending committee hearings and markups; no other lawmaking activity received close to the same dedication. In consuming so much time and attention, committee responsibilities incur significant opportunity costs, yet committee work remains a major legislative preoccupation. In fact, the percentage of freshman (Democratic) legislators requesting two committee assignments has grown from 38 percent in the Eighty-sixth and Eighty-seventh Congresses to more than 80 percent in the Ninety-sixth and Ninety-seventh Congresses (Deering and Smith 1997, 99).

Returns from Committee Service

The attention that legislators devote to their committee work is well warranted: manifold experiences, such as involvement in marking up legislation and learning the rudiments of parliamentary procedure, can be derived from participation in committee deliberations and are undoubtedly useful to future legislator-employees. Here, legislators also learn of informal committee gatekeeping powers and personally put into practice some of the lessons learned about reciprocity, specialization, logrolling, and coalition building. Committees, in essence, provide legislators with a more hands-on approach with respect to congressional decision making. Their reputation as "little legislatures" is well earned (Goodwin 1970).

Some of the returns from committee service come in the form of career mobility and highly competitive postelective salaries. Training on specialized committees, for instance, supplies the expertise required of career changes, whereas service on prestige committees increases employment options, thereby augmenting postelective wages. This is not to minimize the value of committee assignments in serving electoral needs (see, for example, Mayhew 1974; Shepsle 1978); however, committee investments also engender on-the-job training experiences that enhance human capital. In short, congressional committees, much like the larger institution, behave similar to firms in supplying on-the-job training along with the production of public policies.

Like committees, other institutional structures such as informal groups provide settings for learning about Congress, but none of them can rival congressional committees in terms of the variety of skills acquired, the ability to practice these skills on real-life problems, and the depth of knowledge imparted. Perhaps of greater significance, no other learning venue in Congress pairs training with production; hence, other structures lack the reinforcing institutional imperatives and incentives that encourage human capital investments. For these reasons, we have emphasized committees as avenues for on-the-job training in Congress.

Committee Types

For the purposes of our analysis, we specify two types of congressional committees—those that are the most powerful and possess the broadest jurisdictions in Congress, and those that are narrow in terms of jurisdiction, attractive primarily to clientele or special interests. A more comprehensive or
inclusive education (that is, general training) in congressional politics characterizes service on powerful, elite committees, while specialized training is associated with tenure on interest-group committees. We measure human capital investments in these two types of legislative committees in terms of years
of congressional service.[2]

Table 4.1 lists the committees that supply more inclusive perspectives on
congressional politics and the legislative process, at least to a greater degree
than committees in the service of special interests (table 4.2). Table 4.2 lists
the committees that we feel can be considered targets of special interests, and
therefore more specialized in policy interests, jurisdiction, and training. Table
4.3 supports this distinction to the extent that interest group contributions
are targeted at committees dealing with issues relevant to special interests;
most of the committees falling into the category of group serving appear on
this list. We have discussed the substance, knowledge, skills, and experiences
acquired through congressional service, but before examining how training in

TABLE 4.1. Types of
Committees Offering General
on-the-Job Training

Budget
Appropriations
House Rules
Ways and Means
Senate Finance

TABLE 4.2. Types of Committees
Offering Specific on-the-Job Training

Agriculture
Armed Services
Energy and Commerce
Financial Institutions (banking)
Interior
Merchant Marines and Fisheries
Transportation and Infrastructure

Note: Because of some differences in the jurisdictions of committees over time and between
the House and Senate, this list should be considered a general description of the types of committees classified as supplying specialized on-
the-job training.

2. The correlation between prestige and clientele (interest group serving) committees is $r = -.09$
and is not statistically significant at the .2 level; hence, multicollinearity should not be a problem in
interpreting the individual effects of these two variables.

congressional politics translates into skill packages, we turn to a consideration of the factors that influence legislators' investments in training.

Investment in on-the-Job Training

As we have shown, Congress provides numerous opportunities for members to acquire marketable human capital through mere service. However, as we have repeatedly mentioned, not all members avail themselves of these opportunities to the same degree. That is, in acquiring human capital, some legislators will invest greater amounts of time and effort in training than will others. Here, then, we examine the factors that affect legislators' investments in accumulating marketable human capital.

If on-the-job training is central to enhancing human capital, which is valuable in the marketing of ex-legislators, we expect such experiences to be related to postelective employment. We recognize, however, that careers in Congress supply more than just on-the-job training; reputations are formed and votes are taken, for example. And some of the human assets that enhance the prospects of postelective employment—such as party affiliation and previous employment—may be acquired prior to entering Congress. With this in mind, we queried ex-legislators about the importance of the following factors in obtaining their first jobs after leaving Congress: committee assignments,

TABLE 4.3. Committee Targets of Interest Group Money in the House of Representatives

Major Economic Sectors	Congressional Committees Receiving More than 10% of a Sector's Campaign Contributions
Agribusiness	Agriculture (18.42%)
Communications/Electronics	Energy and Commerce (17.83%)
Construction	Transportation and Infrastructure (14.93%)
Defense	Armed Services (23.75%)
	Appropriations (19.10%)[a]
Energy and natural resources	Energy and Commerce (16.94%)
Finance, insurance, and real estate	Financial Services (15.84%)
Health	Energy and Commerce (15.07%)
Transportation	Transportation and Infrastructure (16.03%)
Miscellaneous business	Transportation and Infrastructure (9.98%)
Labor	Transportation and Infrastructure (11.67%)

Source: Authors' calculations based on average amount (%) of all campaign money distributed by interest groups within an economic sector of the economy to House incumbents on individual congressional committees between the 106th and 108th Congresses; data from opensecrets.org.

[a]Members of the House Appropriations Committee Defense Subcommittee are the primary beneficiaries of PAC contributions from the defense industry.

leadership positions, contacts made as a member of Congress, prior political experience, voting record, party affiliation, reputation among voters, employment experiences prior to entering Congress, and expertise gained while in Congress.[3]

Importance of Training to Postelective Employment

Table 4.4 describes the frequencies for these nine survey items. The first column of this table ("very important" responses) shows that congressional training was quite valuable in obtaining employment, especially expertise (45.1 percent), contacts (42.1 percent), and committee assignments (32.5 percent). Evidence also indicates that other forms of human capital were significant—specifically, prior employment experiences (35.6 percent) and reputation (31.2 percent). Conversely, a large number of former legislators felt that voting record (37.6 percent), party affiliation (30.8 percent), and

TABLE 4.4.   The Significance of Elements of Human Capital in Acquiring Postelective Employment (in percentages)

Human Capital	Importance					N
	Very	Somewhat	Little	Not	Dk.	
Committee assignments	32.5	25.5	14.0	26.5	1.5	200
Leadership positions	22.5	26.2	16.6	30.5	4.3	187
Contacts made as a member	42.1	31.2	10.4	15.8	0.5	202
Prior political offices	29.2	29.7	18.8	20.3	2.0	202
Voting record	12.4	22.2	25.3	37.6	2.6	194
Party affiliation	19.0	25.1	21.5	30.8	3.6	195
Reputation among voters	31.2	35.2	12.1	20.6	1.0	199
Prior employment experience	35.6	29.7	13.9	18.3	2.5	202
Expertise gained in Congress	45.1	33.3	11.8	9.3	0.5	204

Source: Authors' survey of former members of Congress, 2004.
Note: All rows total 100 percent. Dk. = "don't know" response.

---

3. The exact wording of the question is as follows: "Thinking of the first job you held *after leaving Congress,* how important would you say the following factors were in obtaining that job—very important, somewhat important, of little importance, not important at all, or don't know." We have used the first job as a reference point for two reasons. First, we want to assure that all members of our sample have the same referent in mind when evaluating the factors important in their obtaining postelective employment. We believe this to be preferable to just asking legislators to identify important experiences. In this way, we follow Kingdon's (1981, 11–12) persuasive argument about the specificity of context in deriving meaningful responses. Second, after the first job, postelective experiences rather than on-the-job training in Congress may be responsible for future employment, thereby confounding the measurement of the effects of training on subsequent postelective employment.

leadership positions held (30.5 percent) did not contribute significantly to obtaining their first postelective jobs.

In sum, evidence shows that investments in committee assignments, gaining expertise, and making contacts—on-the-job training experiences as we have defined them—are significant factors in obtaining postelective employment; we cannot, however, dismiss the relevance of other forms of human capital that are not acquired through congressional training, such as prior employment or political experiences. Both training and nontraining human capital, then, seem to weigh heavily in obtaining postelective employment.[4] Consequently, we expect two dimensions, or factors, to underlie this pool of items, one representing on-the-job training in Congress and the other representing nontraining-derived human capital. This appears to be the case.

Measuring Investments in Training

As table 4.5 shows, the nine variables cluster into two well-defined dimensions, the first representing on-the-job training experiences in Congress—

TABLE 4.5.   Factors Important in Obtaining First Job after Leaving Congress

Questionnaire Item	Investments in Training Factor 1 Loading[a]	Nontraining Assets Factor 2 Loading	Communality
Committee assignment	.843[b]	.141	.730
Leadership position held	.761	.179	.611
Contacts made as a member of Congress	.759	.352	.700
Expertise gained in Congress	.806	.255	.715
Prior political offices	.457	.538[b]	.498
Voting record	.359	.609	.499
Party affiliation	.247	.648	.482
Reputation among voters	.261	.620	.452
Precongressional employment experience	.394	.570	.480

Source: Authors' survey of former members of Congress, 2004.
[a]Principal components for factor extraction; varimax rotation of extracted solution.
[b]Factor loadings >.5 marked in bold.

---

4. The questionnaire concluded with an open-ended question asking respondents whether "any other aspects of your congressional career not mentioned [in this series of questions] played a role in obtaining your first job after leaving Congress." No additional responses were provided, though one respondent felt that "contacts" should be divided into personal and nonpersonal relationships: "Contacts made as a member of Congress, as I stated, are very important, but the emphasis should be placed on the depth of the personal relationship with these contacts."

committee assignments, leadership positions held, contacts made while in Congress, and expertise acquired. The second dimension represents an assortment of factors that also create human capital but are only remotely tied to on-the-job training experiences—prior political experiences, voting record, party affiliation, reputation among voters, and precongressional employment experiences.

We performed the commonly accepted orthogonal rotation (varimax rotation) of the derived two-factor solution (see Rummel 1970, 391–93) for these nine variables to isolate a measure of the relevance of job training (factor 1) to postelective employment that is not confounded by other forms of human capital (factor 2).Table 4.5 describes the factor loadings associated with the individual dimensions. Thus, we obtain a measure of the relevance ex-legislators attach to their training experiences in Congress that is largely divorced from other forms of human capital. In so doing, we spare ourselves the worry that the conclusions we draw about the forces influencing investments in on-the-job training may be flawed because the latter measure captures both training and nontraining human capital.

We conceptualize this dimension of training experiences as measuring investments in on-the-job training, although the question from which this dimension is derived refers to the "significance" of various training and nontraining assets in obtaining employment after leaving Congress. We assume that the importance legislators attach to various congressional activities in obtaining their first postelective jobs reflects the investments made in them. In short, we regard the significance attributed to these activities as a proxy for investments in them: ex-legislators who attribute significance to a whole array of on-the-job experiences can be viewed as investing heavily in those experiences while in Congress; those at the lower end of the scale, who attribute little value to their training, are assumed to have invested less in those experiences during their tenure in Congress. As we demonstrate in chapter 6, there is no evidence that our respondents slanted their assessments of the importance of these skills.

We use this scale (factor 1, *investments in training*) alone and in combination with other measures of legislator skills to estimate the effects of investments in on-the-job training. The remaining orthogonal dimension serves as a measure of human capital derived through nontraining experiences in Congress, or merely *nontraining assets*. One final caveat is in order: our measure of investments in training does not differentiate between investments in specific or general training; it signifies only the investment devoted to the accumulation of human capital through on-the-job training. We leave it to our measures of committee tenure, and our interaction term representing investments in general training (described in chapters 3 and 5), to capture the effects of general and specialized training.

Analysis

The statistical model for explaining investments in on-the-job training is as follows:

$$T = f(X_1 \ldots X_7),$$

where T represents investments in on-the-job training, and

X_1 = number of years of service on interest group committees
X_2 = number of years of service on prestige committees
X_3 = prior political office
X_4 = senator
X_5 = precongressional salary
X_6 = tenure
X_7 = reputational capital

Overall Regression Results

Table 4.6 reports the ordinary least squares regression results. Heading the list of most important influences on training investments is *tenure*, followed by a group of three variables with considerably weaker effects—that is, *prior political office, senator,* and *reputational capital.* Length of service in Congress in-

TABLE 4.6. Explaining Investments in on-the-Job Training

Variable	B	Error	Beta	t	Significance
Senator	−.740	.267	−.180	−2.767	.006
Precongressional salary	−.000	.000	−.026	−.388	.699
Tenure	.038	.010	.303	3.689	.000
Prior political office	.474	.162	.195	2.932	.004
Interest group committee	.015	.010	.114	1.544	.124
Prestige committee	−.004	.011	−.027	−.359	.720
Reputational capital	.143	.063	.144	2.270	.024

Statistics
  R = .421
  R^2 = .177
  N = 218

Source: Authors' survey of former members of Congress, 2004.

creases investments in on-the-job training (beta = .303) because time on the job increases the opportunities for training, which ultimately enhance human capital. This result seems to follow Becker's argument (1993, 113) that time spent investing in human capital is equivalent to the amount invested: "Closely dependent on the embodiment of human capital is the importance of an investor's own time in the production of his own human capital. Own time is so important that an increase in the amount invested in good part corresponds to an increase in the time spent investing: in fact the commonly used measures of schooling and training are years of schooling and training, measures entirely based on the input of own time."

Ability and Endowments

Despite the fact that their previous jobs probably equipped them with some of the necessary political skills, those with prior political experience appreciate the value of and therefore invest in on-the-job training (beta = .195). Perhaps their prior political experience attuned these members to the value of congressional training. It is not merely that those with prior political experience are less naive about the legislative process; they also may be more adept, perhaps even efficient, at producing human capital by hunting down profitable training opportunities. This would not be too surprising since we have suggested that prior political office reflects a flair or talent for politics.

Somewhat surprising is the fact that *precongressional salary* has no statistical effect on investments in training. After all, precongressional salary incorporates important income-earning talents and endowments that should serve as divining rods to finding lucrative ventures in postelective employment. It seems reasonable, then, to expect legislators with lucrative precongressional salaries to minimize their investments in training in congressional politics, preferring instead to be entertained, like "spectators," rather than actively engaged, like "lawmakers" (Barber 1965). Hence, we might expect the wealthy to invest less human capital in congressional training, but such a negative relationship never appears.

Senator

Senators attribute little relevance to training experiences in obtaining employment, and their investments are apropos (beta = −.180), since senators can ride the prestige of their office in obtaining postelective employment to a greater degree than most officeholders; training, therefore, may be of marginal significance. In addition, many senators have served in the House of

Representatives, thereby further reducing the value of training. For senators, then, the returns from investments in on-the-job training are not worth the costs. This is not to suggest that senators eschew on-the-job training because they see no value in it; rather, it is probably more accurate to say that senators already possess many of these political skills long before they reach the U.S. Senate, perhaps as a result of previous employment as members of the U.S. House of Representatives, so further investments yield diminished returns.

Reputational Capital

We have included reputational capital in our analysis because we feel that reputations self-police the actions of politicians (Parker 2004). We might expect legislators with high levels of reputational capital to delve into their training experiences with greater vigor than others because devotion to congressional service is part of the persona of trustworthy and reputable legislators. Such a relationship between *reputational capital* and *investments in training* appears in our data, even if the effect is of only modest proportions (beta = .144).

Skill Sets and Congressional Training

Aside from investments in congressional training, breadth of acquired skills constitutes another consideration in the production of marketable human capital. The training legislators receive pays off in any number of ways, but one overriding concern is the degree to which it prepares legislators for an assortment of jobs, because the more employment options they have, the greater the competition to hire them and thus the higher their postelective salaries. In short, the breadth of skills acquired affects legislator marketability and subsequent postelective career options. For example, those with somewhat narrow skill sets are apt to find a limited number of bidders for their specialized knowledge and skills; consequently, job opportunities will be more restricted. Just the opposite would be true of those with inclusive or broad skill sets—that is, they have greater employment options, which ensures that they job hunt under the most auspicious conditions. Thus, attention needs to be given to the scope or breadth of the skill sets acquired through congressional service.

Skill Set Proficiency

Our measure of the breadth of skill sets is based on the responses of ex-legislators to five survey questions about the extent to which they felt their experiences in Congress provided the necessary skills for various types of generic occupations—that is, high-level corporate executive, midlevel corporate executive, interest group representative, high-level appointed governmental official, and midlevel governmental official.[5] Table 4.7 presents the frequencies for these questionnaire items.

This table clearly shows that ex-legislators feel somewhat shortchanged in acquiring skills appropriate for private sector employment. About two-thirds of former legislators felt that their stints in Congress provided few or none of the skills for corporate jobs. About 43 percent felt ill-equipped for either high- or midlevel corporate positions, while only about 20 percent felt the same about jobs in government.

Most members concede that even experience running all the "enterprises" associated with congressional officeholding (Salisbury and Shepsle 1981) fails to supply a sufficient level of corporate skill proficiency. Also rather stunning, though not unexpected, is the proportion of legislators who felt perfectly qualified to lobby—about three-quarters felt that Congress supplied either all or many of the skills necessary to pursue this vocation. Is it any wonder that so many legislators become lobbyists? This finding is consistent with our earlier point about the skills acquired in Congress and the relatively specialized market for these crafts. We address this point in the next chapter when we deal with the "lobbying trap" and the grooming of lobbyists.

TABLE 4.7. Breadth of Skills Acquired through Congressional Service (in percentages)

	Type of Employment				
Breadth of Skill Set	High-Level Exec.	Midlevel Exec.	High-Level Gov.	Midlevel Gov.	Group Rep.
Provided none of the skills	8.9	9.6	6.5	8.5	5.2
Provided a few of the skills	34.9	33.1	13.0	14.5	12.3
Provided many of the skills	42.6	29.4	52.9	42.7	54.5
Provided all of the skills	7.1	12.5	16.7	15.4	20.1
Don't know	6.5	15.4	10.9	18.8	7.8
Number of cases	169	136	138	117	154
Percentage	100	100	100	100	100

Source: Authors' survey of former members of Congress, 2004.

5. The wording of this question is as follows: "Experience gained in serving as a legislator often helps people to get a job after they hold office. We want to know how much your experiences in Congress helped to prepare you for various types of jobs after your congressional career. For each of the following jobs, estimate how well your job as a legislator prepared you for that type of employment—provided none of the necessary skills, provided a few of the necessary skills, provided many of the necessary skills, provided all of the necessary skills, or can't judge."

Measuring Breadth of Skill Sets

We expected these five questions to form a unidimensional scale reflecting the extent to which congressional service supplied proficiency in a broad range of occupational skill packages, and they did so. Table 4.8 describes the factor loadings associated with each of the individual variables. We interpret this broad skill set scale as measuring the degree to which legislators felt that their experiences in Congress equipped them for a variety of employment opportunities. We consider the variety and diversity of employment possibilities as representing the broad or inclusive nature of the skills acquired through congressional service.

Again, this is not simply a measure of the degree to which legislators dabble in diverse areas, thereby accumulating breadth without skill depth. Skill proficiency is incorporated into the measurement of the *breadth of skill set* and hence reflects not only the range of vocational skill sets acquired but also skill proficiency. At the upper end of the scale are ex-legislators who felt that congressional service provided them with all the necessary skills for jobs that ran the gamut from lobbying to high-level CEOs in the private sector; in contrast, those at the bottom of the scale felt that they had obtained few of the skills necessary for such employment opportunities during their terms of service.

Analysis

The statistical model used to estimate the effects of nontraining capital, precongressional capital, and on-the-job training on the *breadth of skill sets* departs from the basic model of politicians' human capital described in chapter 3. It does so by excluding variables—that is, *general training* and *life cycle investments*—that contain in some manner measurements of skills acquired

TABLE 4.8. Factor Analysis of Breadth of Skill Set Items

Questionnaire Item	Breadth of Skill Set Scale	
	Factor Loading[a]	Communality
High-level corporate executive	.769	.591
Midlevel corporate executive	.807	.652
Interest group representative	.783	614
High-level appointed official	.840	.705
Midlevel appointed official	.809	.655

Source: Authors' survey of former members of Congress, 2004.
[a]Principal component extraction.

through congressional service (that is, *breadth of skill set*); to do otherwise would introduce problems of estimation and specification that would severely undermine the conclusions drawn from these data. Therefore, the model estimated is:

$$S = f(X_1 \ldots X_7),$$

where S represents the breadth of the skill set acquired, and
X_1 = precongressional salary
X_2 = prior political office
X_3 = number of years of service on interest group committees
X_4 = number of years of service on prestige committees
X_5 = investments in on-the-job training
X_6 = nontraining assets
X_7 = reputational capital

Overall Regression Results

Table 4.9 presents the statistical estimates. Our statistical model seems to do a fairly good job in accounting for the *breadth of skill sets,* explaining about 25 percent of the variation in the scope of skill sets among our ex-legislators. It is clear from this table that *on-the-job training* is the single most important factor enhancing the skills of politicians (beta = .423).

The only factors aside from *on-the-job training* that significantly influence the breadth of skills that legislators acquire are *prior political office*

TABLE 4.9. Explaining the Breadth of Skills Acquired through Congressional Service

Variable	B	Error	Beta	t	Significance
Precongressional salary	−.000	.000	−.050	−.802	.424
Prior political office	.331	.153	.138	2.169	.031
Interest group committee	.002	.008	.015	.248	.805
Prestige committee	.009	.009	.065	1.056	.292
Nontraining assets	.117	.061	.117	1.923	.056
Investments in training	.416	.062	.423	6.746	.000
Reputational capital	.081	.060	−.083	−1.359	.176

Statistics
R = .497
R^2 = .247
N = 218

Source: Authors' survey of former members of Congress, 2004.

(beta = .138) and to a lesser degree *nontraining assets* (beta = .117). The relevance of these two variables is not inconsistent with our model since we expect that skills pertinent to private and public sector employment can be acquired through precongressional as well as nontraining experiences. Still, neither *prior political office* nor *nontraining assets* rivals the importance of *investments in on-the-job training* in broadening legislators' political skill packages. Simply put, there seems to be no better alternative in acquiring a broad skill package than training in legislative politics.

Training

Training investments are three times more influential than either of the other significant variables (*prior political office* and *nontraining assets*) in accounting for the breadth of skill sets. Legislators' investments in obtaining firsthand experiences in making bargains, nurturing contacts within the bureaucracy as well as Congress, working within their committees, and gaining expertise as they engage in all of these activities greatly expand their range of political skills.

We cannot, of course, attribute the acquisition of extensive skill sets to investments in general training, as logical as that might seem, since our training measure fails to distinguish between general and specialized investments. Yet the relationship between inclusive skill sets and investments in training implies that investments in a range of training experiences, perhaps even specific ones, may impart a certain breadth to skill sets. Indeed, we might view the accumulation of committee assignments (Parker 1992; Deering and Smith 1997), even rather specialized ones, as a way in which legislators broaden their political skill sets by expanding areas of expertise.

Committees

We have excluded tenure from this equation since its effects are largely subsumed by the variables measuring number of years of committee service.[6] As we observed earlier, committees are good places to acquire specialized or general training, yet the effects of committees in expanding skill set breadth, especially service on prestige committees, seem almost trivial. We can only surmise that committee effects are somehow suppressed in this instance, but are

---

6. The correlations between tenure and the two types of committees are:

Prestige committee service, $r = .47$
Interest group committee service, $r = .36$.

Both correlations are highly statistically significant (alpha < .001).

of greater consequence in supplying occupational versatility and specialization. You might think that working within the confines of committees would provide settings for legislators to expand their skill sets, since as a result of their small size and minimal threats to participation (for example, embarrassment or revelations of ignorance), opportunities for meaningful participation are greatly enhanced. Nonetheless, no evidence indicates that committee service works in this manner. We should not, however, leap to the conclusion that investments in specialized or general training are wasted; as we show in the next chapter, investments in committees help legislators acquire the specialized skills and knowledge that enable them to retool in preparation for changing vocations after exiting Congress. And, of course, since our measure of on-the-job training includes learning experiences that are often derived through committee service, some of the effects of congressional committees could be easily absorbed by our job-training variable.[7]

Summary and Discussion

We have found evidence that supports basic propositions drawn from our human capital theory: tenure in Congress increases the relevance of and therefore investments in on-the-job training; this training, in turn, enhances the breadth of skills acquired during congressional tenure. To put the matter more simply, tenure in Congress creates opportunities for members to gain a variety of skills. Just as legislators are apt to chuckle that the longer they are in Congress, the greater their appreciation of the seniority system, so, too, their regard for on-the-job training is likely to grow with tenure.[8]

What may be of somewhat greater surprise is that although legislators in our sample placed a premium on the skills acquired through congressional service in obtaining their first postcongressional job, many felt rather impoverished in the acquisition of skills relevant to private sector employment. In contrast but not surprisingly, most felt well equipped to become lobbyists. From the perspective of our model, most legislators should indeed feel comfortable stepping into the role of lobbyist after leaving Congress. That is, after all, probably the best use of the human capital they have acquired through congressional service.

---

7. Training investments are, for example, significantly correlated with investments in interest group–serving committees.

8. While these conclusions may not be earth-shattering, they are essential to establishing the important causal connections linking training experiences and the skills they produce (that is, human capital) to postelective returns.

Chapter 5

Returns to Specialized Training: Career Mobility and Grooming Lobbyists

As we have repeatedly argued, legislators invest in on-the-job training because of the expected returns. To judge by media exposés, the returns to officeholding should be equated with lucrative postelective salaries, but the gains from congressional service result in other types of returns. For example, legislators contemplating career changes can acquire specialized training, enabling them to switch vocations after leaving Congress. In labor economics, the term *career mobility* is used to characterize changes between occupations, whereas *occupational mobility* refers to changes in the tasks performed on the job; however, we use these terms interchangeably.

Our examination of legislators' mobility includes tracing their movements from job to job as well as their employment in lobbying along the course of their postelective careers. In addressing the first issue, we also examine the second. That is, most former legislators at one time or another travel down the lobbying road. As a result, we are unavoidably drawn into noteworthy controversies surrounding lobbying employment.

First, we tackle the connected questions of the extent to which former legislators abandon precongressional vocations to lobby after leaving Congress, and whether lobbying merely constitutes a way station for temporarily unemployed ex-legislators. Then, we weigh in on the conventional public choice argument, which holds that lobbying jobs are payoffs for prior legislative favors to special interests. Finally, we explore the possibility of marketlike controls on the penchant for lobbying among former legislators—a sort of lobbying life cycle. That is, lobbying legislators may face prospects of diminished effectiveness and marketability as time goes on and their contacts in Washington dry up. At that point, as cynics might say, lobbying legislators are forced to find "real jobs." While this mechanism is unlikely to lead to across-the-board cessation in legislator lobbying, it merits attention because it offers an alternative to strictly enforced, legally imposed controls or governmental policing of legislator lobbying, two largely ineffective weapons for controlling legislator opportunism (Parker 2004). With such potential, we are rather amazed that this mechanism of lobbying control has for so long remained unexamined.

We conclude the analysis by examining factors that enhance the likelihood of career changes and employment in lobbying. We are particularly interested in the relevance of specialized and general human capital accumulated through congressional training to ex-legislators' ability to: (1) shift vocations after exiting, and (2) take jobs as lobbyists immediately after leaving Congress. We expect both occupational transitions to be fueled by specialized rather than general training, since occupational mobility is an anticipated return from specialized training.

Economic Effects of Specialized Training

As mentioned in chapter 4, legislators have numerous reasons to specialize that relate to the functioning of Congress, including "the bulk and diversity of legislative measures, the pressure of non-legislative tasks, the desire to maximize their legislative impact, pressure from their colleagues, and fear of retaliation if they upset someone else's apple cart" (Matthews 1960, 249–50). While such considerations explain the need for specialization in legislative institutions, they provide little information about legislators' choices regarding specialized training. We might expect legislators' decisions about specialization to revolve around considerations of personal or occupational background and committee assignments, and they do; however, "perceptions of the interests of his present and possible future constituents" also enter into legislators' preferences for specialties (Matthews 1960, 250). So, to some extent, legislators' specialization reflects the interests of prospective employers or expected future employment. Particularly relevant in this regard is specialized training's capacity to prepare legislators for occupational or career changes—that is, to abandon precongressional vocations for new ones.

We have emphasized the importance of developing expansive skill sets in augmenting postelective salaries, but changing occupations necessitates different considerations that are best addressed through specialization. In short, specialized rather than general training is the key investment strategy for career or occupational changes; it supplies the relevant expertise necessary to switch vocations after leaving Congress. With specialized training, legislators have opportunities to acquaint themselves with government and business leaders involved in an issue area; learn the major dimensions of consensus and disagreement within an economic sector; gain familiarity with industry organization, regulations, practices, products, and problems; and above all, acquire industry-specific information of all sorts. We suspect that legislators' investments in specialized human capital during their time in Congress are geared toward these ends.

Paradoxically, career changes by and large lead legislators to the same vocation—lobbying. One legislator, for example, noted on his survey that he was quite disappointed with the career opportunities after he left Congress, writing, "they're all [about] lobbying, and I didn't want to be a lobbyist." This survey respondent's comments provide a real glimpse into the labor market for ex-legislators. While the number of legislators who take up lobbying may seem alarming, lobbying is undoubtedly the best utilization of the human capital accumulated through on-the-job training in Congress.

A large number of groups take part in Washington politics and could use the services of former legislators. Even so, they are usually hired for one thing and one thing alone—lobbying. Politicians consequently end up working for special interests as lobbyists, the most valued use of their skills. Just as Coase (1990, esp. 157–70) wisely notes that economic resources, if left unencumbered, will gravitate to their most valued use, we expect the human capital of politicians to do the same. In this light, lobbying is little more than the vocation that makes the best use of the talents and skills legislators have acquired through their experiences in Congress. It is ironic that congressional service imparts important skill packages, but the relevant jobs—in particular, lobbying—seem to be distasteful to citizens and legislators alike.

Duration of Unemployment

One important question that supersedes issues of career mobility is the length of time legislators need to find their first jobs after leaving Congress. Job mobility is certainly important to former legislators, but like most out-of-work individuals, finding a job frequently takes precedence. We of course do not expect legislators to remain unemployed for very long, but just how long remains a mystery. Thus, we next examine the number of days ex-legislators were unemployed before receiving their first jobs after leaving Congress.

With all the skills that ex-legislators have acquired through service in Congress (chapter 4), and the large number who return to the same vocation, it should not be too surprising that they do not remain unemployed for long; rampant unemployment would be the truly shocking revelation. According to employment chronologies, 58 percent of our sample of ex-legislators found jobs immediately after their terms ended, and just under 10 percent had to wait as long as a year; about 22 percent waited six months or longer to get their first jobs. Generally speaking, former legislators waited something on the order of six months (mean = 192 days) to find jobs.

Democrats

Little can be said about why some former legislators found employment sooner than others except that congressional Democrats seem to have had more difficulty finding jobs ($r = .30$), a result that remains robust regardless of the number or types of variables included in explanatory equations. In fact, it is the only consistently significant factor we can find that influences the time ex-legislators require to find jobs. Democrats might stay unemployed longer because they lack the private-sector business connections of Republicans, which open more doors in the search for employment. Aside from this partisan relationship, we can find no other explanations for the length of time former legislators remain unemployed.

Future Lobbyists

We found absolutely no evidence supporting the contention that postelective employment as a lobbyist represented some sort of a payoff for faithful service while in office. Taken to its logical end, this argument implies that soon-to-be-lobbying legislators should have no problem finding postelective employment, obtaining it sooner than others less connected to special interests. After all, special interests should have jobs lined up for well-connected legislators as soon as they leave office.

Rules prohibiting lobbying by former members of Congress for a one-year period after leaving office may cause lapses in work though not in employment. If lobbying is merely a sinecure, then employing legislators without having them do any work whatsoever should pose no problems. Special interests should have no qualms about employing and paying legislators-turned-lobbyists whether or not they are on the job (performing labor). In fact, soon-to-be legislator-lobbyists report taking their first jobs, on average, well within the 365-day cooling-off period required before ex-legislators can lobby Congress. Thus, if lobbying jobs are payoffs for favors performed while in office, we would expect legislator-lobbyists to experience relatively brief periods of unemployment. Such was not the case.

We performed an independent-samples t-test to examine the equality in the mean number of days spent unemployed by former legislators entering lobbying relative to those pursuing other vocations. This test reveals no significant differences, whether or not equal variances are assumed. Here, the lack of a correlation ($r = .03$) would seem to contradict the claim that postelective employment is an ex post facto payoff for services provided by legislators. The absence of a "lobbying premium" in finding postelective employment foreshadows results presented later in this chapter.

Future legislator-lobbyists appear to spend about six weeks longer (mean = 223 days) searching for their first postelective jobs than other non-lobbying legislators (mean = 181 days). Even if these differences are not highly significant, what kind of a payoff is this? This finding, juxtaposed with those reported later, leads us to question the extent to which postelective employment represents interest group payments to legislators for services rendered while in office. In short, how widespread is this supposed scourge on democracy?

Life after Congress: Reentering the Labor Force

Our primary concern here is to unravel the postelective career paths of ex-legislators. We do so in two ways designed to give the reader a feel for the labor market exigencies facing former legislators. First, we examine the extent to which ex-legislators return to their precongressional vocations. More precisely, we compare precongressional vocations to the types of jobs obtained after leaving Congress to gain a sense of the market for former legislators' services.

Second, we track legislators' postelective occupational changes by examining the effects of postelective jobs on subsequent employment to see whether they stray from their postelective vocations and, if so, the types of occupations they seek. Of particular interest is the frequency with which ex-legislators forsake former vocations for jobs as lobbyists. Our theory leads us to suspect that the limited market for legislators' services will encourage many of them, at one time or another, to seek employment with special interests as lobbyists; hence, we expect to see defections of ex-legislators from their precongressional jobs, or even their initial postelective vocations, to lobbying.

The Lobbying Trap

As a result of the nature of market for their services, legislators find themselves in the grips of a predicament after they leave Congress—what we call the lobbying trap. Lobbying is a trap because it is so enticing to former politicians. But it is not enticing, as many might think, because of the exorbitant salaries paid ex-legislators to lobby former colleagues. It is alluring because it makes such good use of the human capital acquired by legislators, and little additional skill acquisition is normally required; hence, the transferability of skills gives the lobbying profession an undeniable attraction for legislators and their sunken investments in human capital. Simply put, the transition from legislator to lobbyist poses few problems, matters of conscience notwithstanding. Of course, not everyone is so trapped; we expect to find legislators with more altruistic motives gaining suitable postelective employment outside the lobbying trade.

We suggested earlier, perhaps somewhat facetiously, that legislators are not born to be lobbyists. Rather, we suspect that most effective Washington lobbyists are made within the halls of Congress, since there is simply no better education for lobbying than training in legislative politics (chapter 4). This statement seems to contain more than a shred of truth since only a single ex-legislator in our study entered Congress from a job as a lobbyist (table 5.1), but many more left to become lobbyists. And both trends may be on the rise: in 2006, at least eight members of Congress were lobbyists before they won election (Stolberg 2006, A15), and a steady increase has occurred in the percentage of former legislators who turn to lobbying immediately after leaving Congress (table 5.12).

The attraction of lobbying is rather glaring: about one-fifth to one-quarter of former legislators became involved in lobbying during the course of their postelective careers. Lobbying also ranks as one of the most popular vocations at several points along the postelective career paths of ex-legislators (table 5.1). Moreover, a substantial proportion of those who left behind careers in law, education, public service (that is, government), and business found employment as lobbyists after leaving Congress. Indeed, 37.1 percent of our ex-legislators took positions as lobbyists within their first three jobs af-

TABLE 5.1. Vocations of Former Legislators from Precongressional Occupation to Current Job (in percentages)

Vocation	Prior Job	First Job	Second Job	Third Job	Current Job
Lobbying	0.4	23.2	24.3	19.0	19.5
Education/Nonprofit	8.5	12.9	19.1	22.0	9.0
Private sector and financial	35.7	15.6	19.9	23.0	11.8
Law	33.0	25.4	12.5	13.0	14.9
Public service	22.3	16.5	21.3	18.0	3.2
Retired		6.3	2.9	5.0	41.6
Percentage	100	100	100	100	100
Number of cases	224	224	136	100	221

Source: Authors' survey of former members of Congress, 2004.

ter leaving Congress. As table 5.2 indicates, more than a quarter of those who entered Congress from the private sector (28.8 percent), and more than one-third of those previously employed in government jobs (36 percent), found employment as lobbyists in their first job after leaving Congress.

As we noted, legislators are drawn to lobbying because, unlike most professions, it does not require skills that are occupation-specific, and the human capital acquired in Congress is easily transferable. This is one reason why we refer to lobbying as a trap. Lobbying serves as a trap in another way as well: training in politics qualifies legislators only for a narrow range of jobs—in particular, lobbying. It is hardly a coincidence that former legislators, who never thought about what they were going to do after leaving Congress, were considerably more likely than those who did so to go into lobbying within the course of their first three postelective jobs (54 percent). Only ex-legislators citing economic opportunities in the private sector as the reason for thinking about postelective employment exhibited a greater proclivity to enter lobbying (63 percent). These percentages take on even greater significance considering that a little more than one-third of our sample of former legislators assumed positions as lobbyists within the same period. We might conclude, then, that when in doubt about what to do, former legislators find lobbying a straightforward answer.

Lobbying as Interim Vocation

Even if lobbying is a trap, perhaps it is only temporary. We might anticipate that leaving office, perhaps abruptly as a result of electoral defeat, leaves little opportunity for legislators to plan for future employment with any degree of

TABLE 5.2. Movement between Precongressional Vocation and First Job after Leaving Congress by Former Legislators (in percentages)

First Job	Lobbyist	Education/ Nonprofit	Private Sector/ Financial	Lawyer	Public Service
		Precongressional Vocation			
Lobbyist		15.8	28.8	11.1	36
Education/Nonprofit		57.9	10	4.2	14
Private sector and financial		5.3	30	9.7	4
Lawyer			1.3	62.5	22
Public service	100	21.1	17.5	11.1	18
Retired			12.5	1.4	6
Number of cases	1	19	80	72	50
Percentage	100	100	100	100	100

care; hence, jobs as lobbyists might hold some immediate attraction, but only initially. Down the line, however, ex-legislators can be expected to plan better for their second and third jobs and consequently to leave lobbying behind. Simply put, after legislators find better jobs, they quickly abandon lobbying. This could mitigate the problems arising from having ex-legislators lobby their former colleagues, since legislators' interest in lobbying would be short-lived. If so, we would expect to find former legislators leaving lobbying for other occupations. Tables 5.3 and 5.4 address this question.

The evidence seems rather mixed with respect to legislators moving away from lobbying in subsequent jobs after leaving Congress. For example, those who entered Congress from educational or nonprofit institutions showed a decline in their appetites for lobbying between their first (15.8 percent) and

TABLE 5.3. Movement between Precongressional Vocation and Second Job after Leaving Congress by Former Legislators (in percentages)

	Pre-Congressional Vocation				
Second Job	Lobbyist	Education/ Nonprofit	Private Sector/ Financial	Lawyer	Public Service
Lobbyist		6.7	39.5	19.6	20.7
Education/Nonprofit	100	46.7	18.6	10.9	17.2
Private sector and financial		40	23.3	17.4	6.9
Lawyer			2.3	21.7	17.2
Public service		6.7	11.6	26.1	37.9
Retired			4.7	4.3	
Number of cases	1	15	43	46	29
Percentage	100	100	100	100	100

TABLE 5.4. Movement between Precongressional Vocation and Third Job after Leaving Congress by Former Legislators (in percentages)

	Precongressional Vocation			
Third Job	Education/ Nonprofit	Private Sector/ Financial	Lawyer	Public Service
Lobbyist	10	33.3	15.2	12
Education/Nonprofit	70	16.7	12.1	20
Private sector and financial		30	21.2	28
Lawyer			30.3	12
Public service	20	16.7	12.1	24
Retired		3.3	9.1	4
Number of cases	10	30	33	25
Percentage	100	100	100	100

Note: There were no legislators who were lobbyists prior to entering Congress in the data analyzed in this table.

second (6.7 percent) jobs. And the percentage of legislators who held jobs in public service before entering Congress, but took jobs in lobbying after leaving, declines from 36 percent (table 5.2) after the first job to 20.7 percent (table 5.3) by the second job.

Conversely, the percentage of legislators who entered Congress from the private sector and took jobs as lobbyists rises from 28.8 percent to 39.5 percent by the second job. Similarly, an 8.5 percent increase in the percentage of lawyers in lobbying occurs during the second job. In sum, no clear-cut evidence indicates that ex-legislators take up lobbying to fill time until another job comes along; lobbying often is the "other job" that comes along.

Perhaps more telling is the fact that legislators who switch precongressional vocations to become lobbyists spend considerable amounts of time in the job, whether it is their first, second, or third. As we note later (table 5.9), among former legislators who abandoned their precongressional vocations, lobbyists spent anywhere from about five (second job is lobbying) to seven (first job is lobbying) years in the job—not a lifetime, but given the age of most exiting legislators, a sizable segment of their postelective employment livelihoods. Lobbying clearly is not a short-term solution to postelective unemployment.

Returning to Precongressional Careers

One viable alternative to postelective employment as a lobbyist is to return to one's precongressional occupation, which for most members is not lobbying. And, indeed, a large number of ex-legislators returned to the same vocations they held prior to entering Congress. This is not too shocking since considerable resources are consumed in learning a new vocation and perhaps in abandoning already accumulated human capital (and accompanying sunk costs) relevant to a previous occupation.

We do not want to belittle the pull of prior occupations, but only about one in three ex-legislators who left employment in law, the private sector, or government returned to these vocations during their second or third jobs (tables 5.3 and 5.4). Precongressional employment in either the private or public (government) sectors has the greatest difficulty in enticing former practitioners to return. For example, 62.5 percent of lawyers returned to practice law after leaving Congress, while only 18 percent of government workers and 30 percent of private sector employees returned to their precongressional vocations (table 5.2). Legislators from precongressional private and public sector occupations were also more likely to take jobs as lobbyists after leaving Congress. From the vantage point of these legislators, then, lobbying was more lucrative than returning to precongressional jobs in either the private or public sectors. Or perhaps more accurately, the returns from taking jobs as lobbyists were significantly greater than those obtained from returning to prior occupations in government and the private sector, despite the costs of retooling or learning a new vocation. But then again, lobbying entails little retooling for most ex-legislators, who have already incurred many of the necessary costs through their job training in Congress.

Public-Spiritedness and Postelective Employment

Another obvious alternative to lobbying jobs requires financial sacrifice on the part of former legislators—that is, trading salary for job prestige or philanthropic employment. Such employment is commonly found in charitable and nonprofit organizations, such as universities. Here, then, we address the issue initially raised in chapter 2—namely, that legislators might be driven by public-spiritedness to seek training appropriate for employment reflective of their altruistic motives. Given an earnest commitment to broader social goals, as reflected in prior public-service employment, we expect public-spirited legislators to seek training experiences equipping them for employment in charitable, educational, or philanthropic institutions, which represent perfect outlets for their nonmonetary interests.

Generally speaking, little evidence supports the idea of any major movement on the part of ex-legislators from jobs in government to educational or charitable organizations (tables 5.2–5.4). A mere 18 percent of legislators who entered Congress from the public sector returned to governmental employment, and only 14 percent found their way into employment with educational or philanthropic organizations. Indeed, twice as many legislators who left public service for Congress took their first jobs as lobbyists (36 percent) as found employment with educational or philanthropic organizations.

Still, we cannot ignore the 57.9 percent of legislators who entered Congress from prior positions in educational or nonprofit institutions and returned to the same vocations after leaving Congress. This certainly lends credence to the possibility that those motivated by less material returns found training experiences befitting postelective employment. However, this relationship may be confounded by the attraction of returning to a prior profession or the costs of not doing so, since few public-spirited legislators considered their postelective employment prospects appealing. That is, those who found postelective employment in educational and nonprofit organizations were more likely than others to be disillusioned with their employment prospects (figure 6.1). Public-spiritedness clearly comes at a price, a cost that most of those with training in government seem reluctant to pay and one that results in impoverished job prospects for those with prior experience in non-profit institutions. Our study of human capital in politics, then, stumbles across the same conclusion as many economic studies of rational behavior: public-spiritedness is treated rather poorly, economically speaking.

Are Lobbying Jobs Payoffs?

Many postelective career paths appear at some point to go through lobbying. For example, with the arguable exception of education and other nonprofit institutions, lobbying has attracted sizable percentages of legislator-employees from every vocation: 25 percent of those who assumed positions in public service immediately after leaving Congress were employed as lobbyists in their second jobs (table 5.5), and 19.2 percent found such employment in their third jobs (table 5.7); 45.5 percent of those previously employed in the private sector or by financial institutions took jobs as lobbyists the second time around (table 5.5).

The pervasiveness of lobbying along the postelective career paths of ex-legislators could easily lead to the popular inference that lobbying jobs are payoffs for faithful service to special interests while in office. This is something of a stylized fact in the rent-seeking literature, and anecdotal evidence certainly makes this hypothesis believable. However, this argument has rarely been subjected to empirical testing (for an exception, see Eckert 1981). Tracing the postelective careers of legislators furnishes evidence relevant to assessing the validity of this proposition. Specifically, if lobbying jobs are payoffs for

TABLE 5.5. Movement between First and Second Jobs after Leaving Congress by Former Legislators (in percentages)

	First Job after Leaving Congress					
Second Job	Lobbyist	Education/ Nonprofit	Private Sector/ Financial	Lawyer	Public Service	Retired
Lobbyist	36	10	45.5	11.4	25	
Education/Nonprofit	16	45	4.5	8.6	25	50
Private sector and financial	24	30	40.9	8.6	9.4	
Lawyer	4			31.4	15.6	
Public service	20	10	9.1	34.3	25	
Retired		5		5.7		50
Number of cases	25	20	22	35	32	2
Percentage	100	100	100	100	100	100

previous services performed at the behest of special interests, lobbying legislators should exhibit little occupational mobility since they definitely have no reason to abandon their lucrative lobbying sinecures.

Lobbying jobs' attractiveness to ex-legislators is no surprise, but as we noted, the attraction or pull may result from skills acquired in Congress as easily as from payoffs for previous legislative assistance rendered. As one ex-legislator volunteered,

> Knowing the right people in government agencies, and knowing the Chairman of House and Senate committees and subcommittees, and committee staff, having worked with all of these people, has helped significantly in my lobbying work. Having served as chairman of three Appropriations subcommittees helped [me] to know how and where to obtain money for clients. Also knowing the process of government and Congress has been extremely helpful.

This legislator clearly has amassed valuable (that is, marketable) human capital that would warrant top price, and special interests would gladly pay it, whether or not he personally had performed favors for them in the past.

If lobbying jobs represent some form of quid pro quo transaction, we would expect ex-legislators to take positions as lobbyists with the special interests they so faithfully served while in office, and to hold on to these sinecures until they retired or died. In short, former legislators would rarely stray beyond their first lobbying jobs, which would be the explicit payoff for aiding group causes during their tenures in Congress. More precisely, we would expect a lack of occupational mobility beyond the first job. Nothing could be further from the truth, however: lobbyists change jobs and occasionally even careers.[1] Tables 5.5 through 5.7 describe the patterns of ex-legislators' employment in their first, second, and third jobs after leaving Congress.

Despite the constant hoopla about politicians taking jobs as payment for services rendered while in office, our data offer little evidence in support of this argument. In fact, findings contradicting this proposition readily crop up. For example, many former legislators move from their initial (first job) posi-

---

1. Those who contend that postelective employment is a payoff by special interests might argue that since legislators deal with multiple interest groups, they have a series of jobs to go to after leaving Congress; hence, having a number of jobs is to be expected when legislators exit. However, since ex-legislators remain in their first and subsequent jobs for a considerable period of time (seven or more years), agreements on employment beyond the first job are likely to be subject to if not to magnify problems inherent in incomplete contracts, such as the inability to anticipate future contingencies and moral hazards.

tions as lobbyists, and few retire from them. In addition, although lobbyists may continue to lobby, they do so at the very least with different employers and are not averse to leaving lobbying for other professions.[2]

We are also not persuaded that economic-minded employers would find hiring slothful legislators—just there to collect a check—particularly good for

TABLE 5.6.   Movement between Second and Third Jobs after Leaving Congress by Former Legislators (in percentages)

	Second Job after Leaving Congress					
Third Job	Lobbyist	Education/ Nonprofit	Private Sector/ Financial	Lawyer	Public Service	Retired
Lobbyist	24	10.5	11.8	18.2	29.2	
Education/Nonprofit	16	47.4	23.5	18.2	12.5	
Private sector and financial	28	26.3	35.3	27.3	8.3	
Lawyer	8	5.3		27.3	20.8	
Public service	20	10.5	29.4	9.1	20.8	
Retired	4				8.3	100
Number of cases	25	19	17	11	24	2
Percentage	100	100	100	100	100	100

TABLE 5.7.   Movement between First and Third Jobs after Leaving Congress by Former Legislators (in percentages)

	First Job after Leaving Congress					
Third Job	Lobbyist	Education/ Nonprofit	Private Sector/ Financial	Lawyer	Public Service	Retired
Lobbyist	42.1		29.4	4.3	19.2	
Education/Nonprofit	15.8	75	5.9	4.3	26.9	50
Private sector and financial	26.3	16.7	23.5	17.4	30.8	
Lawyer	0		5.9	43.5	3.8	
Public Service	10.5	8.3	35.3	17.4	19.2	
Retired	5.3			13		50
Number of cases	19	12	17	23	26	2
Percentage	100	100	100	100	100	100

2. There is, perhaps, another argument about why lobbying jobs do not constitute payoffs for favors performed while in office. Even if a narrow range of vocations matches their skills, the training experiences of ex-legislators still assure them a comparative advantage in the hunt for these (lobbying) jobs; thus, there is no shortage of employment opportunities. As a result, the rational, enterprising politician wishing to maximize returns would not find it beneficial to restrict the job search to a single employer, employment search and matching costs aside. Ex-legislators have cornered the market for lobbying services and can increase their returns through competitive bidding for their services rather than by merely committing to one buyer or special interest without testing the waters. In contrast to theories suggesting that postelective employment as a lobbyist is a quid pro quo exchange for previous favors, we see the on-the-job training experiences of legislators and the resultant human capital they accumulate as contributing causes at a minimum.

business. It seems rather odd that rational employers would allow any erosion of their profits by condoning featherbedding by lazy ex-legislators. Even if lobbying positions were part of the bounty ex-legislators collected for past services performed, employee shirking would set a bad example, destructive of organizational morale and the efficient functioning of the organization (Downs 1967, chapter 6, esp. 63–71). The bottom line is, of course, employer profits, but gains must be balanced against outlays, some of which come in the form of long-run organizational costs. Can there be any doubt that indolent legislators drive up organizational costs?

This is not to naively assert that lobbying positions are never handed out, like sinecures, to former legislators who have enriched company profits by extraordinary amounts while in Congress. Unfortunately, that type of hiring persists. Even so, we suspect that it is less common than assumptions in economic and political research or media exposés imply.

These arguments, in conjunction with empirical findings about the duration of unemployment for soon-to-be-lobbying legislators and other results reported later in this chapter, give us reason to pause before embracing the notion that ex-legislators are hired as lobbyists as a reward for favors delivered while in office. Indeed, it seems more rational to employ ex-legislators as hired guns because their congressional training and connections will efficiently and effectively boost employer profits in the here and now. Perhaps we have underestimated the linkages between lobbying jobs and favors for special interests because our statistical analysis is too gross to pick up the nuances operating in this veiled, favor-trading market; then again, media infatuation with major exposés of corruption may have jaded us toward this perception.

Does Lobbying Have a Life Cycle?

Lobbying has an appeal that former legislators find difficult to avoid, especially given the specialized market for their services. This conclusion is not too startling, since even the unsophisticated would have probably predicted it. What is rather unique about these results is that they reveal legislators' willingness to abandon precongressional vocations for jobs as lobbyists. Perhaps more important, lobbying is not a job that politicians take lightly, just because they are temporarily out of work; on the contrary, ex-legislators leave their second and third occupations to become lobbyists. You can take men and women out of lobbying, but all too frequently, it seems, you cannot take lobbying out of them. Indeed, their training in Congress has seen to that all too well.

Our first reaction is that this conclusion does not bode well for our political system. But things may not be as bleak as they seem at first glance because the lobbying activities of legislators may be naturally curtailed by mechanisms aside from their retirement, death, or impairment—specifically, a life cycle to the influence of legislator-lobbyists. That is, lobbying by ex-legislators could be naturally constrained by time and legislative turnover. Considerable legislative effort has been directed at controlling lobbying—for example, through passage of laws requiring lobbying registration—but little attention has been given to the market dynamics associated with lobbying, and in particular, to the fact that the demand for the lobbying services of individual legislators may decline with time.

If former legislators market to special interests knowledge of and contacts with officials inside Washington in addition to substantive expertise, then as time passes, these contacts disappear with turnover in Congress and the bureaucracy. Similarly, the influence and access they possess dissipates. For that matter, legislators' knowledge of policies and the policies themselves may become outdated within a few years after leaving Congress. Evidence indicates that issue familiarity and knowledge decay with time among former legislators turned lobbyists (Heinz et al. 1993, 125–26). As a result, the demand for ex-legislators' lobbying services may diminish over time. In short, there may be a life cycle to the lobbying activities of ex-legislators: they may prosper in the early years after their departures from Congress, when their knowledge and contacts are fresh, but decline with time.

One former legislator alluded to such a cycle: "Most ex-members living in D.C. are engaged in various forms of lobbying. Their specialized committee assignments help, but mainly their overall access [is what matters]. This diminishes over time because of turnover in Congress." This does not necessarily mean that lobbying is naturally constrained if enough time passes, since it is doubtful that special interests will have difficulty finding and cultivating replacements for these used-up lobbyists. Nonetheless, the possibility of a life cycle to the lobbying activities of former legislators makes a lot of sense. If this life cycle indeed exists, we should expect to see lobbyists move into other vocations over time because their diminished congressional contacts and knowledge become less valuable to special interests. The evidence certainly seems suggestive of such a mechanism.

For example, by the third job, close to 60 percent of the ex-legislators who took positions as lobbyists in their first job after leaving Congress were doing something else (table 5.7). Just over a third (36 percent) of those who were lobbying in their first postelective jobs continued as lobbyists in their second jobs (table 5.5). Between the second and third jobs, this figure drops to just 24 percent (table 5.6). Former legislators clearly are not confirmed lobbyists. They may do more than take a stab at this vocation, but they are not in any way wedded to this profession by will as much as skill.

We do not deny that legislators are attracted to lobbying; however, it would be an exaggeration to contend that lobbying is the only vocation for which legislators have a flair. Lobbying may best suit the talents of ex-legislators, but it is not the sole outlet for their human capital. Simply put, legislators do not have to make a beeline to the headquarters of interest group organizations after leaving office; they have other employment possibilities beyond returning to their precongressional vocations, although such opportunities are more problematic than employment as lobbyists.

There is, of course, the other side to the coin—that is, legislators seem manifestly drawn to lobbying, whether or not their contacts and knowledge have dried up. Like all vocations, lobbying requires sunk investments, so weaning ex-legislators from this activity altogether is likely to be a fool's errand. Indeed, almost 60 percent of those legislators who chose to lobby immediately after leaving Congress were also lobbying in their present jobs (table 5.8), and 42.1 percent of those who were lobbyists in their first jobs after leaving Congress were still lobbying in their third jobs (table 5.7).

Nonetheless, we suspect that journalists and congressional critics exaggerate the number of legislators who become lobbyists as soon as they leave Congress—the figure is 22.7 percent in our sample of former legislators. Still, a far greater number (37.1 percent) have taken jobs as lobbyists within their first three employment opportunities. And further complicating the issue, former legislators retire from lobbying at lower rates than in other professions; for ex-legislators, apparently, the job is too much fun, too lucrative, or

TABLE 5.8. Movement between First Job after Leaving Congress and Current Job by Former Legislators (in percentages)

	First Job After Leaving Congress				
Current Job	Lobbyist	Education/ Nonprofit	Private Sector/ Financial	Lawyer	Public Service
Lobbyist	58.8	7.4	9.1	5.4	13.9
Education/Nonprofit	5.9	33.3	3.0	1.8	13.9
Private sector and financial	5.9	7.4	30.3	5.4	16.7
Lawyer	2.0		9.1	50.0	2.8
Public Service		3.7	3.0	3.6	8.3
Retired	27.5	48.1	45.5	33.9	44.4
Number of cases	51	27	33	56	36
Percentage	100	100	100	100	100

just too easy to permit retirement (table 5.8). With these facts in hand, we cannot be too sanguine about life cycle controls on the lobbying activities of former legislators. Legislators clearly can find their way into lobbying at any point along their postelective career paths and have incentives to do so.

Factors Promoting Career Changes

We have now described the postelective career paths legislators commonly follow, but aside from insinuating the dynamics underlying these occupational transitions, we have done little to empirically tie legislators' specialized human capital to career mobility. That is, we have yet to demonstrate that specialized human capital is, in fact, linked to the career changes we have previously described—for example, abandoning precongressional occupations and taking jobs as lobbyists. Next, therefore, we examine the forces promoting these career changes and the role of specialized training.

We analyze first the variables leading ex-legislators to move to different vocations after leaving Congress, and then those that drive ex-legislators to choose lobbying as their first postcongressional job. In contrast to the way in which many observers portray exiting legislators, these career decisions are not one and the same, although the two variables are interrelated ($r = .35$). In conjunction, they supply complementary perspectives on the forces underlying the occupational mobility of former legislators. In both situations, we expect factors associated with specialized training to increase the likelihood of career transitions.

Methods

For this section of the analysis, we categorize ex-legislators with respect to whether they returned to their precongressional vocation during subsequent postelective employment. If they switched vocations, they are coded as 1; if they returned to the same vocation within the first three jobs they held after leaving Congress, they are coded as 0.[3] This provides a measure of job mobil-

---

3. We use the span of three jobs as the interval for recording whether ex-legislators returned to their first postelective jobs. Our reasoning is that beyond the third job, other labor market factors, such as subsequent job and postelective experiences, may intervene to confound the relevance and significance of congressional training on job mobility. That is, if we include, say, their fourth or current jobs as expressions of the accumulation of human capital in Congress, these latter jobs may not be related to the human capital acquired in Congress but rather may result from a buildup of postelective experiences. One result of expanding the number of postelective jobs examined might be to exaggerate the capacity of congressional training to equip ex-legislators with the human capi-

ity—that is, the ability of ex-legislators to move to new vocations. Confining our measurement of career change to the first three postelective jobs may seem a rather short span of time for making inferences about the postelective employment of legislators. However, this job span encompasses the vast majority of the remaining income-earning years of ex-legislators, in light of the number of years they spend in these jobs (table 5.9) and the age at which legislators generally exit Congress.

We use a similar convention for analyzing the decision to become a lobbyist—that is, former legislators are coded as 1 if they became lobbyists immediately after leaving Congress and 0 otherwise. Since both measures of occupational change are dichotomous dependent variables, we use logistic regression to estimate the effects of the independent variables. We use the basic human capital model (see chapter 3) to account for legislators abandoning prior vocations and taking jobs as lobbyists.[4] The only major deviation is that we include *postelective salary* to predict the move to lobbying, since the argument is often made that the lucrative salaries associated with lobbying entice legislators into this trade. Our objective is to assess the extent to which training in Congress and the human capital produced pave the way for postelective occupational changes. We include all aspects of human capital, aside from

TABLE 5.9. Mean Number of Months Spent in Postelective Occupations among Legislators Who Switched Vocations[a]

Vocation	First Job	Second Job	Third Job
Lobbying	82.50	58.00	71.00
Education/Nonprofit	72.65	48.00	59.73
Private sector and financial	92.79	78.93	124.20
Law	82.14	108.00	
Public service	56.48	52.71	73.50
Number of cases	102	60	39

Source: Authors' survey of former members of Congress, 2004.
[a]Defined as legislators who never returned to their precongressional vocation in three subsequent postelective jobs.

tal necessary to pursue new and different vocations. We feel that limiting the span of employment to three jobs ensures an adequate time period for ex-legislators to draw on congressional training and experiences to find new vocations; a reasonable period for human capital acquired through congressional training to remain potent; and a limited enough time period to reduce the likelihood that postelective job experiences would intervene to confound occupational changes resulting from on-the-job training in congressional politics.
4. We refer to ex-legislators as abandoning precongressional occupations for postelective positions as lobbyists because only one of the respondents in our sample listed his precongressional vocation as lobbyist. Therefore, for all practical purposes, former legislators taking postelective jobs as lobbyists are indeed leaving behind precongressional vocations.

that derived through training, to ensure that the effects of training on career changes do not capture stocks of human capital produced through other means.

Switching Careers

Our theory suggests that investments in human capital increase the marketability of political skills, thereby equipping politicians with the wherewithal to find new vocations. Career changes are quite difficult and taxing: moving to a new vocation or embarking on a new career often entails learning new skills, terminology, information, and the like, which necessitates specialization. And lobbying aside, abandoning one's precongressional vocation is normally an economically perilous and personally costly venture. These risks are hard to ignore, but ex-legislators overcome these barriers through specialized training in Congress.

Congress is unique in this regard since it provides rich opportunities for legislators to specialize in diverse and numerous policy areas, thereby enabling legislators to familiarize themselves with and gain expertise in a variety of economic sectors. Indeed, the congressional process encourages legislators to specialize in this manner. Expectations of career changes underlie investments in specialized human capital; consequently, we expect legislators who make investments in specific rather than general human capital, and specialized rather than general training, will more likely change careers after leaving Congress. In fact, we might expect general training to reduce the chances of career changes since it fails to supply the necessary specialized capital underlying career changes—a negative relationship between the two variables.

Analysis

"Individuals obtain returns to human capital investment by achieving both higher prices for the rental of their human capital services, that is, increased wages, and greater opportunities to rent these services, that is, increased employment in the labor market" (Bloch and Smith 1977, 550). Consistent with this argument from labor economics, we find that investments in human capital increase the likelihood of legislators changing vocations after leaving Congress. And a large number of legislators apparently make the necessary investments, since 42.6 percent of our sample switched vocations from their precongressional occupations after leaving Congress. This is a fairly high level of occupational mobility, especially given that we are measuring occupational change, not merely taking another job in the same occupation. Table 5.10 reports the estimates for the various variables in our human capital model as they affect legislators changing vocations.

Abilities and Endowments
Two factors leading ex-legislators to switch to different occupations are precongressional salaries (the higher that salary, the greater the likelihood of changing vocations) and prior political officeholding (previous employment in politics increases the likelihood of switching occupations). Training in Congress helps engender occupational changes, of course, but given the nature of the transition—switching occupations, not merely jobs—human capital in the form of abilities and endowments seems essential. Perhaps more perplexing is why large precongressional salaries fail to tempt ex-legislators to return to their former occupations. After all, given the obstacles facing occupational changes, the sunk costs already invested in precongressional vocations, and the financial value of existing human capital relevant to the latter, what would motivate officeholders to gamble by switching occupations? We offer three explanations that are consistent with both these data and our arguments.

First, to the extent that economic talent is incorporated into precongressional salaries, high earners are exceptionally capable and therefore adept at mastering new occupations. For them, occupational change represents a challenge, not a barrier. Second, having attained monetary success as well as high

TABLE 5.10. Human Capital and Decisions to Switch Vocations

Variable	B	S.E.	Significance
Precongressional salary	.000	.000	.014
Prior political office	.778	.397	.050
Service on prestige committee	.023	.024	.333
Service on interest group committee	.053	.024	.023
Broad skill set	.306	.225	.174
Investments in training	.358	.182	.050
Life cycle investments	.033	.019	.080
General training	−.872	.396	.028
Nontraining assets	−.201	.170	.237
Reputational capital	−.182	.160	.255

Statistics
Number of cases = 200
Percentage correctly predicted = 69.0
Log likelihood = 230.467
Chi-square = 43.403 (10 d.f.)
Nagelkerke R^2 = .262

Note: Coefficients are derived from a logistic regression. S.E. = standard error.

political office, ex-legislators may simply want to explore other challenges, such as new vocations. Finally, precongressional salaries are shorthand representations for legislators' stores of human capital, so the higher the salaries, the larger the stocks of human capital that can be devoted to career changes, which consume considerable capital. Simply put, sizable precongressional salaries can be thought of as proxies for human capital accumulated prior to entering Congress, and such abilities and endowments fuel occupational changes. As Sicherman and Galor (1990, 178) observe, "individuals acquire skills and experiences in one occupation in order to be able to move to another occupation."

Specialized Training
Despite the significance of abilities and endowments, on-the-job training also surfaces as important in inducing ex-legislators to change occupations. Here, too, we finally see some evidence that investments in committee specialization pay off: the number of years served on committees servicing clientele groups increases the likelihood of switching jobs; in fact, judging from levels of significance, it is one of the most reliable factors in this regard. Human capital acquired within the confines of specialized congressional committees provides bases for retooling and acquiring skills necessary for leaving old vocations for new ones. Indeed, we suspect that the specialized nature of committee business facilitates ex-legislators' capacity to switch vocations after leaving Congress. In short, specialized training derived from service on committees with narrow policy jurisdictions enables ex-legislators to move to different vocations beyond their precongressional jobs.

While we might expect such specialized (human) capital to lead former legislators to take jobs as lobbyists after leaving Congress, no significant relationship exists between service on interest group committees and taking jobs as lobbyists after exiting Congress (table 5.11). Lobbyists are indeed specialized, but legislators pursuing specialized training are not destined to become lobbyists. Evidence also shows that training in congressional politics itself promotes occupational mobility: investments in on-the-job training increase the likelihood that ex-legislators will move to different vocations some time in their first three jobs after exiting Congress, and the relationship between life cycle investments and occupational change approaches statistical significance. We will say more about life cycle investment in acquiring inclusive skill sets in the following pages.

We feel confident in concluding that training in congressional politics enhances career mobility among legislators. In terms of our theory, then, legislators anticipating career changes after leaving Congress invest heavily in training while in office—in particular, training within the confines of specialized legislative committees. At this point, we introduce a new variable into the statistical analysis—namely, *general training*—that is theoretically and empirically relevant to our analysis and represents an important element in the politicians' human capital model.

General Training

While specialized training appears to influence career changes, no evidence indicates that the breadth of skills acquired through congressional service has any impact whatsoever on career mobility. In fact, some evidence shows that *general training,* a variable closely associated with broad skill packages, may reduce the likelihood of career transitions. On the surface, the negative relationship between *general training* and career changes (table 5.10) implies little more than that general training reduces the likelihood of career transitions. We believe, however, that this relationship is relevant to the broader issue of the differences between specialized and general training.

As we noted, specialization is the route for legislators envisioning career changes, and general training is of little use in changing professions, perhaps because acquiring expertise sufficient for a lateral move into another profession—legislators are generally too old to start from the bottom and work their way up—requires skill specialization. Neither an expanded skill set nor extensive investments in general training provides the necessary (specialized) capital to foster career changes. We might speculate that in contrast to specialization, general training reduces the likelihood of successful career transitions because of its failure to supply the requisite human capital, like expertise. Simply put, career changes require investments in training, but it is primarily intensive, specialized training, such as occurs within narrowly defined legislative committees. This negative relationship between career changes and general training supports our argument that specialized rather than general training provides the human capital underlying career changes.

In sum, we find considerable evidence suggesting that investments in specialized human capital ease transitions to new or different vocations. This relationship arises—assuming that the occupational change is not to lobbying—because switching vocations requires a lot of preparation in terms of time and skill acquisition. Hence, training in congressional processes translates inputs of personal time and specialized human capital into the development of the necessary skills, information, knowledge, and experiences facilitating career changes. We offer one small caveat about occupational mobility: 60.7 percent of the vocation switchers turned to lobbying at some time during their subsequent jobs, while 25.8 percent of those who returned at some point to their precongressional occupations took jobs as lobbyists sometime during their first three postelective jobs. These findings may indicate job mobility, but there is certainly little evidence of occupational variety.

Lobbying

As we have shown, occupational changes frequently result as legislators take positions as lobbyists. There is, of course, a large demand for lobbying skills, and few are as well equipped as are former members of Congress, whose day-to-day experiences have inescapably prepared them for just such opportunities. However, if we are to believe journalistic reports, job training and skill acquisition play a minor role if any in attracting legislators to lobbying after they leave office. They are portrayed, like Pavlov's dog, as merely lured away by their insatiable appetites for saliva-inducing salaries.

While perhaps an accurate depiction in a few instances, far more is involved in the process by which legislators, or politicians in general, turn to lobbying—the proverbial dark side of politics. Volumes of training alone push them in that direction. This state of affairs arises out of the most innocent of circumstances: on-the-job training equips officeholders with unique political skills that are primarily of value to those who seek some governmental benefit or program—that is to say, special interests. Therefore, we expect training to underlie decisions to become lobbyists. Table 5.11 reports our findings with respect to the movement to lobbying immediately after leaving Congress.

Analysis

We introduce three additional variables into our model that are of scholarly interest: *membership in the U.S. Senate, party affiliation,* and *year of entry into Congress.* The first two variables probably need little discussion since they address simple descriptive statements about the association of Democrats, Republicans, and senators with lobbying, and none of these variables is significant. Year of entrance into Congress is statistically significant and therefore warrants explanation. In fact, *year of entry* is one of the most important variables affecting the likelihood of ex-legislators taking jobs as lobbyists after exiting Congress.

Cohort Effects

We have argued elsewhere (Parker 1996) that Congress's membership is undergoing transformation. Members who cherished the intrinsic returns of officeholding, such as power and national prominence, are being replaced by others who relish officeholding for the wealth that can be expropriated through congressional service. The latter are attracted to legislative service because of Congress's capacity to manufacture and dispense rents to economic interests. This has resulted in adverse selection in the membership of Congress, as more recent generations engage in rent-seeking activities to a greater degree than earlier cohorts—for example, raising and spending more money on their congressional campaigns.

For this reason, we included an indicator of the year legislators first entered Congress. The adverse-selection argument leads us to expect a significant, positive relationship with lobbying: the later a legislator entered Congress, the more likely he or she will be interested in financial gain, and the greater the likelihood that he or she will take a job in the highest-paying postcongressional vocation—lobbying—after leaving Congress. We were not disappointed: lobbying is exceptionally appealing to recent legislative cohorts (table 5.11).

Recent generations might turn to lobbying because their brief tenure has deprived them of opportunities to obtain the training necessary for acquiring expansive skill sets. And, indeed, recent generations do invest less in training than earlier cohorts ($r = -.15$)[5] and are less active than earlier cohorts in such congressional activities as speech making and offering legislative amendments (Hibbing 1991, 417). But as table 5.11 shows, the effects of year of en-

TABLE 5.11. Human Capital and Decisions to Become Lobbyists

Variable	B	S.E.	Significance
Precongressional salary	.000	.000	.265
Prior political office	.384	.490	.434
Service on prestige committee	.008	.029	.791
Service on interest group committee	.003	.026	.917
Broad skill set	.212	.304	.485
Investments in training	1.008	.262	.000
Life cycle investments	.073	.026	.005
General training	−1.604	.597	.007
Nontraining assets	−.232	.211	.270
Postelective salary	.000	.000	.066
Reputational capital	−.533	.283	.059
Party affiliation	.345	.376	.359
Senator	.602	.812	.458
Year elected	.062	.021	.003

Statistics
Number of cases = 201
Percentage correctly predicted = 82.1
Log likelihood = 173.219
Chi-square = 52.289 (14 d.f.)
Nagelkerke R^2 = .340

Note: Coefficients are derived from a logistic regression. S.E. = standard error.

5. This correlation is statistically significant at the .02 level in a two-tailed test of significance.

try do not merely capture the lack of training or skills resulting from a short tenure in Congress; even when these variables are controlled for, generational effects persist.

Generational Changes

In table 5.12, we examine further this question of adverse selection by presenting data on the percentage of ex-legislators taking jobs as lobbyists, organized by decade to make trends more readily discernable. As this table demonstrates, a rather pronounced increase has occurred in the percentage of ex-legislators who entered the lobbying trade right after leaving Congress. For example, 28.2 percent of the legislators who left Congress in the 1990s chose to lobby, while only 14.9 percent of those who exited before 1980 arrived at the same decision, nearly a 100 percent increase. Looking at these data in terms of decade of arrival rather than departure, more than one-third of those who entered Congress in the 1990s chose lobbying as their first job, while only 12 percent of those arriving before the 1970s made that decision, almost a 300 percent increase in lobbying legislators.

We might gain some solace from the fact that the percentage of former legislators choosing lobbying after leaving Congress dips from 30.4 percent to 21.2 percent among congressional cohorts arriving between the 1970s and the 1980s, respectively. However, this figure rebounds to all-time highs in lobbying-bound ex-legislators (34.8 percent) for those entering since 1991. These data point to the fact that recent generations of legislators, however defined, display a greater penchant for lobbying than those in the past.

We do not want to minimize the effects of the overall growth in the demand for lobbyists, which could account for the proclivity of recent generations of ex-legislators for lobbying. After all, the increased demand for lobby-

TABLE 5.12. Generational Growth in Lobbying as First Job after Leaving Congress (in percentages)

Decade of Departure	Lobbyist	Decade of Arrival	Lobbyist
Before 1970	0 (19)[a]	Before 1970[b]	12 (75)
1971–80	14.9 (47)	1971–80	30.4 (79)
1981–90	19.7 (66)	1981–90	21.2 (52)
1991–2000	28.2 (78)	1991–2000	34.8 (23)
2001–3	52.6 (19)		

Source: Authors' survey of former members of Congress, 2004.
[a]Figures in parentheses represent the number of cases in the category.
[b]Before 1961, 12% of our former legislators chose to lobby in their first job after leaving Congress.

ists means that legislator-lobbyists should be able to obtain higher salaries, thereby making the vocation even more attractive. But we doubt that market dynamics alone can account for this rise: as we show in the next chapter, despite the growing market demand for lobbyists, recent generations of legislator-lobbyists receive lower salaries than past generations. We will say more about this generational relationship later, but at this point it will suffice to simply note that generational differences in preferences for lobbying suggest that symptoms of adverse selection are afoot in Congress.

Training
Here again we find evidence that there is a payoff to investments in training, even if it is only related to becoming a lobbyist. Although it is not readily apparent, we suspect that this relationship between investments in training and lobbying employment reflects the specialized training underlying career changes. This finding supports both our early argument about the limited market for the skills acquired through congressional service and findings from labor economics that "the probability of occupational change increases with the transferability of skills: the greater the transferability, the greater the incentive to change" (Shaw 1984, 324). In short, congressional training provides skills that ease the occupational transition to lobbying.

This result also echoes a point we have made repeatedly: lobbying is not just welfare for legislators or a golden parachute for past service to special interests. Put more bluntly, lobbying jobs are not merely sinecures awarded for helping special interests. Like all employers, special interests are always on the lookout for competent individuals who are well trained, and avoid employing potential shirkers. This is why special interests are effective and powerful in politics—they employ competent, well-trained former politicians who know their way around Washington and the state capitals rather than inexperienced, inept, and lazy people.

Life Cycle Effects
Those who choose lobbying may be well trained in many respects, but their behaviors are also marked by declining investments in expanding the scope of their skill packages, a consequence of life cycle effects. These individuals are not slothful or even slovenly; rather, they just long ago lost the burning desire to significantly expand their existing skill sets. Lobbying may be the perfect employment option for ex-legislators wishing to capitalize on past congressional experiences without expanding or enhancing political skills since it requires little additional training due to the close functional similarity between the jobs of legislator and lobbyist. This variable represents the third-degree

interaction between *breadth of skill set, investments in training,* and *tenure;* it is not only highly statistically significant but also theoretically relevant.

Life cycle effects in acquiring human capital are important to Becker's (1993, 108–16) arguments and likewise are incorporated into our treatment of politicians' investments in human capital. The logic behind this measure is consistent with propositions drawn from human capital theory—specifically, that demand curves for human capital are negatively inclined:

> The principal characteristic that distinguishes human capital from other kinds of capital is that, by definition, the former is embedded or embodied in the person investing. This embodiment of human capital is the most important reason why marginal benefits decline as additional capital is accumulated. One obvious implication of embodiment is that since the memory capacity, physical size, etc. of each investor is limited, eventually diminishing returns set in from producing additional capital. The result is increasing marginal cost of producing a dollar of returns. (Becker 1993, 112–13)

This nonlinear variate reflects legislators' investments in general training during the normal course of their congressional careers, which diminish with legislative tenure because of down-sloping legislator demand for these skills.

This diminished demand for broadening or extending existing skill packages seems to be a common feature in the behavior of legislators. "As the years wear on, the typical representative develops a more focused (and usually more successful) legislative agenda. There is a detectable decrease in legislative breadth" (Hibbing 1991, 418). This decline in "breadth" makes a lot of sense: legislators have probably already learned quite a lot after several years of congressional service, so additional skills and information may not be worth the marginal gain. With tenure in office, then, legislators have less incentive to acquire more human capital, and therefore make smaller subsequent investments in expanding their skill bases.

Incentives for human capital investment also decline because long tenure in office usually means a shorter period to cash in returns. "Since the property rights to human capital cannot be transferred, the finiteness of life plays a central role in human investment" (Blinder and Weiss 1976, 450). "With finite lifetimes," Becker (1993, 114) writes, "later investments cannot produce returns for as long as earlier ones and, therefore, usually have smaller total benefits." This variable in essence discounts the investments made in general training over the course of congressional careers, which is consistent with the well-repeated observation that legislator learning is most rapid in the early stages of congressional careers (Asher 1973).

General Training

No evidence shows that general training increases ex-legislators' propensity to lobby; indeed, the negative relationship between general training and lobbying suggests that inclusive skill sets reduce the likelihood of lobbying. Yet investments in training work in just the opposite direction, increasing the odds that legislators will take jobs as lobbyists. This pattern is consistent with the differential effects of general and specialized skill packages. That is, training's positive relationship to lobbying, and general training's negative relationship to lobbying, suggest that the training variable captures the effects of specialized training, which enhances the odds that legislators will change careers. Investments in (specialized) training count more than the acquisition of inclusive skill sets in preparing legislators for career changes, and lobbying seems no exception, since it, too, represents an occupational shift for legislators.

Becoming a lobbyist may involve the acquisition of human capital through on-the-job training experiences and the investments that go along with that training, but apparently it is not even remotely related to the acquisition of inclusive skill sets. But this should not be construed to mean that inclusive skill sets are worthless to lobbying firms. More likely, broad skill sets provide greater employment versatility and thereby drive up rental prices, making this human capital too costly for lobbying firms to afford. We therefore interpret this relationship to mean that general training reduces the incentives to become a lobbyist because this human capital is better marketed elsewhere—that is, the costs to special interests of hiring those with general training (for example, higher salaries) to lobby normally exceed the benefits from doing so.

Postelective Salary

Self-reported salary approaches statistical significance (alpha $< .066$) as we have defined it here in explaining postelective employment as lobbyists. Claims about the relevance of salary in luring legislators into lobbying—as if they needed encouragement beyond their specialized political skills—seem to carry more than a shred of truth. Still, salary has nowhere near the impact we expected in turning ex-legislators into lobbyists. Nonetheless, those taking jobs as lobbyists after leaving Congress have distinct economic motives: they were more likely, by nearly a three-to-one margin (14 percent to 5 percent), to cite economic opportunities as stimulating them to think while in office about what they would do after leaving. In sum, postelective salary is an important inducement to enter lobbying, but its effects may be exaggerated, and in any event, far more significant factors lead ex-legislators down that path.

Political Party

The insignificant effects associated with party affiliation might give some observers cause for concern, since then–majority leader Tom DeLay insisted that K Street lobbying firms hire only Republicans after the party gained control of the House of Representatives in 1996. This dictum surely ensured greater lobbying opportunities for Republicans leaving Congress (see, for example, Kornblut 2006a). However, journalistic arguments notwithstanding, we find no evidence (table 5.11) that party has any effect whatsoever on legislators' decisions to become lobbyists after leaving Congress.

We have entertained the possibility that this relationship may be confounded—that is, suppressed—by the fact that recently departing House Republicans may have exploited their K Street political advantage in becoming lobbyists to a greater degree than legislators who exited earlier without the comparative political advantage of DeLay's K Street requirement. After controlling for year of exit, the relationship between party and lobbying should become clearer. However, we examined the partial correlation between party and former legislators whose first postcongressional jobs were as lobbyists, controlling for year of exit, and the relationship remained statistically insignificant. Even including in a our equation an interaction term representing year of exit from Congress and party failed to produce a significant relationship. While the absence of a relationship between party and lobbying is unexpected, it is not beyond comprehension, since most successful special interests do business through the bureaucracy, where partisanship is at a minimum, rather than through the more partisan-charged legislature. In a number of respects, such an approach is less costly to special interests. Groups are well aware that passing legislation in Congress requires far more greasing of wheels than does extracting a friendly regulation or exemption from a federal agency.

Reputational Capital

Finally, we find evidence that reputational capital does indeed constrain potential opportunism, in the sense that it reduces former legislators' inclination to take up lobbying (table 5.11). To put the matter differently, those with the least amount of reputational capital, and therefore less to lose if reputations go sour, are more likely to take jobs as lobbyists after leaving Congress. Whether or not lobbying's unseemly reputation is well deserved, many ex-legislators obviously believe that taking jobs as lobbyists threatens their reputational capital. Given these findings about reputation, lobbying seems akin to Akerlof's (1970) depiction of the used car market, inundated with mechanically deficient cars, or lemons, with one proviso: whether or not the lobbying trade tends to attract the worst or least reputable people, most observers, including many politicians, believe that such is the case.

Summary and Discussion

One factor undeniably works in the favor of former legislators: they do not stay unemployed for very long. Given their talents, is it any wonder? Undoubtedly more surprising is the fact that soon-to-be legislator-lobbyists obtain their positions no faster than others less connected to special interests. Legislators receiving postelective employment as compensation for their help to interest groups should move into lobbying positions right after leaving Congress, but they apparently do not. Thus, if lobbying jobs were actually payoffs for services performed while in Congress, the length of time between leaving Congress and obtaining lobbying positions would not be lengthy. However, no relationship whatsoever exists.

We also observe a surprising level of career mobility in the postelective employment of members of Congress. It is surprising because, given the costs associated with accumulating human capital in another vocation, many legislators are nonetheless willing to abandon their precongressional occupations. Experience in Congress appears to pave the way to new careers, or at least to strengthen ex-legislators' resolve to face the risks and uncertainties that switching occupations entails.

Still, the lobbying trade remains a major outlet for such occupational mobility. While many legislators return to their precongressional occupations, a large number find employment elsewhere, and at one time or another, lobbying is often that employment. Most ex-legislators find lobbying an attractive occupation, and few can avoid the temptation to ply their accumulated human capital in this trade: 49.4 percent change vocations by taking jobs as lobbyists immediately after leaving Congress. Given the ubiquitous nature of government, those willing to ply this trade encounter no shortage of jobs.

Legislators take jobs as lobbyists because of the skills acquired through training in congressional politics, not because of any quid pro quo arrangement between special interests and politicians. In fact, a persuasive argument could be made that from the perspective of rational politicians, such quid pro quo deals would only constrain the price their services could command in the market. They would probably prefer to have an auction-type situation set the price of their wares. They have accumulated a marketable portfolio of political skills, so let the bidding begin. Rational politicians, with a comparative advantage in political skills, would be wise to encourage open bidding for their services to maximize their earnings, even if only to leverage preferred employers.

We can also conclude from these results that lobbying is not merely an interim vocation until a better job comes along, since ex-legislators leave precongressional vocations, despite the costs in doing so, for positions as lobbyists; moreover, no evidence indicates that the profession of lobbying loses its attraction over time, since each (precongressional) vocation or occupational grouping retains large numbers of lobbyists within its ranks through the second and third jobs. However, we found some evidence that the lobbying trap might be constrained by a life cycle effect in which lobbyists gravitate to other vocations over time. Even so, lobbying will always remain an attractive vocation for ex-legislators simply because their on-the-job training creates many suitors for their skills but limits the types of jobs that can make best use of their acquired talents. If the resources and talents of legislators gravitate to their most valued use, like unfettered economic resources, we should expect legislators to take jobs as lobbyists. To do otherwise should raise eyebrows.

Legislators can of course find jobs other than as lobbyists, or in their prior vocations, by acquiring specialized skills through years of service on clientele committees. Training in legislative politics, and in particular specialized training, underlies career changes (table 5.10) and triggers employment as lobbyists (table 5.11). We might surmise, then, that the acquisition of specialized skill packages would provide diverse employment venues in which former legislators could ply their talents. But given the nature of the rent-seeking society, most businesses need ex-politicians for lobbying and probably little else, to the chagrin of many members of Congress.

Chapter 6

Returns to General Training:
Competitive Wages—But at a Price

In the previous chapter, we demonstrated that the returns from specialized training primarily took the form of career changes. General skill sets were either inconsequential or negatively related to this objective. With respect to postelective wages, however, general skill packages are far more relevant. We conclude our statistical analysis by examining the remaining two hypotheses derived from our theory: the economic value of training in terms of postelective salaries, and the effects of investments in general training in securing special interest subsidies for campaign debt.

Investments in on-the-job training differ from normal investments in that the latter produce returns in the form of assets, but with investments in training, "the return comes—not in the form of assets—but *as a price change.* The investor purchases with his investment—not an income or service stream in the future—but the option of selling his holding of one item (that is, his labor services) at a higher price" (Lindsay 1971, 1196). Investments in general training equip legislators with skill sets that are highly versatile, thereby ensuring a broad range of employment options. As a result, general skill packages boost postelective wages, but of course do so at a price.

Although general training is highly marketable, it also has costs—in particular, the costs of funding reelection campaigns. All legislators, generalists or specialists, must pay such costs, but specialists' campaign costs are subsidized to a greater degree by special interests. Special interests view campaign support as serving two objectives: investing in potential employees and encouraging legislator specialization, thus equipping legislators with outlooks on policies coinciding with those harbored by the interests. As a result, special interests do not spread their largesse indiscriminately—in particular, they shy away from supporting those pursuing general training. Special interests may do so because the competitive salaries broadly trained legislators command in the market exceed the benefits most special interests can derive from employing them. Whatever the reason, this practice complicates simple estimates of the returns from inclusive skill sets. Gains in postelective earnings must be balanced against unsubsidized campaign costs in gauging the net returns derived from general training.

We start our analyses of these questions by describing the economic effects of general training and skill set breadth. Campaign subsidies aside for the moment, a general education in congressional politics is a highly profitable investment venture, since it expands employment options, thereby ensuring that job hunting occurs under the most auspicious conditions.

Economic Effects of General Training and Inclusive Skill Sets

Legislators unwilling or ill-prepared to take employment in such lucrative occupations as lobbying or law can still improve their postelective wages by acquiring inclusive skill sets and engaging in general training opportunities whenever possible. Such actions produce highly versatile skill sets. Skill versatility, in turn, enables ex-legislators to entertain a wider assortment of employment possibilities, thereby ensuring highly competitive salaries. In addition, inclusive skill sets afford legislators the option of taking advantage of the best earning opportunities at the most propitious times—that is, when earnings and wages are at their height and political skills are in greatest demand.

We have suggested that the narrowness of the market for the services of former legislators determines, in part, subsequent postelective earnings; accordingly, the specialized suffer and the generally trained gain because the latter have more and better employment options. But more than just the breadth of the skill set acquired through congressional service determines postelective earnings; the scarcity of that skill set also comes into play. There are just very few opportunities within Congress to acquire the types of skills and knowledge that translate into general training skill sets. Matthews and Stimson (1975), like many congressional scholars, point to the strong emphasis on specialization in the House and Senate, which narrows the market for the services of legislators while placing a premium on those securing a general education in congressional politics. As a result, those with general training have a comparative edge in the labor market, enabling them to better distinguish their human capital from more prevalent specialized skill sets. Skill scarcity, then, should be considered in determining the rental value of skill sets; when it is, the value of inclusive skill sets is obvious.

We can gain an even better appreciation of why general training is so important by examining the occupational wage schedule facing exiting legislators. By expanding employment options, legislators' occupational skills place fewer restrictions on postelective employment choices. That is, general training helps legislators counter the natural constraints on postelective employment resulting from precongressional occupational background.

Occupational Wage Structure

Exiting legislators encounter an implicit schedule of wage rates for various occupations that shapes their expectations about the financial returns they can expect as a result of congressional service. They know they can realize generous postelective salaries if they can find the right venues in which to rent their political capital and then just settle in. It is, of course, no secret where these job opportunities can be found—they are normally situated in occupations with the largest postelective salaries. Hence, rational legislators sift through employment prospects in terms of the most financially rewarding occupations—that is, those where their human capital will command top dollar. Even for less economically minded legislators, this is as good a starting place as any in fashioning postelective job-hunting plans. We construct a reasonable facsimile of this tacit wage structure by calculating salary statistics for the specific occupational categories of postelective employment.

While locating in profitable vocations is impeccable financial advice for augmenting postelective salaries, it is far easier said than done. In many cases, legislators lack the qualifications, expertise, or credentials to assume high-paying jobs such as lawyers. Nonetheless, information about occupational salary schedules is not useless, since members of the same occupation should have approximately the same qualifications and income-earning skills. Comparing the postelective salaries of lawyers, for example, entering other occupations thus provides an indication of where legislative service by former lawyers commands its greatest economic return. It also provides a closer look at how changing occupations or returning to prior fields affects postelective salary gains and losses.

As a starting point, we examine the postelective salaries associated with specific occupations. This information provides a rough indication of where the best and worst postelective salaries can be found, qualifications and expertise aside. Some readers may think our findings predictable, yet the underlying questions—that is, where are the best- and worst-paying jobs for former legislators?—have never been subjected to empirical inquiry. Our findings, therefore, are not startling but are nevertheless fresh, and will fill some of the lacunae in the literature surrounding this topic.

Postelective Salaries and Occupation

The postelective wages of former legislators have a clear structure. In table 6.1 we present the mean salaries (in 2004 dollars) for the more extended classification of postelective employment. In some instances, these means are based on small numbers of cases; consequently, we have combined comparable vocations in analyses of these data in chapter 5. Those taking jobs in educational or nonprofit institutions unquestionably suffer the most since they are among the poorest paid ex-legislators; not surprisingly, they were also the least satisfied with their employment prospects after leaving Congress.

In the preceding chapter, we suggested that skills acquired in Congress made lobbying an attractive profession for ex-legislators. There is an additional reason for turning to lobbying after leaving Congress—it is a highly lucrative occupation. As table 6.1 indicates, lobbyists and those who represent trade associations garner some of the highest starting salaries; their wages are rivaled only by those of partners in law firms. We suspect that such six-figure salaries prompt critics to believe that the wages ex-legislators receive to lobby is cause enough for them to do so. As we have shown in chapter 5, concerns other than postelective salary generally drive the decision to become a lobbyist.

Still, we cannot fail to notice that lobbying ex-legislators collect the jaw-

TABLE 6.1. Mean Salaries for First Job after Leaving Congress, by Occupation

Occupation[a]	Mean Salary	S.D.	N
Lobbying	$325,190	$213,231	17
Private sector employment	291,495	160,399	28
Public sector (government)	213,286	206,554	36
Education	128,121	67,056	20
Nonprofit/Philanthropy	150,183	104,983	4
Consultant	222,356	117,484	31
Lawyer	268,570	145,477	38
Trade association	356,656	24,728	2
Law partner	353,072	155,754	17
Retired	84,836	43,926	4
Financial institution	228,291	52,495	3
Not classified	285,755	93,639	3

Source: Authors' survey of former members of Congress, 2004.
Note: Figures in the table are in 2004 dollars. S.D. = standard deviation.
[a]When using the original five-category classification of vocations (table 1.1) and adding a sixth category for retirement from Congress, the reported salary differences are statistically significant in an analysis of variance (ANOVA) test (alpha < .000) and the Levene statistic for homogeneity of variances is insignificant (alpha > .409).

dropping salaries we assumed they received. Indeed, on top of the ease of transition from legislator to postelective lobbyist, the wages are highly competitive, perhaps bordering on lavish. Even though salary plays a small role in why legislators take up lobbying, it is hard to believe that salary plays no role whatsoever in their high levels of job satisfaction (figure 6.1). Thus, we should not pity those falling prey to the lobbying trap that all too frequently ensnares ex-legislators. Given these employment benefits, it is hard to second-guess their bliss.

Occupational Skill Sets and Profitable Employment

We describe these salary data further in table 6.2 by examining the differences between pre- and postcongressional wages (that is, postcongressional wage minus precongressional wage). As a result of the small number of cases on which these mean salary differences are sometimes based, we focus primarily on those table entries based on five or more observations, since means calculated from a smaller number of cases are more problematic.

While prevailing occupational wage rates provide legislators with an idea

TABLE 6.2. Pre- and Postcongressional Salary Differences by Entering and Exiting Occupation

		Precongressional Occupation			
First Job after Exiting	Lobbyist	Nonprofit and Education	Private and Financial	Lawyer	Government
Lobbyist		$N = 3$	$N = 22$	$N = 7$	$N = 18$
Mean		−65,621	**11,248**	**66**	**98,337**
Median		−38,482	**40,597**	−17,210	**145,342**
Nonprofit/Education		$N = 8$	$N = 7$	$N = 2$	$N = 6$
Mean		−790	−165,111	−154,539	−55,436
Median		−12,090	−185,260	−154,539	−43,486
Private/Financial		$N = 1$	$N = 19$	$N = 7$	$N = 2$
Mean		**36,166**	−104,503	**48,524**	**1,099**
Median		**36,166**	−23,447	**98,095**	**1,099**
Lawyer			$N = 1$	$N = 43$	$N = 10$
Mean			**217,314**	−89,178	**204,223**
Median			**217,314**	−41,305	**170,841**
Government	$N = 1$	$N = 4$	$N = 14$	$N = 8$	$N = 9$
Mean	−104,807	**74,790**	−9,942	−152,512	**152,145**
Median	−104,807	**88,700**	−13,249	−118,053	**29,743**
Retired			$N = 3$	$N = 1$	
Mean			−294,115	−49,586	
Median			−63,860	−49,586	

Note: Entries are mean salary differences between precongressional and postcongressional salaries. Positive salary gains are shown in bold.

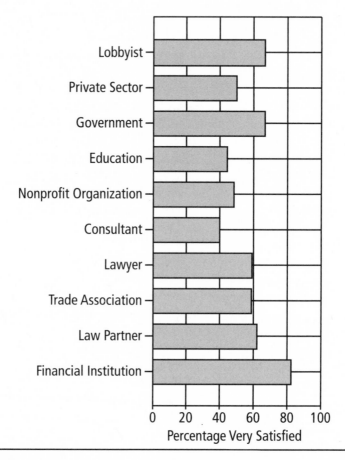

QUESTION: How satisfied were you with the employment opportunities you encountered upon leaving Congress—very satisfied, somewhat satisfied, slightly disappointed, very disappointed?

The figure shows those who gave the response "very satisfied" to this questionnaire item.

FIG. 6.1. Job satisfaction of former members of Congress with employment opportunities. (Data from authors' survey of former members of Congress, 2004.)

of where the best salaries can be obtained, qualifications and skills may preclude particular legislators from taking jobs in these areas. Table 6.2 identifies the most lucrative vocations for exiting legislators with particular occupational backgrounds. In this way, we can spot the most profitable employment suited to the occupational skills of former legislators. For example, although the number of cases (four) on which this relationship is based is rather small, ex-legislators with prior employment in nonprofit organizations obtain their highest earnings by taking jobs in government. For former legislators from the private sector, lobbying is clearly the best bet; to do otherwise ensures large losses in postelective salary. And with respect to legislators from careers as lawyers, financial institutions and private sector employment provide the highest-paying returns. Any other occupational alternative results in salary losses.

What stands out most from this table is the fact that those with prior service in government find numerous profitable outlets for their human capital. They raise their precongressional salaries in every occupation they enter, employment in nonprofit foundations notwithstanding. Some observers may see this finding as indisputable evidence of the economic value of public-service employment and the usefulness of the human capital it creates in conjunction with congressional service. We, too, are firm believers that just about every organization needs people with knowledge of the inner workings of government, but before we herald the economic virtues of public service, we need to remember that governmental employment is one of the poorest-paying precongressional vocations (table 1.1); hence, far less is required to increase the salaries of former government employees.

Lucrative and Not-So-Lucrative Postelective Employment

Next, we winnow this list down to the few occupations that appear to consistently generate salary losses and gains for legislators. By now, most of the results should be predictable. Whereas very few postelective vocations exhibit any salary gains whatsoever, lobbying and postelective governmental employment show indications of earning power (table 6.2). However, in both instances, salary gains depend on prior occupational skills. For example, only those from prior employment in government or nonprofit institutions experience salary gains when taking jobs in government; similarly, only those with prior employment in the private sector and government gain financially when taking jobs as lobbyists. Unfortunately, in other cases, the number of respondents within an occupational category is just too small to permit any inferences.

Even though postelective salary fails to strongly attract legislators to lobbying (table 5.11), the job provides one of the best guarantees of salary gains after leaving Congress. For the risk-averse, lobbying is a no-brainer. We should probably count our blessings that even more ex-legislators are not attracted to this trade.

Not surprisingly, jobs with philanthropic and educational institutions result in losses in postelective wages across all precongressional occupations, but ex-legislators taking these sorts of jobs are probably inclined to trade salary for prestige, or are less motivated by the former than the latter. Once again, public-spirited legislators pay a price for their altruism. The lesson is clear—simply put, future lobbyists and governmental employees are the closest to being wage winners in obtaining salaries beyond their precongressional wages, but there are plenty of exceptions; the public-spirited, by contrast, are destined to absorb financial losses in most cases.

Put another way, former legislators best leverage their experiences in Congress into competitive postelective salaries by entering occupations where their political skill sets are most appropriate for the job. This is exactly how we expect the returns on investments in congressional training to work out. Legislators acquire marketable political skills, and two areas where those skills are in greatest demand are in lobbying and government. As a result, these occupations deservedly yield the greatest financial returns to political skill sets.

Returning to Prior Occupations

Given the large number of legislators incurring salary losses in postelective employment, would they be better served by returning to their previous vocations? Even this scenario does not present inviting prospects for financial gain, however. Our findings here follow a common refrain—a second career in politics is costly. In nearly every case, legislators resuming former vocations—that is, the main diagonal in table 6.2—encounter lower wages. Aside from lobbying, the other notable occupational exception to losses in postelective wages is government employment, where returnees experienced salary gains; however, these increases are not statistically different from zero (paired-samples t-test), although we recognize that with only nine cases, obtaining significance is quite demanding. In short, merely returning to precongressional occupations after a stint in Congress appears to do little to enhance postcongressional salaries.

The salary losses experienced by ex-legislators returning to the same vocation are in some cases sizable. Lawyers, for example, experience statistically significant declines on the order of five figures in postelective wages after service in Congress (alpha < .028). This finding is somewhat odd since the conventional wisdom has long held that forays into politics, and especially legislative politics, represented a form of professional advertising for lawyers and resulted in income gains. Unlike doctors and engineers, attorneys can move in and out of their jobs without jeopardizing their practices (Barber 1965, 68–69; Davidson and Oleszek 2002, 124–25). In short, congressional service was thought to be all profit for lawyers. We are not prepared to dismiss the validity of this characterization, but the postelective salaries of former legislators resuming their law practices prompt questions regarding whether lawyers are so advantaged. Our data certainly suggest otherwise.

Legislators' Human Capital and Occupational
Wage Rates

Three conclusions can be drawn from this discussion and analysis. First, regardless of whether they are changing occupations or resuming prior vocations, legislators face genuine prospects of lower postelective wages. They have vacated lucrative income-earning vocations for a second career in Congress, and this hiatus can result in the atrophy of occupational skills and therefore demand for their talents. Moreover, some legislators chose to enter Congress during their peak productive years. This is why the acquisition of marketable political skills is extremely important to legislators, and why they devote time to accumulating human capital in Congress.[1] We elaborate on our earlier point that legislators invest in on-the-job training because of the expected returns by adding that to do otherwise poses real threats to postelective livelihoods.

Second, given the financial incentives, former legislators are likely to stay

---

1. The question could be raised as to whether legislators are truly rational since they spend extensive amounts of time and money to get to and stay in Congress but are then rewarded with diminished earnings when they leave. The issue of the rationality of politicians certainly transcends our analysis, though we emphasize that nothing in our findings should be construed as fodder for a frontal assault on the notion that politicians are rational or even as support for a small insurrection on this matter. First, salary figures ignore the personal benefits individuals derive from officeholding and may thereby minimize the relevance of service in high elected office to the utility incomes of politicians; prestigious political office alone is a lifetime accomplishment for most people. This phenomenon could easily offset economic losses incurred through officeholding. Second, on a more cynical note, salaries also do not incorporate all the benefits derived from officeholding—not merely the perquisites but those off-budget items and proceeds so difficult to monitor, such as foreign travel, jobs for family and friends, and insider information designed to produce large financial returns. Hence, salary "supplements" may need to be taken into account.

active in politics either as lobbyists or as government officials. We suspect that accumulated human capital has a lot to do with ex-legislators' attraction to these jobs. We must abandon the idea that legislators are irrelevant after they leave Congress because their days as influential policymakers have ended; they are likely to retain a significant say in running government, and their legislative skills magnify that influence.

Finally and perhaps most noteworthy, lobbying and government employment represent the two areas of profitable postelective employment where legislators can best rent their human capital, since jobs situated in these occupations take full advantage of legislative skills and know-how. In these occupations, political skills earn salary premiums, for obvious reasons. The market for legislative skills is, however, noticeably specialized and seems to limit legislators' job choices to a few occupations. Legislators may have few other attractive employment outlets for their talents. As one legislator volunteered,

> I am fortunate to be a lawyer, so I had a readily available occupation when I returned to private life. Knowledge of this gave me great independence while in Congress, as I wasn't worried that electoral defeat would spell economic ruin. I believe most ex-Congressmen and women have a much more limited range of options than commonly believed.

This legislator's comments seem right on target: employment alternatives are indeed limited. The advantages of more inclusive skill sets seem quite evident, since legislators possessing these skills can always avail themselves of standby jobs in lobbying and government but also have other employment possibilities. In a sense, then, general training mitigates the occupational constraints on legislators seeking competitive postelective salaries by expanding employment options.

Previous Literature on Legislators' Earnings

While very few studies have examined the postelective employment of legislators (Lott 1990; Borders and Dockery 1995; Parker 1996, 137–40), until the classic work of Diermeier, Keane, and Merlo (2004, 2005), none had tackled the question of postelective salaries. Our study differs from the Diermeier, Keane, and Merlo analysis in important respects and generates contrasting conclusions that we believe are related to these differences. Here we highlight some of the major differences.

Salary Data

Diermeier, Keane, and Merlo (2004) do not directly obtain information about ex-legislators' salaries. Instead, they assign postelective salaries based on wage function estimates derived from surveys of Chicago lawyers conducted in 1975 and 1995, adjusting these salaries by billing rates to account for geographic location of law practices. The assumption—probably valid in many instances—is that ex-legislators are hired by law firms as either lawyers or lobbyists. With respect to public sector employment, the authors obtained the annual salaries of officeholders by scanning state statutory codes and/or directly contacting the relevant offices. While this is quite an impressive and ingenious job of computation, we believe that it creates problems in subsequent analyses since these wage calculations are more than a step or two removed from actual legislators' salaries.

Truncated Sample

Another major problem with their analysis of postelective earnings is that it ignores large groups of ex-legislators. In particular, occupations in the business and financial sectors would escape classification as employment in lobbying or law, as would vocations in education or philanthropic institutions; these groups together represent 28.5 percent of the postelective employment of former legislators (table 5.1). Although the proportion of ex-legislators who find employment as lobbyists, lawyers, and governmental officials (65.1 percent) is considerably larger than those entering vocations in business and nonprofit institutions such as universities and colleges, Diermeier, Keane, and Merlo's analysis ignores the wages of the final two groups—those that receive the lowest postelective salaries (table 6.1). Thus, by neglecting the salaries of these occupational groups, Diermeier, Keane, and Merlo (2005) have biased their analysis in important respects by excluding the most poorly paid former legislators.

Specification Errors

Third, Diermeier, Keane, and Merlo (2005) fail to include *precongressional salary* in their equations predicting postelective wages, despite the fact that this store of human capital affects postelective earnings because it represents the capitalization of the value of precongressional human capital. As such, it is essential that this variable be included in estimating equations; otherwise, the impact of training on postelective wages will also capture the influence of the stock of human capital that legislators possessed prior to entering Congress, thereby confounding the measurement of legislative training. Moreover, precongressional salary supplies a theoretically useful and relevant baseline for comparing the effects of job training in congressional politics.

In addition, Diermeier, Keane, and Merlo's (2005) measure of committee influence, simply conceptualized as membership on major congressional committees, ignores the basic human capital premise that returns are based on investments. Thus, the really important consideration is not whether they served on major legislative committees but how long they served. In sum, Diermeier and his colleagues may have misspecified their explanatory equations by excluding an important variable—*precongressional salary*—and inappropriately calculating the influence of committees, all of which can lead to faulty interpretations of the role of congressional service in enhancing postelective wages.

Salary Estimates

Finally, there are questions surrounding the validity of their derived postelective salary estimates. We noted earlier that their salary estimates would be distorted just because they have excluded a large number of former legislators who chose postelective vocations outside of law, lobbying, and government. We now suggest that these salary estimates are flawed. As we alluded earlier, their wage function extrapolations for ex-legislators may be a poor proxy for actual wages. For example, the authors assign legislators who left Congress before 1985 the estimates for the 1975 wage function, and all others estimates from the 1995 wage function. Such calculations seem rather gross. We can demonstrate that their salary calculations (Diermeier, Keane, and Merlo 2004) are indeed suspect by comparing the salary estimates they computed for ex-legislators with self-reported postelective wages.

We can identify fifty-one former legislators in our study who also have had their salaries computed by Diermeier, Keane, and Merlo (2005). We have transformed these estimates into 2004 dollars and then correlated them with the self-reported salaries for the same legislators. Not surprisingly, considering that the variables are measuring the same thing, the two estimates are positively correlated but at an unexpectedly modest level ($r = .39$). When we examine further these salary estimates, using a paired-samples t-test and employing a one-tailed test of significance since we can anticipate a positive relationship a priori, the differences between our salary estimates and those derived by Diermeier, Keane, and Merlo are statistically significant (alpha $< .056$). Even though both estimates are related, the Diermeier-Keane-Merlo

estimates provide a biased view of the self-reported salaries of former legislators, even for those who fall within the narrow range of occupations (that is,
lawyers and government officials) they examine.

Thus, in addition to their truncated sample and the possibility of specification errors in their equations, the Diermeier-Keane-Merlo estimates differ
from the salary estimates supplied by legislators themselves, exhibit considerably less variation than the latter, and tend to underestimate self-reported
postelective wages.[2] We would prefer to compare both wage estimates to more
objective information, such as income tax filings or statutorily required reports, to better assess which procedure comes closest to actual salary figures.
But in the absence of such information, self-reporting in an anonymous survey seems an arguably better second-best solution to obtaining valid representations of postelective salaries than through wage function extrapolations.

Contrasts between our findings and those of Diermeier, Keane, and
Merlo (2005) can be expected to arise from divergence over matters of theory,
research design, data, variable measurement, and equation specification. We
are not being picayune, since these are not minor issues, but that should not
detract for one moment from the incredible modeling and data collection
that Diermeier and his colleagues accomplished; we do not want to undercut
their effort in the least. Nonetheless, we believe that their analysis has resulted
in an incomplete characterization of the effects of congressional training on
the postelective wages of former legislators and that our analysis represents a
significant improvement over their treatment of this question.

Analysis

In this segment of the analysis, we also include measures of *party affiliation,*
tenure (years of congressional service), and *membership in the Senate* because
of the intriguing questions associated with each: Do senators, because of their
broader representational and institutional responsibilities, earn more than
House members? Do Republicans, as a result of their attachments to business,
receive higher salaries than Democrats? And does merely staying in office
(that is, tenure in Congress) ensure a lucrative postelective salary? However,

---

2. The estimated mean for the fifty-one former legislators in both studies, derived from self-reporting of postelective salaries, is $277,878, with a standard deviation of $232,437; the comparable
salary estimates from Diermeier, Keane, and Merlo (2005) are a salary mean of $229,406 and a stan-
dard deviation of $93,652. For our entire sample, the mean is $247,062, with a standard deviation
of $165,155.

we have not included a variable representing *retirement from Congress* in this present salary equation (table 6.3), although others have found a relationship between the two (Diermeier, Keane, and Merlo 2005). This factor is statistically insignificant in the equation, perhaps as a result of the incomplete salary data provided by retirees. As a consequence, we hesitate to suggest that retirement from Congress has no effect whatsoever. We now turn to a calculation of the economic effects of legislators' human capital, and in particular the impact of on-the-job training experiences.[3]

Statistical Model

The conclusions reached in this section are based on a research design appropriate for testing the effects of congressional training on postelective wages. In particular, by including *precongressional capital* in our wage equation, we obtain measurements of changes in the market value of human capital resulting from service in Congress. Consequently, our analysis represents a sort of quasi-experimental, before-and-after approach to congressional service, where we have pre- and postelection measurements of salary, controlled for relevant aspects of legislative service, and distinguished theoretically between the contrasting effects of general and specialized training on postelective salaries (see Cook and Campbell 1979, esp. 124–26). Such research designs are at their best in dealing with problems of internal validity.

The conventional model of human capital accumulation assumes that individuals invest in themselves to maximize their discounted lifetime incomes. Our model starts with the same assumption and incorporates measures of precongressional office capital (abilities and endowments), along with nontraining human capital, and indicators of congressional training—such as breadth of skill sets and investments in training—to create a quasi-experimental design where we can examine the change in salaries that results from going to Washington and engaging in on-the-job training. We again use the politicians' human capital model to estimate the postelective salaries of former legislators:

---

3. Becker (1993), among others, has used the differences in wage earnings among those with and without investments in training as measures of the returns to training. Despite the popularity of this measurement among early human capitalists, it is extremely biased: "The 'difference between net earnings' of trained and untrained individuals describes merely the increase in the investor's command over a subset of the items in his consumption bundle. It ignores the fact that one of the most important items in that bundle, leisure, has become costlier in the process. Considered as an estimate of the wealth effect . . . this income-difference measure systematically overstates the value of this return" (Lindsay 1971, 1196–97).

$$W = f(X_1, \ldots X_{14}),$$

where W represents the postelective wages of legislators in their first job after leaving Congress, and

Abilities and endowments:

X_1 = precongressional salary

X_2 = prior political office

Nontraining capital:

X_3 = nontraining assets

X_4 = reputational capital

On-the-job-training in Congress:

X_5 = years of service on interest group committees

X_6 = years of service on prestige committees

X_7 = investments in on-the-job training

Breadth of skills:

X_8 = skill acquisition, or breadth of skills acquired

X_9 = general training (breadth of skills acquired × investments in on-the-job training)

X_{10} = life cycle investments in general training (breadth of skills acquired × investments in on-the-job training × tenure)

TABLE 6.3.   Explaining Legislators' Postelective Salaries

Variable	B	Error	Beta	t	Significance
Precongressional salary	.176	.045	.268	3.930	.000
Prior political office[a]	47.160	28.533	.119	1.653	.100
Interest group committee[a]	.835	1.695	.038	.493	.623
Prestige committee[a]	3.886	1.795	.167	2.164	.032
Nontraining assets[a]	−17.303	11.031	−.104	−1.569	.118
Investment in training[a]	8.561	12.646	.053	.677	.499
Reputational capital[a]	6.345	10.306	.040	.616	.539
Broad skill set[a]	37.985	12.885	.224	2.948	.004
General training[a]	34.852	15.376	.236	2.267	.025
Life cycle investments[a]	−1.522	.905	−.187	−1.680	.095
Party[a]	−3.159	20.670	−.010	−.153	.879
Senator[a]	−2.529	44.104	−.004	−.057	.954
Year of entry[a]	−4.644	1.121	−.308	−4.143	.000
Tenure[a]	−7.241	2.061	−.351	−3.512	.001

Statistics

$R = .508$

$R^2 = .258$

$N = 201$

Source: Authors' survey of former members of Congress, 2004.

Note: Legislators retiring after leaving Congress are included in this table.

[a]These coefficients are per $1,000 in salary.

Equation-specific variables:
X_{11} = year of entry into Congress
X_{12} = senator
X_{13} = party affiliation
X_{14} = tenure

Overall Regression Results

Table 6.3 describes the regression results. This equation accounts for a respectable 26 percent of the variation in the postelective salaries of ex-legislators, with four factors significantly influencing wages—precongressional salaries, year of entry into Congress, tenure, and two variables associated with the acquisition of political skills. One way of thinking about the relative influence of these variables is by rank-ordering the absolute magnitudes of the standardized regression coefficients from lowest to highest. By this method, the least influential (significant) variable on postelective salaries is years spent on prestige committees (beta = .167), followed in influence by a group of three variables with similar effects—specifically, *breadth of skill set* (beta = .224), *general training* (beta = .236), and *precongressional salary* (beta = .268).

Economic talent and acquired training/skills seem to play a greater role in boosting postcongressional wages than does service on powerful committees, despite the latter's relevance to internal legislative influence.[4] The effect of precongressional salary is to be expected since it represents the value of human capital acquired prior to congressional service, and such capital will undoubtedly affect subsequent earnings. "Each person forms a separate human-capital 'market.' Rates of return to him depend on the amount invested in him as well as on aggregate stocks of human capital" (Becker 1993, 263). Still, *tenure* (beta = −.351) and *year of entry* (beta = −.308) are by far the most important variables in the equation, with effects about twice the size of those attached to *prestige committee service*. How long legislators stay in Congress and when they arrived shape postelective salaries to a far greater degree than either training or economic talent.

---

4. To examine the effects of training in individual committees on subsequent earnings, we started by including within our analysis variables—that is, years spent on individual committees—representing each of the committees in the House and Senate. Since working in congressional committees—for example, on bill markups and on formulating public policies—produces both information and skills (human capital), we wanted to identify those experiences that contributed the most in this regard to the postelective earnings of ex-legislators. Because of the small number of legislators assigned to any one committee, however, the committees had to be combined into prestige and interest group–servicing committees.

Ability and Endowments versus Training

Considering the powerful effects of abilities and endowments, the influence of training is indeed impressive. For instance, the skills acquired through on-the-job training—that is, *broad skill sets* and *general training*—rival the effects of economic talent (*precongressional salary*) on postelective wages and in this regard are almost twice as influential as political aptitude (*prior political office*, beta = .119). Taken as a whole, training seems to be at least as influential as ability in shaping postelective wages. The impact of these training variables is most remarkable because they noticeably increase the market value of human capital beyond precongressional levels. In terms of legislators' postelective wages, endowments certainly matter, but training seems to constitute an equalizer.

Tenure

Spending time in Congress clearly is inadequate to raise postelective wages, as there is a strong negative relationship between tenure and postelective salary (beta = −.351). It is reasonable to envision legislative tenure as a by-product of a sorting process that operates through elections to eliminate from office legislators who are poor agents—for example, legislators at odds with the preferences of their constituents (Lott 1987; Dougan and Munger 1989; Lott and Reed 1989). As a consequence, surviving legislators possess characteristics (for example, campaign skills) that differ from those who are screened out. In this way, survival of the fittest may result in legislators who are unusually qualified for office and are extremely adept at staying in office.

Such sorting might also affect postelective earnings by producing legislators with talents and characteristics highly valued in the market and therefore heavily compensated. If such a process were at work, senior legislators, who have repeatedly survived the electoral sorting process, should earn more than those who were earlier sorted out of office; however, we observe a robust negative relationship between tenure and postelective wages (table 6.3). That is, those successfully surviving the sorting process appear to earn less than those exiting after far less time in Congress. The sorting process may produce electorally able politicians, but no evidence indicates that the process manufactures legislators who can translate their resulting office longevity into postelective income.

Legislators have to do something with their time in office—invest in job training—to have it count toward their postelective salaries; otherwise, employers are likely to discount legislative service as an income-earning trait and accordingly offer lower wages. It may be, as Woody Allen has wryly observed, that "80 percent of success is showing up," but from a look at the salaries paid ex-legislators and the effects of tenure, far more is expected of their service in Congress. Although perhaps an unexpected result, this negative influence of tenure has been observed elsewhere (Diermeier, Keane, and Merlo 2005).

Of course, this does not mean that tenure has no positive effects whatsoever on legislators' earning power. Tenure is the most important factor explaining investments in congressional training (beta = .303), because with seniority come more opportunities for additional legislative training, thereby encouraging legislator investment. For example, with increasing seniority, opportunities to chair legislative committees and join the party's leadership corps fall within reach. Thus, a positive, indirect effect of tenure on postelective salaries seems plausible: tenure increases investments in congressional training, which, in conjunction with the acquisition of inclusive skill packages (that is, general training), enhances wages.

Prestige Committees

The important influence of membership on elite congressional committees on postelective wages (beta = .167) raises two important issues. First, membership on prestige committees requires approval of party leaders, and their consent is often predicated on considerations such as party loyalty and electoral safety. Thus, we must consider party leaders' decisions regarding appointment to prestige committees. Second, we have to entertain the possibility that those assigned to these elite committees are already well-skilled; hence, prestige committees may independently do little to augment the salaries of those with prior general training. Even if party leaders have a large say in appointments to prestige committees, and service on such committees is predicated on political skills, it does not negate the influence of prestige committees on postelective salaries.

Party Leaders' Assignment Practices
The consent of leaders is, of course, necessary for appointment to elite committees, but rational party leaders are far from capricious in these matters. Granted, party leaders consider such factors as party loyalty, electoral safety, and legislative experience in making committee assignments, but they also have every incentive to assign their most skilled members to these important committees. Worming one's way into the good graces of party leaders may work in obtaining assignments to some committees, but leaders have a whole lot more at stake with respect to elite committees. Given the impor-

tance of these committees to the productivity of the legislature—governing, among other things, the raising, spending, and budgeting of tax monies—party leaders cannot afford the luxury of shirking or ineptness on the part of committee members. Therefore, appointments to prestige committees are unquestionably conditioned by considerations of legislator ability and perhaps even general skills. In so doing, leaders can enhance the efficiency and effectiveness of the legislature, which increases their political profits in clearing the market for legislation. In short, leadership compliance is essential for legislators to obtain the general training that goes along with elite committee assignments, but party leaders' decisions include consideration of the skills legislators have acquired. Indeed, we believe that political skills and know-how—that is, legislators' human capital—are some of the first things considered.

Prior Training

If we accept the argument that some element of legislative skill is necessary for appointment to elite committees, a second issue readily emerges: the effects of prestige committees may merely capture levels of general training necessary for legislator assignment to these committees. That is, general training in elite committees may be exaggerated since such training is necessary just to obtain these committee assignments. We have addressed this issue by introducing separate measures of inclusive skill sets and general training into our explanatory equation, thereby controlling for such possible effects on postelective salaries. The effect of time spent on prestige committees consequently captures the specific effects of investments within these committees, not the general training obtained or the inclusive skill sets acquired during the course of congressional careers. In addition, we do not consider simple appointment to a prestige committee as the linchpin of a lucrative postelective salary; time spent on the job is what really counts in accumulating human capital, and our measurement of investments in elite committees emphasizes this fact.

Inclusive Skill Sets

General training increases the postelective salaries of ex-legislators (beta = .236), and the breadth of skill sets is only marginally less important in this respect (beta = .224). Likewise, institutions specializing in general training, such as prestige committees, function in a similar manner but to a lesser degree (beta = .167). On the whole, then, increasing the breadth of skill sets through congressional service and training of some sort increases postelective wages. Specialized training does not provide a salary boost, as is the case in la-

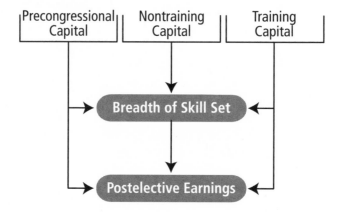

FIG. 6.2. The relationship of human capital to postelective earnings

bor economics (see, for example, Topel 1991; Williams 1991). This result is nonetheless compatible with our theoretical perspective: legislators with inclusive skill sets have a larger market in which to rent their human capital, thereby ensuring highly competitive wages.

Inclusive skill sets can be thought of as encompassing what Grossman and Shapiro (1982, 1068) have termed the "option value" of general training. "A worker with general training has the option of choosing in which industry to seek employment. This allows him to work in a very risky industry when conditions are favorable there, while avoiding the industry if times turn bad." That is, generally trained legislators can pick and choose their employment opportunities, therefore avoiding the necessity of taking jobs in industries or economic sectors where the wages are lower, at least for the moment.[5]

So, in politics, ex-legislators equipped with wide-ranging skill packages obtain higher salaries than other legislators because they can be selective in choosing their jobs, thereby ensuring employment under auspicious conditions. For instance, broadly trained legislators may be able to secure top posi-

---

5. Another possible explanation of course exists for the higher salaries associated with general training and broad skill sets: because specialized training and assets are beneficial in changing vocations, the lower salaries offered specialists may be a consequence of leaving one's occupation for a different one. That is, those with general training may simply return to their precongressional vocations and therefore forgo the salary losses normally associated with changing careers. In contrast, those changing vocations incur a salary loss, perhaps only temporarily, until they can reach the same level of expertise as those more experienced in the occupation. This argument, though tempting, is not supported by our data: although a negative relationship exists between career changes and postelective salary, it is not statistically significant (see chapter 7, note 2).

tions in large corporations—for example, as CEOs—when stockholders find political experience and talents alluring and profitable. But when those opportunities are foreclosed, perhaps as a result of public skepticism or disdain for politicians, such legislators can take refuge elsewhere, as in the many avenues of governmental employment. When the time is again ripe, they can dart back into private sector employment. From this perspective, general training—or broad skill sets, for that matter—constitutes self-insurance for legislators. The interrelationships among the various components of human capital as they relate to postelective salaries are described in figure 6.2.

Alternative Explanations of Training Effects

As we noted in chapter 1, there are, of course, other interpretations for our findings, although we do not believe other explanations can account for the diversity and breadth of the findings reported here. Nonetheless, we have encountered a couple of arguments that offer sensible explanations for some of the effects of training on postelective salaries. For that reason, we examine two alternative explanations for these effects, in the process bolstering confidence in the validity and significance of our results.

Biased Retrospective Evaluations
The skeptical might contend that our results simply reveal that former legislators who have done well congratulate Congress on supplying the necessary skills for them to do so; conversely, ex-legislators who have fared poorly belittle their experiences in Congress. This seemingly devastating critique of the effects of training runs into difficulty, however, when subjected to empirical testing. For example, this contention implies that the effects of training are biased, thereby exaggerating its influence on postelective wages. However, training investments have no statistically significant influence on postelective wages; only in conjunction with skill set breadth does (general) training influence salaries.

We might pursue this "bitterness" argument further from another angle. Perhaps less accomplished legislators rationalize that they indeed acquired extensive skill sets, but that the effort was pointless since they were poorly compensated after leaving Congress. In this instance, the effect would be to wash away the influence of skill set breadth in augmenting postelective salaries. Yet such also is not the case, since skill set scope has a highly robust positive relationship to postelective earnings. In short, the argument that slanted respondent perceptions of the value of congressional activities account for our results about postelective wages, when juxtaposed with other reported findings, reveals readily apparent contradictions. Therefore, we doubt that such a rationalization effect is a rampant, widespread phenomenon within our data.

While certainly provocative arguments, they cloud the basic issue—that is, rationalizations aside, what did (wage) gainers and losers do differently during congressional service to yield these salary differences? Controlling for tenure clearly demonstrates that salary differences cannot be attributed merely to time in the institution; legislators did something with that time. Nor are abilities and endowments factors, since we have controlled for these variables as well.

The straightforward answer is that since service in Congress was full-time employment, some ex-legislators made more out of their congressional experiences, financially speaking, than others. But why did training boost salaries in one case, yet do so to a lesser extent or not at all in the other? The answer seems clear: differences in the training received. Given that all experiences in Congress entail training of some kind, those whose human capital increased in market value after their stints in Congress invested in training experiences different from those invested in by legislators suffering losses. In sum, while in Congress, those who failed to achieve postelective salary increases did not invest in skill sets as highly marketable as those receiving larger wage gains.

We have theorized that diverse institutional experiences engender differentials in postelective wages, and we have found evidence consistently supporting this proposition. Furthermore, less obtrusive or reactive measures, such as prestige committee service, tell the same story: a general education in congressional politics pays off in higher postelective salaries. It is therefore unlikely that systematic biases in survey responses can explain the income-earning effects of inclusive skill sets and training. Our instincts, then, lead us to trust the observed relationships between institutional investments and wage changes because they are reasonable, consistent with economic theory, supported by less obtrusive data, resilient in the face of alternative explanations, and follow our theoretical predictions.

If less well-to-do former legislators in fact disparage the value of their congressional training, since it failed to boost their postelective salaries while augmenting the wages of others, they have no valid reason to feel that way. Congressional training per se is not to blame; rather, legislators' deliberate decisions about investing in training during their congressional careers affect postelective wages.

Leadership Position versus Training

The relationships among broad skill sets, general training, and postelective salaries might be said merely to reflect the significance of holding leadership positions in Congress. Former political leaders always seem to be in demand as consultants, speakers, professors, and the like. Such demand easily translates into earnings. We offer two observations with regard to this point.

First, the relationship between postelective wages and past service as a congressional leader (party leaders coded as 2, committee leaders coded as 1, and nonleaders coded as 0) is statistically insignificant when entered into our wage equation. Moreover, the introduction of this measure into the wage equation does nothing to disturb the effects of legislator investments in broad skill sets on postelective salaries. Therefore, the effects of inclusive skill sets and general training are not proxies for positions of congressional leadership.

Second, party leaders are, by the nature of their offices, equipped with broader and more variegated views of politics and policy-making. Their positions put them in contact with a variety of officials within the governmental and private sectors, all of them promoting different policy packages and objectives. Thus, leaders' skill sets, in contrast to those of regular party members, are likely to be more general in makeup because of their exposure to a broader assortment of interests. In addition, they have made the necessary long-term investments in congressional training ($r = .20$) to warrant elevation to positions of party leadership—for example, developing a mastery of parliamentary procedure and serving long periods on prestige committees ($r = .23$).

These correlations are not so daunting as to imply that no differences exist between service in congressional leadership positions and the acquisition of general training skills. In fact, we might say that these correlations only reinforce our contention that the acquisition of inclusive skill sets is frequently associated with leadership experiences; this is why these skill sets are so uncommon and costly to acquire, and why they engender such large postelective salaries. Yet even though leadership positions provide fertile settings for acquiring broad-based skill sets, they do not ensure legislator investment, effort, or proficiency.

The question of the economic effects of leadership position on postelective wages really should be considered in these terms: Which counts more in setting postelective wages, service in and occupation of positions of party power, or the human capital acquired while in these offices? For the rational employer, the answer is obvious: honorific positions are of little economic value unless they are coupled with the skills necessary to enhance company or industry profits. If so, then, the human capital acquired through service as a party leader, rather than the mere occupation of such a position, is what counts in boosting postelective salaries. The observed negative relationship between tenure and postelective salaries supports this contention.

In short, we do not believe, and can find no evidence to support the idea, that the relationships we have uncovered between the acquisition of expansive skill sets and postelective salaries is purely an artifact of party leaders obtaining large salaries because of powerful positions formerly held. This is not to deny that party and committee leaders can draw fat salaries after leaving Congress. But they may do so because of the skills and human capital they have acquired while on the job.

Life Cycle Discount

As expected, senior legislators are penalized for their diminished investments in general training during the later course of officeholding (beta = −.187). Although this relationship only flirts with statistical significance, it is consistent with our expectations. While the statistical significance of this variable is worrisome, its close conceptual and computational association with tenure (that is, tenure is one of the factors used in computing life cycle investments) accounts for some of this variable's apparent unreliability. Not surprisingly, excluding tenure[6] from the equation enhances considerably the significance of this variable (that is, alpha < .003), with only a marginal loss in the explanatory value of the equation. Thus, we offer a discussion of this quasi-significant but theoretically important variable.

Senior legislators have undoubtedly accumulated large amounts of general training from their on-the-job congressional experiences during the course of their long careers; however, as time goes on, we have speculated, they invest less in that endeavor. For example, they may have minimized efforts to keep abreast of the latest developments in their policy areas, reduced the time spent maintaining and nurturing personal contacts with bureaucrats, or curtailed involvement in the legislative life of Congress. And as noted, abundant rationales exist for reducing investments in general training, such as the finite lifetimes and earning streams of legislators and the declining marginal value of additional political skills with tenure.[7]

---

6. We have included *tenure* in our estimating equation because the variable influences postelective salaries and improves the fit of the model to the data, increasing the R^2 from .46 to .51.

7. This raises an interesting if only tangential point: legislative scholars highlight new members' ability to exercise considerable power in the contemporary or modern Congress, but offer little recognition of the fact that many senior members seem to exhibit so little overt resistance to the eclipse of their powers. From the perspective of human capital theory, senior members may do so because there are diminished returns to plying these skills with each successive endeavor. In short,

Such reduced investments are unlikely to escape the notice of employers, since, as many economic models of information accumulation suggest, an individual's job experiences or investments in human capital create information about their skills relevant to the performance of various tasks (see, for example, Macdonald 1980, 1982; Harris and Weiss 1984). Thus, prospective employers should be able to assess the future productivity of ex-legislators by observing their recent investments in human capital. Consumers (Akerlof 1970; Nelson 1970; Klein and Laffler 1981) and voters (Downs 1957; Stigler 1971) may be rationally ignorant of the goings-on in Washington, but special interests find that a less cost-efficient strategy in their dealings with politicians. For example, unlike voters, employers have the incentives and wherewithal to spot legislator incompetence or lack of interest in policy questions during committee deliberations.

Diminished investments in expanding or acquiring skills during later stages of congressional careers may signal those contemplating hiring senior ex-legislators that their skills have declined and do not warrant premium dollar. Employers consequently discount the human capital acquired by senior ex-legislators and pay them accordingly.

The Generational Tax

Recent generations of ex-legislators appear to suffer in their postelective salaries, commanding far lower salaries than those entering Congress decades earlier (beta = −.308). We infer from this that newer legislative cohorts unknowingly chance upon a hidden tax when looking for employment after leaving Congress. This tax is linked to adverse selection in the composition of Congress (Parker 1996), which has resulted in recent cohorts exhibiting unusual levels of avarice and opportunism. Characterizing them as ferreting financial gain out of every nook and cranny in the legislative process may seem cruel and callous, but the empirical data all too often lead to that sad conclusion. Such a drive for economic profit is not lost on those hiring legislators, and far from finding it an attractive employee trait, employers implicitly tax the wages of those exhibiting these qualities, paying lower salaries. Ironically, then, precisely their appetites for wealth may prevent them from parlaying their years in Congress into lucrative postelective salaries.

It is unquestionably bizarre that the wealth-maximizing preferences of recent generations should prevent them from obtaining top dollar for their

---

the costs of fighting back attempts to muscle in or encroach on the prerogatives of senior members may not be worth the returns, given that the latter are far less interested than more junior legislators in enriching their training in congressional politics.

services after they leave Congress. Yet the dramatic ways recent congressional cohorts differ from their predecessors with respect to their appetites for wealth could easily diminish their attractiveness as employees, and consequently the salaries they receive in postelective employment. We might say, therefore, that recent legislative cohorts' efforts to enrich themselves while in office cost them dearly when they leave, as they receive lower starting salaries. A generational tax is thus applied to postcongressional salaries, with those recently entering Congress suffering the heaviest tax burden.

Rationale behind Generational Tax

Recent generations receive lower postelective wages for at least four reasons. First, as we have alluded, their wealth-pursuing behavior may be all too transparent to potential employers. For example, shaking down special interests for campaign funds is a sure indicator of more than business acumen—it conveys information about character to potential employers. This inability to shroud or conceal their penchant for financial gain diminishes their appeal to employers as well as their bargaining leverage.

Second, employers rightfully fear that with all the asymmetries in information, and the attendant coordination problems endemic to politics and the legislative process, it is easy to be cheated. In light of their demand for wealth, recent generations of legislators may be viewed as more likely to exploit the costs of employer monitoring and policing. If employers do in fact harbor such concerns, they may offer lower wages to cover expected losses from employee unreliability and opportunism, thereby reducing the salaries offered recent generations of legislators.

Third, aware that competitive bidding for the services of these ex-legislators is certain to result in higher costs, either in salaries or in employee turnover, employers may be less disposed to pay top wages to hire recent generations of ex-legislators whose job loyalty is always up for sale. Thus, employers may hire others who are less likely to be persistently on the prowl for higher-paying jobs. This may reduce the salaries that recent generations of legislators can command in the market, as economically wise employers factor potential disruption to the organization into the salaries offered.

Fourth, employers are sensitive to employee characteristics in trying to create a good job match, but their efforts are stymied because recent generations are unlikely to excel at any of the important traits. For instance, job turnover looms important in this regard, but recent generations have a penchant for spending less time in their first ($r = -.21$) and second ($r = -.17$) postelective jobs; controlling for tenure in Congress does nothing to diminish the significance of these relationships. In addition to job turnover, recent gen-

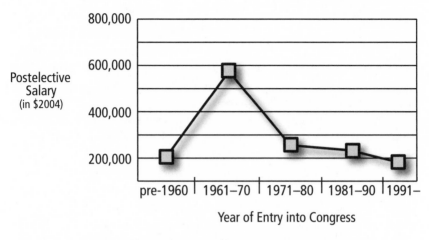

FIG. 6.3. Postelective salaries of lobbyists by decade of arrival

erations are less well trained, if their levels of investment are any indication (r = −.15); they are also less constrained by threats to their reputations because they have invested so little in them (r = −.12). Recent congressional cohorts clearly do not share the traits employers cherish in valued employees. All of these factors probably play a role in structuring the salaries recent generations of former legislators collect, since all are important employee characteristics.

The Lobbying Paradox
Figure 6.3 addresses what may seem something of a paradox: Why should recent generations obtain lower postelective salaries (table 6.3) when they are so inclined to find lucrative employment as lobbyists (table 5.11), the highest-paying occupation for ex-legislators? We believe that the explanation rests in the lower wages that recent generations of legislator-lobbyists receive. As figure 6.3 reveals, lobbying ex-legislators arriving since the 1990s received lower starting salaries than those elected before 1960, continuing a steady decline from the high point in postelective wages obtained by the 1961–70 cohort of former legislators. While recent generations of legislators may gravitate to high-paying positions as lobbyists, the salaries they receive are often lower than those obtained by legislator-lobbyists entering Congress in earlier periods. As table 6.3 shows, regardless of the tenure accumulated, the generational relationship persists.

This paradox might have less to do with the characteristics of recent congressional cohorts and more to do with the narrow or specialized market in which legislators rent their human capital. Over time, we might expect congestion to set in as former legislators gravitate to this profitable trade to earn the supernormal returns associated with this occupation. Even Capitol Hill staff members are entering the trade in increasing numbers, providing competition for lobbying positions (Kirkpatrick 2006a; Kornblut 2006a), and greater competition for these jobs could result in lower salaries for ex-legislators. We offer two observations relevant to this argument.

First, the rent-seeking society continues to generate enough business to employ tens of thousands of lobbyists, as the growth in government regulations shows (Ornstein, Mann, and Malbin 1996, 165). And even if the market for their services is specialized, confined to those dealing with the federal government, many groups find themselves in the position of seeking to extract benefits from government in the form of subsidies, control over complements and supplements, price fixing, or influence over the entry of rivals (Stigler 1971). In short, the market may be specialized in terms of the types of jobs available for former legislators, but the demand for the services they supply remains high.

Second, no matter the size of the market, ex-legislators still have a comparative advantage as a consequence of the nature of their political training and accumulated human capital. "Congressional experience conveys more value than does employment in the executive branch or with independent agencies. Broader substantive expertise is gained in Congress, and gained more quickly. The same is true of contacts" (Heinz et al. 1993, 127). Thus, it is unlikely that the specialized and arguably congested market for legislators' services can account for the decline in the salaries of recent generations of legislators; legislative skills, as noted earlier, are matchless.

Senators

Finally, no bonus seems to be attached to service in the Senate: the postelective earnings of ex-senators do not differ statistically from the salaries of House incumbents. Senators have an easier time finding employment (Parker 2004), but their postelective salaries are not in keeping with the higher status of their office relative to that of members of the House. However, because of the small number of senators in our analysis, we are reluctant to dismiss the possibility of a relationship.

Subsidizing Training in Congressional Politics

It is often difficult if not impossible to find any trace of political action committee (PAC) contributions affecting roll-call votes and the like. This is something of a paradox: special interests pour money into the reelection coffers of incumbent officeholders, but few scholars have uncovered a substantial linkage between PAC contributions and legislator behavior, such as congressional votes (see, for example, Chappell 1982; Wright 1985; Grenzke 1989).[8] Should we then conclude that since empirical findings always trump anecdotal evidence, we have grossly exaggerated the influence of special interests in politics? If special interests are not influential after spending billions for that purpose, the joke is really on them, is it not? Laughter is the wrong response, however, since only the politically naive could envision special interests as having no influence on public policy.

We feel that studies of interest group influence in politics concentrate too much on PAC money per se. In so doing, they have ignored the often-repeated observation that incumbent officeholders can probably raise as much money as they need to defeat most electoral competition. Plus, incumbents routinely face underfinanced challengers, so large war chests are not electoral imperatives. But this does not mean that no relationship exists between group PAC money and legislator behavior; we may just be looking in the wrong places.

This is not to deny that campaign funds serve all the sinister and perverse ends envisioned by political scientists and economists—and then some. We would only add that a number of the nefarious and quasi-nefarious outcomes can also be explained by assuming that legislators are enticed or encouraged to specialize in policy areas rationally trolled by special interests. Legislative votes, for example, are an area of congressional behavior in which we expect the worst, but see the least in terms of firsthand observation of the surreptitious exchanges between special interests and legislators. Yet this does not prevent legislators' votes favoring special interests from being interpreted as evidence that these legislators are in these groups' pockets. The alternative characterization—that is, legislators support special interest positions because they see the policy solutions, alternatives, and choices from the same perspective—seems an equally plausible explanation, but it receives little play.

Special Interest Money as Educational Subsidies

From our perspective, PAC money subsidizes the on-the-job training of politicians returned to office so that they can continue to invest in the skills and information that enhance their human capital. This makes them valuable commodities to special interests both during and after congressional service.

8. A few studies find some consistent measure of influence for interest groups (see, for example, Silberman and Durden 1976; Welch 1980; Kau and Rubin 1982; Evans 1986) but even then, the influence is rather modest at best.

Indeed, it would not be too far afield to characterize PAC contributions as evidence that "industries follow investment oriented-goals in political activity" (Grier, Munger, and Roberts 1994, 921). PAC contributions provide the tuition and fees associated with elected office, thereby subsidizing the costs of returning to office and undertaking further specialized training. Officeholders are like most employees in the sense that some of the most attractive training opportunities are those where the costs can be effectively transferred to others. Legislators thus pursue specialized training because they can easily find sponsors to underwrite the costs.

Rational politicians must listen to interest groups because they provide the type of expert knowledge required in formulating governmental policy (Downs 1957, 247–58); in so doing, however, they become as specialized in their information and outlook as the specialized interests—that is, the legislators tend to see things in the same way as the special interests. Specialized training, then, is one factor leading legislators to develop policy views that parallel those of special interests. In short, legislators support interest group causes not only out of debt or to fulfill a deal but in addition, and perhaps even more frequently, because their specialized training has led them to view public policy issues from the same perspective as special interests. This may explain the virtual invisibility of interest group influence on many matters of public policy: little difference exists between the views of specialized legislators and interest groups operating in that specialized policy area—in a real sense, the legislators *are* the special interests.

From this theoretical angle, legislators do not merely swing their office doors wide open to interest groups because they have supplied campaign monies, as some models assume; rather, special interests gain access to legislators because they tend to see problems and policies from the same vantage points. The analogy frequently used to characterize interest group–legislator contact is that of an encounter between buyers and sellers. While special interests and the legislators they seek to influence may not be kindred spirits, we suspect that their interactions are far less stressful than such market transactions—perhaps more akin to fans getting together to talk about their favorite teams.

The Cost of a General Education

Even though specialists draw lower postelective wages than generalists, their training is subsidized to a greater extent by interests expecting to benefit from the acquired specialized knowledge and skills. Here, type of training almost certainly affects the level of campaign subsidy. "Persons receiving general training would be willing to pay these costs," Becker (1993, 34) writes, "since training raises their future wages." Conversely, special interests have few incentives to subsidize job-training experiences less specialized to group needs but generally useful to many firms. Consequently, we expect that investments in general training will be less subsidized by special interests (a negative relationship). Politicians undertaking general training must make this trade-off: general training and capital ensure a wider breadth of employment options, but recipients must be willing to pay a greater proportion of the training costs—that is, the tuition and fees, or campaign costs, necessary to hold office.

Analysis

We have employed the standard politicians' human capital model here, although our interest focuses on a single theoretical relationship within it: the effects of general training on the subsidization of campaign costs through PAC contributions. We include additional sources of human capital (political and economic talents and endowments, for example) to ensure that the effects of general training do not merely capture some unspecified stock of human capital absent from the explanatory equation. Our dependent variable is the extent to which legislators' election costs are subsidized through interest group campaign contributions (that is, PAC money) during the course of their congressional careers. This variable is calculated as the sum of the total amount of PAC money received during the course of congressional service divided by the total campaign disbursements during the same period. Our analysis here is noticeably restricted to less than half of our original sample— that is, 101 ex-legislators—since data on campaign expenditures were unavailable before the late 1970s.

Statistical Model

In this segment of the study, we focus on the last of our major hypotheses: special interests are less inclined to subsidize the campaign costs of legislators pursuing general training. We have also added several additional variables so that our equation would not suffer from threats of misspecification because important variables are absent. Hence, we include measures of *party affiliation, service as a senator, future career change, future position as a lobbyist, year of exit from Congress,* and *year of entrance to Congress.*

Party affiliation is included under the hypothesis that Democrats are more likely to have their campaign costs subsidized by special interests than

Republicans are because their mass electoral basis is generally composed of the less well-to-do, thereby necessitating financial support beyond personal contributions and money derived from mass fund-raising events. The notion underlying the inclusion of a dummy variable in the equation representing employment as a senator is simply that the high costs of Senate elections, relative to most House campaigns, requires a greater degree of subsidization from special interests.

Years of entrance and departure from Congress capture the effects of adverse selection that seem apparent at just about every corner of our analysis: the newly arrived are more likely to become lobbyists, display a reticence toward investing in training, behave opportunistically, and raise and spend campaign money rather lavishly (Parker 1996, 107–13); those exiting Congress more recently are likely to become lobbyists ($r = .27$). It is certainly not beyond imagination that such generations would also find ways to lay off their campaign debts onto special interests. Thus, we have included a simple measure of (the year) when legislators entered and left Congress; we expect recent generations to have a larger proportion of their campaign costs financed by special interest money.[9]

In addition, we include two occupational change variables—specifically, career change after leaving Congress and employment as a lobbyist. Both of these variables are measured over the course of the first three jobs ex-legislators took after leaving Congress. That is, if ex-legislators did not return to their precongressional occupations within their first three jobs after leaving Congress, they are classified as having changed occupations and coded as 1; otherwise, they receive a 0. Similarly, if ex-legislators took jobs as lobbyists sometime during the course of their first three jobs after leaving Congress, they are categorized as lobbying and coded as 1; otherwise, they, too, receive a 0.[10] As we noted in chapter 5, career changes and

---

9. A strong correlation exists between year of entry and year of departure ($r = .70$), which indicates the obvious—more recent entering congressional cohorts also left Congress later; consequently, year of departure remains a useful, complementary generational marker. In most of the other equations (see, for example, table 6.3) we have avoided using both of these generational markers since expressions of multicollinearity arise when both variables are present in the same equation as a consequence of this strong intercorrelation. No problem arose, however, with respect to this equation (table 6.4).

10. Substituting a variable representing employment as a lobbyist in the first job after leaving Congress—that is, a dependent variable in chapter 5—for this variable does nothing to improve the model's fit to the data and is statistically insignificant. We feel that the variable that we have used—whether ex-legislators turned to lobbying within their first three jobs after leaving Congress—is a better representation of the underlying argument that campaign contributions represent in-office payoffs, since legislators contemplating future lobbying positions can over time be expected to shift their campaign costs onto prospective employers.

lobbying necessitate specialized training, which interest groups enthusiastically support with PAC funds. For this reason, we might expect that legislators aspiring to some sort of career change would have their campaigns subsidized at a higher level than those expecting to return to their precongressional occupations.

Two relevant variables missing from this equation—*precongressional salary* and *electoral safety* (average margin of victory during congressional service)—were initially examined, but their effects proved statistically insignificant, and they were removed from the results displayed in table 6.4. In addition, their inclusion confounded the reliability of other factors of greater substantive and theoretical significance without any measurable gain in prediction.

The model estimated is as follows:

$$C = f(X_1 \ldots X_{15}),$$

where C represents the percentage of the total campaign costs (that is, disbursements) of legislators during the course of their careers in Congress that were subsidized through PAC contributions from special interests, and

Political ability:

X_1 = prior political office

Nontraining capital:

X_2 = nontraining assets

X_3 = reputational capital

On-the-job-training in Congress:

X_4 = years of service on interest group committees

X_5 = years of service on prestige committees

X_6 = investments in on-the-job training

Breadth of skills:

X_7 = skill acquisition, or breadth of skills acquired

X_8 = general training (breadth of skills acquired × investments in on-the-job training)

X_9 = life cycle investments in general training (breadth of skills acquired × investments in on-the-job training × tenure)

Equation-specific variables:

X_{10} = year of entry into Congress

X_{11} = year of exit from Congress

X_{12} = career change within first three jobs after leaving Congress

X_{13} = turned to lobbying within first three jobs after leaving Congress

X_{14} = senator

X_{15} = party affiliation.

Overall Regression Results

The results of our analysis are described in table 6.4. A few things stand out about this equation. First, our model provides an extremely good fit to the data (R = .75), explaining more than half of the variation in special interest group subsidization of legislators' campaign costs during the course of their careers in Congress.

Second, contrary to much speculation about how postelective jobs for legislators are merely an extension of special interest support—but after rather than during officeholding—no significant relationship exists between PAC subsidies and taking jobs as lobbyists during the course of postelective careers. We might expect prospective lobbyists to cultivate special interests to smooth the way to future jobs, but if they do, we find no evidence of a linkage between that employment and interest group support while in office. If employment is a payoff for service to special interests, we would expect a highly statistically significant relationship between campaign support and future

TABLE 6.4. Explaining PAC Subsidies of Legislators' Campaign Costs

Variable	B	Error	Beta	t	Significance
Career change	.041	.041	.091	1.008	.316
Lobbying in first 3 jobs	−.051	.039	−.113	−1.312	.193
Prior political office	−.047	.048	−.086	−.988	.326
Interest group committee	−.002	.003	−.075	−.845	.400
Prestige committee	.000	.002	.013	.129	.898
Nontraining assets	.015	.019	.062	.763	.448
Investment in training	.001	.021	.005	.050	.960
Reputational capital	−.012	.015	−.065	−.800	.426
Broad skill set	.012	.020	.053	.614	.541
General training	−.049	.026	−.252	−1.878	.064
Life cycle investments	.001	.001	.153	1.073	.286
Party	.057	.032	.140	1.796	.076
Senator	−.137	.110	−.104	−1.240	.218
Year of exit	.024	.004	.526	5.278	.000
Year of entry	.007	.003	.283	2.529	.013

Statistics
R = .745
R^2 = .554
N = 101

Source: Federal Elections Commission, 1980–2004; authors' survey of former members of Congress, 2004.

employment as lobbyists, since both campaign support and postelective jobs are compensation for favors performed for special interests. The lack of a relationship casts further doubt on how widespread the bartering of postelective lobbying positions actually is.

General Training

PAC support appears to be conditioned less by future employment as a lobbyist and more by the specificity of legislators' training. Simply put, as predicted, special interests penalize general training in the sense that legislators opting for such training have their reelection campaigns financed to a lesser degree by special interests than do legislators with more specialized training in congressional politics. Thus, the third conclusion that can be drawn from this table is that special interests subsidize a smaller percentage of the campaign costs incurred by those pursuing a more general education in legislative politics.

We recognize that our measure of general training only approaches statistical significance (alpha < .064). The sign of this variable is in the proper direction, however, and ignoring this variable's close proximity to our established level of significance (alpha < .05) would certainly blind us to its relevance, and therefore increase the likelihood of falling prey to the equally distasteful *type-II* error that thwarts exploratory research of this nature. For these reasons, we conclude that this hypothesis is reasonably valid.

Generational Effects

Aside from general training, only two other relationships are of substantial importance in influencing levels of PAC support—our generational markers. That is, those who recently entered (beta = .283) and left Congress (beta = .526) have been the most successful in obtaining special interests' campaign support. Once again, we see these results as further expressions of adverse selection: recent congressional cohorts again seem to be behaving opportunistically, this time shifting their campaign debt to special interests. We characterize this behavior as opportunistic because transferring campaign costs has nothing to do with investments in specialized training, which PAC contributions naturally support—that is, the positive relationships persist even when we control for such investments (table 6.4).

While some might suggest that such entrepreneurial shrewdness is worthy of applause, we see it simply as further indication that recent generations of legislators have found governmental employment amenable to their wealth-maximizing motives. There has never been reason to be sanguine about the flow of special interest money into congressional campaign coffers, but the opportunism of recent generations, as exhibited in part by their fondness for passing their campaign costs onto special interests, gives cause for even greater concern. Pawning off campaign debts onto interest groups invites trouble, as numerous exposés of campaign fraud and influence buying and peddling testify. Perhaps equally disquieting is the fact that these generational variables are so important.

Alternative Explanations for Generational Effects
The appetite of recent generations for special interest subsidies might stem from high levels of electoral insecurity, which recent entrants always experience. This is a reasonable argument; however, generational differences persist even when a measure of electoral safety—average margin of victory during the course of one's congressional career—is introduced into the equation (not shown). Fear for electoral survival is surely not what leads recent generations of legislators to lay off their campaign debts onto special interests.

The relationship between congressional cohorts and campaign subsidization also might simply result from the higher costs of contemporary elections—that is, recent generations of legislators face higher campaign costs and need to have these soaring costs subsidized in some manner; special interests are all too willing to do so. Congressional campaigns undeniably cost considerably more today than they did decades ago. We suspect that some of the escalating costs of congressional campaigns are reflected in the strong association between year of departure and level of campaign subsidization: those who exited more recently endured the most costly campaigns, thereby necessitating rather substantial PAC subsidies. Yet after we have controlled for this variable, generational differences still remain—that is, recent generations of legislators transfer more of their campaign debt to special interests regardless of when they exited. It is doubtful, then, that merely the rising costs of congressional campaigns have led recent generations of legislators to reallocate the debt incurred in their campaigns to special interests.

Senators and Democrats

Two additional variables warrant mention, if only because their effects address important contemporary issues about politics. First, senators display no greater cunning than representatives in having their campaign costs subsidized by special interests. Senators may run more expensive campaigns, but no evidence indicates that doing so leads to greater campaign debt being shifted to special interests. The considerable personal fortunes of many sena-

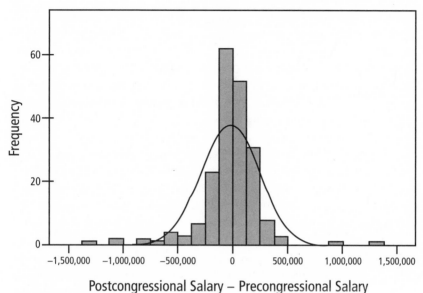

Postcongressional Salary – Precongressional Salary

FIG. 6.4. Wage gains and losses for ex-legislators

tors, and their willingness to devote substantial portions of it to getting elected, may reduce their need to depend on PAC money to cover campaign debts. Second, Democrats seem to be more successful at having campaign costs subsidized, but the relationship falls short of statistical significance.

Summary and Discussion

During our survey, several ex-legislators in our sample beseeched us to awaken the public to the financial sacrifices associated with public office. Given our public choice roots, and journalistic accounts of the gain expropriated through officeholding, we were skeptical about these self-serving entreaties. However, when we examined the differences between postelective and precongressional salaries (that is, postelective salary minus precongressional salary), we were startled to find that this was no ruse.

Legislators—at least those in our sample—had in fact suffered financial losses. Given the level of postelective salaries, the losses do not qualify as spectacular by any means—the median loss in salary was $11,044—and although there is a modest skew, it is not excessive (figure 6.4). Still, the mere fact that wages declined at all, rather than increased, is a bit startling. Perhaps we have been too harsh in taking our legislators to task for the lucrative employment they obtain after leaving Congress: public office is itself a financial sacrifice, and no matter how handsome the pay, postelective wages for the most part do not measure up to preelective salaries.

We have also uncovered evidence that adverse selection may be emerging within the composition of Congress, as recent generations of legislators try to slough their campaign costs onto interest groups. Do some prospective employers perceive these attempts to have campaign costs subsidized as extortion in the sense discussed by McChesney (1987). If so, we might expect a reduction in the wages these legislators command when exiting Congress, as employers reap some measure of revenge by adjusting present wages to compensate for preemployment bonuses distributed in the form of PAC contributions. We have found evidence of such a tax applied to the wages of recent congressional cohorts, and to their postelective salaries as lobbyists. Recent generations of legislator-lobbyists are by and large the most poorly paid of this highly compensated lot of employees, with their salaries differing statistically and falling in a significant and noteworthy linear fashion since the 1960s (figure 6.3).

We have suggested that employers seem to be sensitive to the characteristics of their legislator-employees, paying lower wages to those who have recently reduced their investments in general training and to more recent generations of legislators. In both cases, shirking problems may provide the rationale. We have found that general training and the broad skill sets it produces redound to the benefit of former legislators by enhancing their postelective salaries. However, general training and the acquisition of broad skill packages are less subsidized by special interests, since such general human capital serves a wider assortment of markets and is of course less specialized to group needs.

Chapter 7

Summary of Findings and Implications

Table 7.1 summarizes the major findings about human capital and politics uncovered in our inquiry. Investments in on-the-job training clearly pay off handsomely for legislators, whether they anticipate changing careers or earning lucrative postelective salaries. In this sense, our study reaches the same conclusion as Becker (1993) and other human capitalists: job training increases future returns. We might take a step further by suggesting that although ability, talent, and endowments go a long way in determining legislators' fortunes in later life, training seems equally powerful in this regard. In the following pages we recount and discuss our major findings and the implications that can be derived from them.

General and Specialized Training

The salary boost engendered by general training and the acquisition of expansive skill sets result from the scarcity of these skills and the option value associated with general training capital. These assets allow former legislators greater choice in deciding which economic sectors will be most profitable to enter. These skills are scarce in part because they are so costly to acquire within Congress, like membership on the House Rules Committee or service in a succession of political leadership posts. Similarly, we found that investments (years of service) on committees providing general training increased postelective salaries (table 6.3).

Training also helps legislators acquire specific skill packages through their committee assignments and other congressional experiences. If legislators have tired of their precongressional occupations, for whatever reason, Congress provides manifold opportunities for specialized training that equips legislators with skills necessary for career changes. Three factors encourage legislator specialization: legislators' desire to find someone to foot the bill for their elections, the expectation of future career changes, and the cost of acquiring broad skill sets. Specialized skills, though perhaps of little value in enhancing postelective salaries, are particularly important in supplying the human capital necessary for subsequent career changes.

This may seem something of a paradox: general training and inclusive skill sets enhance postelective salaries, but legislators are by and large specialists. This seeming contradiction can be explained by considering a few points. First, postelective salaries do not take into consideration the costs of an education in politics. Specialists have the costs of their campaigns subsidized to a greater degree than do generalists; hence, nonsubsidized campaign costs must be deducted from generalists' postelective earnings or amortized across postelective lifetimes. The result would certainly be a lower level of real postelective earnings for generalists.

Second, legislators may have no alternative but to specialize, at least in the short run, since few can afford to finance their own reelections; being beholden to special interests for campaign money assures specialization in politics. And, after all, legislators need to keep getting reelected just to accumulate the human capital that enhances the marketability of political skills. Pragmatism, if nothing else, leads legislators to specialize because they know that special interests will cover their campaign costs if they do so.

Third, salary premiums may be paid to those who have acquired broad skills because such skill sets are so rare; scarcity affects value and price. Hence, even if members preferred general training to specialization, the opportunities to invest in the latter are far greater. Legislators' investment strategies con-

TABLE 7.1. Summary of Findings: Human Capital Factors

Dependent Variables	Precongressional Capital: Abilities/Endowments	Nontraining Capital	On-the-Job Training	Breadth of Skill Set
Breadth of skill set	Prior political experience[a]	X	X	
Job mobility	X		X	
Choosing to lobby		Reputational capital[a]	X	
Postelective earnings	Precongressional salary[a]		X	X
Campaign support			General training[a]	

[a]This is the only factor within this category of variables that significantly influences (or approaches statistical significance with) the dependent variable.

sequently emphasize specialized training because of its greater availability and lower cost.

Finally, specialization is extremely important for those ex-legislators interested in changing vocations; hence, some of the economic effects of specialization may not be readily apparent just from computing salary differences. The ability to switch vocations is one significant economic factor that may encourage legislators to specialize despite the financial loss they may suffer in postelective salary.[1] For many employees, a better or different job—indeed, a new career—is worth taking a lower salary. Some ex-legislators may be of the same mind.[2]

We might still say that, all things equal, it probably does not pay for legislators to specialize since doing so jeopardizes postelective salaries. However, rarely are all things equal in politicians' eyes: campaign costs make specialization a necessity of life for most politicians, especially members of Congress; gaining expertise in a narrow policy area is a good vehicle for switching occupations; and the opportunities for specialization are more readily within reach than those providing general training. Therefore, legislators' decisions about investments in human capital necessarily incorporate cost-benefit considerations beyond postelective salary.

Adverse Selection

We do not want to dwell on this point, but one of the most intriguing results is the extent to which adverse-selection predictions explain generational differences in the postelective salaries of lobbying legislators, the inclination to take a job as a lobbyist, and a fondness for shifting campaign debts to special interests. We have intimated that recent congressional cohorts may be more inclined toward opportunism, and the returns on investments they pursue (for example, jobs as lobbyists) suggest that this characterization has some validity. In earlier research (Parker 1996) we suggested that recent generations of legislators were less interested in service in the institution and more concerned with enhancing their personal economic wealth. Our findings here, a

---

1. A large number of legislators change careers—42.6 percent never returned to their precongressional careers within their first three jobs after leaving Congress. Given the large number of legislators who change vocations, it is easy to understand specialization's importance not merely to congressional operations but also to legislators' future livelihoods.
2. A negative correlation exists between changing careers and one's salary after leaving Congress ($r = -.13$); the relationship is significant at the .078 level in a two-tailed test of significance. As might be anticipated, changing vocations is somewhat costly, but the relationship is not highly reliable.

decade later, have done little to persuade us otherwise. This information, juxtaposed with our earlier observation about their penchant for raising and spending large amounts of campaign monies (Parker 1996), lead to the inescapable conclusion that, at a minimum, the behavior of recent generations of legislators bears watching.

Implications

The marketability of skills and talents, then, shapes the investment strategies of politicians while in office. For example, legislators anticipating career changes after leaving Congress invest more heavily in specialized human capital, while those hoping to boost postelective salary or earnings invest in general training and in acquiring inclusive skill sets. In sum, human capital investments depend on the costs associated with acquiring particular skill sets, relative to the anticipated economic gains obtained in terms of career changes or lucrative postelective wages. This is a simple characterization of political life—politicians make decisions on the basis of expected returns and the associated costs—but a number of important implications can be derived from this premise. We now turn to a discussion of a few of these systemic implications, some of which are intermingled with our hypotheses taken to their logical ends.

Campaign Contributions

Most political scientists consider PAC funds to be attempts by groups to support like-minded candidates or to ensure access to incumbent officeholders—that is, those most likely to win election. For public choice economists, campaign funds represent rents that politicians extract from monopoly-hungry special interests for present and future favors (see, for example, McChesney 1987). We do not deny that campaign funds serve these purposes, but we add that PAC money can be viewed as a subsidy for acquiring and continuing to acquire specialized assets (human capital) that are economically valuable to groups in society.

For politicians, the costs of an education in politics necessitate a fairly steep level of tuition and fees, which normally exceeds the income and perhaps fortunes of most politicians. Subsidizing the costs of elections no doubt covers only some of the job training expenses incurred in politics. Still, it undoubtedly offsets a significant proportion of the out-of-pocket expenses that politicians encounter in trying to obtain public office—on average, about 24 percent (see appendix).

Our approach to campaign financing should be contrasted with Mc-Chesney's (1987) insightful analysis of "rent extractions." He contends that legislators extort money from special interests by threatening to impose costs on them—for example, in the form of additional federal regulations. To avoid these costs, groups pay the tribute demanded of them. This political black-mail often is paid through campaign contributions. Simply put, politicians hold up special interests to obtain large campaign contributions by threatening to harm their livelihoods and profits through regulations. While McChesney's argument is both novel and provocative, it ignores legislator demand for postelective employment. Opportunistic behavior may enable politicians to keep special interests at bay while in office, but the shoe is on the other foot when politicians leave public service. Then, politicians are beholden to special interests for postelective employment.

If politicians are planning for the future, therefore, they need to consider how their treatment of special interests while in office might affect their job prospects after they leave.[3] Taking advantage of special interests, even if it could be done with electoral immunity, makes for really poor employee-employer relations in the future.[4] Thus, with respect to the demands of special interests, rational expectations of future returns implicitly police the behavior of politicians while in office. But such opportunistic behavior is unlikely to arise in any event for the simple reason that factors contrive to promote a cooperative relationship, perhaps even a friendly one, between special interests and lobbyists.

---

3. From the perspective of a rent-seeking model, future employers can always change their minds about hiring ex-politicians when the time to do so arrives; hence, politicians need some indication on the part of economic (special) interests that they do indeed intend to keep that commitment. Special interests demonstrate such commitments through their over-time transactions, many of which are obviously hidden from public view. These transactions signal politicians that future employers can be counted on to keep their promises of postelective employment. Equally effective in this regard is the fact that should special interests later decide to renege on such promises, they would probably be blacklisted and unable to "buy" politicians in the future without paying rather large up-front bonuses.

4. If the job market is especially narrow, as it is for the skills of most politicians, such behavior might be devastating in terms of future employment prospects. Even if employers required the services of politicians, they might exact a measure of revenge for past extravagant holdups by paying prorated (lower) salaries. Far-fetched? As we noted, those legislators most successful at shifting their campaign debt onto special interests—that is, recent generations of legislators—also tend to receive lower postelective salaries even when taking lucrative jobs as lobbyists (chapter 6).

Rent Seeking

Another implication of our theory is that rent seeking occurs because it is a highly marketable skill that legislators can add to their repertoire and that undeniably whets the appetites of special interests. The legislator's rationale for manufacturing rents or facilitating their formation is quite simple: rent-seeking groups subsidize on-the-job training as well as provide a market for ex-legislators' services. Accordingly, legislators devote considerable time to rent seeking, not merely to do some group's bidding in Washington, but because they know skill proficiency requires practice; hence, we should not be the least surprised at the amount of rent seeking that occurs in Congress. In short, rent seeking is one of those skills that legislators also acquire and practice on the job.

Moreover, rent seeking and the results from it are observable to future employers, especially those working in particular policy areas. Unlike many expressions of competence, which are easily confounded by asymmetries in information, moral hazards, and the like, rent seeking is more readily discerned. Consequently, it is more difficult to fool special interests about rent-seeking talents. This implication provides an alternative explanation for the prevalence of rent seeking in politics and especially why rent seeking is so ubiquitous in the U.S. Congress: it is an acquired skill; it is derived from daily on-the-job training; its success or failure can be observed (for example, by special interests); and it is highly valued by groups.

Decentralization

More than a few scholars have attempted to explain decentralization within Congress (see, for example, Huntington 1965, esp. 18–22; Polsby 1968; Davidson and Oleszek 1977). Our theory offers another explanation: legislative decentralization results from the demand for on-the-job training opportunities with which to accumulate human capital.

Congressional leaders accommodate or accede to the demands of their members for such training experiences because investments in training are likely to occur along with productive legislative activities. And the demand for training should be greatest among the youngest members (with regard to tenure) since they have the most to gain from a decentralized environment in terms of the acquisition of additional human capital. In contrast, senior legislators, having already accumulated extensive skill sets through their years of on-the-job training, have less need of and demand for such training. Thus, the demand for decentralization comes largely from those who most value the added training. This echoes an often-repeated refrain in congressional reform efforts: junior members spearhead changes in decentralizing the institution's structure, and in the process assume larger policy-making roles within the institution.

Some observers have termed such trends "democratization" within political institutions. We prefer to think of it as an upshot of legislators' desire to accumulate marketable human capital. That is, changes designed to democratize or reform congressional procedures have the surprising latent effect of increasing the opportunities to amass human capital or reduce the costs of doing so. For example, two close observers of arguably the most important institutional reform effort to date, the 1965–75 Democratic Caucus reforms designed to reduce the power of seniority, concluded,

> In one sense, the seniority principle emerged even stronger with the 1965–1975 innovations. True, the caucus was not committed, at least in principle, to the idea that seniority should not be followed inflexibly in selecting committee chairmen. Yet, the thrust of the reforms was to spread the benefits of seniority beyond the standing committee chairmen to the more than 130 subcommittee chairmen. Ironically, there were in 1975 more seniority leaders than ever in the House of Representatives; and, within the committees, the seniority principle was extended to apply to subcommittee chairmanships. (Davidson and Oleszek 1977, 50)

Thus, the reforms resulted in extending the opportunities to acquire important human capital to a greater number of individuals in the majority party. More recent reforms introduced by House Republicans following the 104th Congress and Senate Republicans in 1997, which limited committee and subcommittee chairs to six-year terms, can be seen in this light as well. Like the Democrats decades earlier, the Republicans' approach to committee leadership not only decentralized influence and power more widely within the party but at the same time increased membership access to marketable skills and valuable human capital.

Specialization

Our take on specialization among legislators differs from conventional treatments as well (see, for example, Matthews 1960, esp. 95–97; Polsby 1968). Few scholars ever question why specialization materializes so easily within legislatures; usually, most are content to appeal to "efficiency" and perhaps even to give a nod to Adam Smith's conclusions about specialization's benefit in "pin" production. In fact, the impression is that those who choose to be generalists are bucking institutional demands and incentives. Norms, for example, heartedly encourage specialization within the institution (Matthews 1960; Asher 1973; Weingast 1979). Generalists could be institutional outliers, but they are not legislative oddities, too idiosyncratic to warrant mention, little less analysis. Legislators choosing this career route are not simply irrational—far from it. There are distinct incentives to becoming a generalist rather than a specialist, such as the greater options for postelective employment and institutional power.

Most legislators specialize in only a few policy areas, but the rationale for such specialization extends beyond the efficiency it induces. As we noted earlier in this chapter, campaign support provides incentives for specialization. Special interests pay reelection costs for those who are willing to specialize in policy areas important to these interests, and for most legislators, shelling out huge sums of campaign money just to gain the latitude to be a generalist does not make sense. Specialization, then, arises in part from the fact that narrow interests subsidize the training costs of legislators, which prompts the latter to specialize in policy areas valuable to these interests. The specialized assets of legislators thus become sunk costs, thereby encouraging future specialized investments. Specialization also has its own attraction for legislators: specialized training leads to the acquisition of expertise and skills necessary to change careers.

Organization of Political Structures

We see political structures, such as committees, as serving purposes beyond merely promoting efficiency (Dodd and Schott 1979, 71–72) or coordination as a result of multiple decision makers (Lindblom 1965, 151–57). Nor do we envision institutional organization as enhancing electoral security solely by generating particularistic and distributive benefits (Ferejohn 1974; Mayhew 1974; Fiorina 1989), locked into serving the collective needs of the party (Rohde 1991; Cox and McCubbins 1993), or wholly dedicated to furthering institutional interests (Krehbiel 1991). Rather, we view institutions as coupling training with production, creating in the process opportunities for economically minded officeholders to enhance human capital. This is not to question, even tangentially, whether legislative structures exist for all of the aforementioned reasons. Our point is that such structures may also survive (or experience changes) for reasons related to their capacity to augment legislators' human capital.

The Seniority System and Marketable Human Capital
The seniority system rewards longevity in Congress and committees. According to Polsby, a noted legislative scholar (Polsby, Gallagher, and Rundquist 1969), the growth of this enduring congressional feature resulted from an in-

surgent revolt against the dictatorial behavior of then-Speaker Joseph Cannon. Conversely, the rise of the seniority system could be attributed to legislator demand for more opportunities to build and amass human capital within Congress and especially within the committee system—a good place to acquire important legislative skills. The seniority system in essence protects legislators' investments in human capital acquired through committee membership. Indeed, a closer look at some of the external conditions existing prior to the emergence of the seniority system supports the notion that the desire to accrue human capital may have played a role in its development.

Preceding the establishment of the modern-day seniority system in the early 1900s, legislators accumulated little human capital because of the short tenure of most members as a result of high turnover. Service in Congress was neither highly valued nor marketable. The 1896 partisan electoral realignment changed this state of affairs by reducing the number of competitive congressional seats, thereby lengthening terms of legislative service. "For the House there could be no question of modern-type 'seniority' until membership turnover was reduced to a level such that there was substantial continuity of committee service. Such *de facto* stability tends to generate demands for *de jure* seniority" (Price 1975, 14). As congressional service increased, so did the buildup of human capital. With the growth of government and its role in the economy (for example, tariffs), the marketability of this political capital ultimately also rose.

To protect the accumulation of such capital, members sought assurances that their investments in committee service would be secure: the result was the seniority system. Party leaders acquiesced for the simple reason that increased opportunities for acquiring human capital through training would increase Congress's productivity. Increased legislative productivity, in turn, increases the political influence of party leaders because of their pivotal position in clearing the market for legislation and in obtaining favors for doing so. Coupling training with production provides strong institutional incentives for expanding opportunities for human capital acquisition through legislative service.[5] This, we believe, is a critical factor in explaining why party leaders seem so receptive to increased job training in politics.

Governmental Growth

The promotion of job training experiences has its own systemic consequences. For example, the demand for political training opportunities could

---

5. We emphatically agree with Weingast and Marshall (1988) that Congress is organized like a firm to control opportunism in upholding legislative bargains. But we add that Congress resembles a firm in another respect: it couples on-the-job training with production (of laws).

give rise to governmental growth for at least a couple of reasons. First, the demand for training, and the fact that Congress couples training in politics with lawmaking, results in increases in the production of laws along with increased training; as a consequence, the size of the federal government may also grow.

Second, legislators have incentives to create federal programs, since their knowledge and familiarity with such programs increases the value of their human capital and therefore their marketability to those special interests that depend on these programs, those hoping to muscle in on them (Tullock 1967), or those wishing to influence their future implementation (see, for example, Olson 1982, 70–71). Legislators exhibit little reticence about intruding into the affairs of agencies. They do so not merely to intimidate, cajole, or threaten these agencies into acceding to the demands of the legislature but to hone their bureaucratic fix-it skills. And legislators could not care less if their intrusions into agency affairs create red tape, since such bureaucracy only further enhances the value of tape-cutting services. In addition, the cozy triangles among congressional committees, bureaucracies, and special interests (Lowi 1969; Fiorina 1989) provide opportunities for legislators to learn how to manipulate bureaucrats into fashioning regulations favorable to constituency interests. Thus, legislator demand for opportunities to acquire human capital through training could result in growth in the complexity of laws, the number of federal programs, and the regulations applicable to both—all features of governmental growth.[6]

The Good, the Bad, and the Ugly Sides to Legislators as Lobbyists

Our analysis addresses a number of questions about the behavior of legislators after they leave office—in particular, how and why legislators become lobbyists. We now focus on this issue because of its enduring interest among political scientists and economists alike. We think of our inquiry as reaching good, bad, and rather ugly conclusions about lobbying by former members of Congress. We have found some positive features about lobbying by ex-legisla-

---

6. While inquiry into most of these implications lies far beyond the range of this study, we have found evidence supportive of the basic premise underlying them all: political institutions, like firms, couple on-the-job training opportunities with production. Specifically, we have found empirical evidence that increased investments in congressional training enhanced the over-time productivity of the institution: the growth in the number of committee assignments held by members of the House of Representatives (investments in training) resulted in subsequent increases in the production of laws (Parker 1992).

tors—for example, lobbying jobs are not payoffs for service while in Congress, and some marketlike controls on this activity may exist. We have also reached some conclusions that give us cause for concern, like the myriad of loopholes in congressional reforms designed to constrain legislator lobbying. And, finally, we have arrived at some disturbing conclusions about the ability of congressional training to enhance legislator skill sets while engendering economic losses for society.

The Good

One of the conclusions reached in our study is the conventional if not time-worn finding that many ex-legislators become lobbyists when they leave Congress. We believe, however, that the scary, off-the-cuff estimates reported in the mass media exaggerate the number. And we need to revise our beliefs about lobbying being the last resort for hapless politicians: given their levels of job satisfaction, lobbyists seem quite content with their job choices; they require no solace, for they do not feel doomed. That legislators seem to end up as lobbyists is noncontroversial and may add little to what we already know. Why legislators turn to the proverbial dark side of politics when they leave office remains, nonetheless, an issue of contention.

The prevailing argument is that the salary offered prospective lobbyist-legislators, or the execution of promises between interest groups and legislators, results in the latter becoming lobbyists. Lobbying certainly pays well, and anecdotal evidence indicates that special interests hire former legislators who have demonstrated support for group policies. Still, many legislators become lobbyists because a specialized market exists for their services, with the major employment responsibilities involving lobbying. And of course, specialized training points legislators in precisely that direction. This is not to deny that some legislators opportunistically trade policy influence for lucrative post-elective jobs in something akin to spot-market transactions; the spectacular media exposés of corruption in Congress and rent-seeking transactions between lobbyists and legislators provide adequate evidence of such unfortunate happenings. Systematic empirical research suggests, however, that the number of legislators engaging in such unsavory activity is relatively small (Heinz et al. 1993).

While the argument that lobbying jobs are payoffs for services performed on behalf of special interests is quite seductive, this line of reasoning encounters several inconsistencies with our findings. First, former legislators do not treat their postelective lobbying jobs as sinecures, rarely retiring from them. Second, lobbying legislators move to other jobs during the course of postelective employment, sometimes even abandoning lobbying. Third, training in congressional politics noticeably matters more than prospective salary in obtaining lobbying positions. Fourth, future lobbyist-legislators receive no higher levels of special interest subsidies for their campaigns than other legislators. Finally, ex-legislators obtain lobbying jobs with no greater alacrity than those pursuing other postelective employment opportunities. To accept then that lobbying jobs are payoffs to legislators requires a coherent explanation for these apparent anomalies. Legislators unquestionably perform favors for special interests—for example, influencing bureaucratic rules and rulings. However, their objective is often to demonstrate, at least in part, their proficiency at these enterprises, thereby enhancing their stock of human capital, building up their résumés, and increasing the marketability of their skill sets.

Another positive conclusion is that although legislative reforms seem incapable of effectively constraining ex-legislator lobbying, two naturally occurring mechanisms seem to have been ignored in this regard. First, for whatever reason, ex-legislators are not committed to lobbying in terms of postelective employment. Lobbying is not a short-term solution to postelective employment, but it is also not the only thing that ex-legislators do after leaving Congress. Indeed, during the course of their postelective careers even legislator-lobbyists find other vocations more enticing and change occupations. The second mechanism is something analogous to a life cycle of lobbying activities, where legislators move from lobbying to other vocations as their government contacts and expertise fade. Each of these noncoercive solutions has numerous empirical anomalies, however, so we are cautious about heralding them as marketlike answers for controlling ex-legislator lobbying.[7]

The Bad: The Frantic Rush to Reform

The recent scandals surrounding lobbyists, such as the now-infamous Jack Abramoff who pleaded guilty to fraud, tax evasion, and conspiracy to bribe public officials, and a number of members of Congress, including Representative Randy "Duke" Cunningham (R-Calif.), who was sentenced in 2006 to

---

7. A more obtrusive means of minimizing postelective lobbying would be to increase opportunities for legislators to acquire inclusive skill packages—for example, by expanding the membership of committees offering general training. A greater availability of opportunities to acquire broad skills would seem to be more effective in reducing former legislators' fondness for lobbying. At the same time, however, such a change might adversely affect legislator investments in specialization, which many scholars see as an important if not essential ingredient in congressional decision making (Mayhew 1974; Weingast 1979; Krehbiel 1991). Indeed, support for legislator specialization through congressional norms, procedures, and committee assignments may paradoxically promote conditions conducive to the training of lobbyists.

eight years and four months in federal prison for taking $2.4 million in bribes from two defense contractors, have resulted in a surge of interest in reforming lobbying practices.[8] Something akin to an ethical arms race has erupted on Capitol Hill, with Democrats and Republicans tossing ideas back and forth, each trying to trump the other's reform efforts. This rush to reform has resulted in hasty solutions that could result in significant external costs for Congress, and at the same time prove ineffective in constraining legislator lobbying.

One reform effort that has picked up steam in both political parties is the demand for restrictions on lobbying by former members of Congress. For instance, members of Congress from both sides of the aisle have called for public disclosure of negotiations regarding private sector jobs by incumbent officeholders. Such a reform was stimulated by the publicity associated with the 2003 dealings by W. J. "Billy" Tauzin (R-La.), chair of the House Energy and Commerce Committee, that led to his hiring as president of the Pharmaceutical Research and Manufacturers of America in January 2005. Congressional training and the resulting human capital equip legislators all too well for lobbying. Constraining this employment outlet in any way can be expected to jeopardize legislators' investments in job training and the accumulation of human capital.

First, we might expect less specialization on the part of legislators. Unable to lobby, legislators could be expected to expend less human capital in acquiring specialized skills, or perhaps even in investing in on-the-job training. Simply put, the returns from, and therefore the investments in, specialization would be diminished. In some scenarios, such circumstances could result in greater policy-making influence for bureaucrats rather than elected officeholders, an alarming situation about which economists working in government have had their suspicions for decades (see, for example, Niskanen 1975). In addition, the financial burden of campaigns would now fall more directly on the shoulders of legislators, so that only the extremely wealthy could afford the costs of political office. If lobbying groups cannot benefit from hiring former legislators, they are less inclined to supply campaign money, so legislators will finance more of their own campaigns.

These externalities notwithstanding, no assurances exist that such reforms would provide effective control of lobbying in Congress since rational legislators can be expected to find ways of circumventing controls on this attractive vocation. In the same sense that robbery increases efforts by victims

---

8. While much of the focus has concerned lobbying in Congress, special interests are exceedingly active at the state level, where decisions are made daily on issues such as drug policy, utility regulation, road construction, and the like. Indeed, in most state capitols, lobbyists outnumber lawmakers by an average of five to one (Broder 2006, A19).

to prevent future thefts and equally dedicated efforts by thieves to overcome these preventive measures (Tullock 1967), we might expect the high returns from lobbying to lead legislators to fashion rules allowing exemptions to restrictions on this profitable trade. Although former House members and congressional aides presently are barred from lobbying on Capitol Hill for one year after departing, no rules bar lobbyists turned legislators from lobbying on behalf of former clients, and none are currently contemplated. This has led to some sobering examples of how this loophole might be exploited. For example, in 2005, his first year in the Senate, John Thune (R-S.D.) wrote language into a transportation bill that expanded the amount of loan money available to small railroads, one of which just happened to be a former client, the Dakota, Minnesota, and Eastern Railroad (Stolberg 2006, A1).

Another loophole difficult to close is lobbying by spouses. "Marriages to lobbyists are increasingly common among Capitol staff members and even members of Congress" (Kirkpatrick 2006b, A17; see also Shenon 2006b). This may not sound at first like much of a loophole for lobbyists to ply their craft, but measured in dollars, the effect can be quite significant: "in 2005 alone, appropriations bills contained about $750 million for projects championed by lobbyists whose relatives were involved in writing the spending bills" (Kelley and Eisler 2006, 1). The issue of spousal lobbying has never received much notoriety until it became intertwined with the ill-fated 2006 deal to put several American ports under the control of a company owned by the United Arab Emirates.

The political controversy stirred by this policy decision created a great deal of consternation on Capitol Hill, leading Dubai Ports World, the company in question, immediately to hire former Senate majority leader Robert Dole (R-Kan.), whose wife, Elizabeth Dole (R-N.C.) is a U.S. senator, to lobby on the company's behalf. Bob Dole has sworn that he never lobbied members of Congress, including his wife, on this issue, but only lobbied the Bush administration. His testimonial may have some credibility since, almost simultaneous with Bob Dole's hiring by Dubai Ports World, Elizabeth Dole wrote a letter to the chair of the Senate Armed Services Committee, John W. Warner (R-Va.), voicing concerns about the transfer of the ports (Kornblut 2006b, A10).

The visibility of this issue may have made it difficult for Elizabeth Dole to side with her husband's clients even if she wanted to, or perhaps her letter to Warner is the public posturing in which most politicians engage when they sense public outrage and potential political fallout. In any event, this situation certainly places the issue of spouse as lobbyist in a very real context, complete with ethical and personal predicaments. Thus, politicians face a real dilemma: they invest in job training to acquire marketable human capital, but it is saleable within a narrow range of vocations—lobbying. Moreover, to salt the wound, public outrage and political sensibilities require restrictions on this trade, with politicians designing the rules to do just that. Even if politicians are not rational, they are also not angels; nor, for that matter, are they stupid.

Some loopholes are virtually impossible to close. For instance, it is exceedingly hard to police the benefits diverted to family and children by lobbyists as compensation for legislator assistance.[9] Consequently, in their dealings with interest groups, some legislators have given new meaning to the term *family man*. Representative William Jefferson (D-La.), for example, faces federal indictment for moneymaking schemes involving his wife, two brothers, five daughters, and two sons-in-law:

> Over dinner with business partner and FBI informant Lori Mody, [Jefferson] furtively scrawled the letter "c" on a sheet of paper, and next to it wrote some numbers indicating that he was demanding a much larger personal stake in an African business deal than previously agreed to. "The 'c' is like for 'children,'" the congressman told Mody, as an FBI tape recorder rolled. "I make a deal for my children. It wouldn't be for me." (Lengel and Weisman 2006, 1)

If, more often than not, legislators merchandise their human capital rather than trade favors for postelective employment, reforms designed to reduce gift giving to legislators, such as tickets to cultural or sporting events, should receive widespread support in Congress. Conversely, reforms aimed at constraining the already narrow market for their skills by reducing the attractiveness of hiring former legislators seem destined to failure. To expect legislators to do more in terms of lobbying reforms is to ask them to behave without self-interest, which is a lot—probably too much—to ask of any politician. This may be one of those problems of social cost where the costs of removing the nuisance exceed the benefits of doing so (see Coase 1990, 131–32).

Critics might scoff at this conclusion by pointing out that the Honest Leadership and Open Government Act (2007) was designed to reform such potentially corrupt congressional practices; it was, in many respects, the culmination of efforts to enhance ethical standards in Congress, curb certain lobbying customs, and bring greater transparency to the relationships be-

---

9. For example, in the case centering on the bribing of Representative William Jefferson (D-La.), in return for promoting technology products to federal agencies (for example, the Defense Department) as well as African companies and governments, a company owned by Jefferson's family was paid $367,500 over a four-year period. In addition, his children received jobs with the technology corporation (Shenon 2006a, A14).

tween lawmakers and lobbyists. This far-reaching legislation tightened ethics guidelines, restricted lawmakers' interactions with lobbyists, increased lobbying disclosures, and imposed new requirements on earmarking federal funds. Despite its sweeping proportions, the act does little to remedy many of the problems associated with legislator-lobbyists. Indeed, tightening restrictions on (and increasing the transparency of) lobbying Congress may actually magnify legislators' training in furtively navigating the political process and circumventing legislative barriers to the provision of special interest benefits, such as the parliamentary obstacles to earmarked appropriations created by the Senate.

While this reform legislation increased the time senators have to wait before lobbying Congress to two years, it left untouched the one-year limitation on legislative lobbying by House incumbents. But even for senators, this reform amounts to little since senate membership has nothing to do with the probability of becoming a lobbyist (table 5.11). Likewise, prohibiting former senators from access to the Senate floor seems rather meaningless given this statistically insignificant relationship between taking a lobbying position after leaving Congress and being a senator. Furthermore, House reform efforts regarding the floor privileges of former members were neither as exacting nor precipitous as those in the Senate; consequently, former House members retained their floor privileges. And while both the House and Senate attempted to address the thorny issue of spouse-as-lobbyist, their efforts were of marginal consequence. For example, the House provision only prohibits staff from having contact with their boss's lobbying spouse or family, and is silent on the matter of spouses lobbying other House members and their staffs. The Senate goes a step further on this issue by prohibiting spouses and immediate family from lobbying other members and their offices, but the prohibition does not apply to spouses who were serving as lobbyists at least one year prior to the recent election of their spouse, or a year prior to their marriage. This is not to contend that this act will have no effect whatsoever on congressional ethics. We wish merely to point out that these reforms only tangentially tackle many opportunistic legislative practices, and may, in fact, actually boost the value of legislative skills in lobbying, thereby further enhancing the demand for legislator-lobbyists.

The Ugly

For those alarmed by the influence of lobbyists, the most disconcerting aspect of our study is probably that as a result of acquired training and skills, legislators find lobbying an attractive vocation in which they have a comparative advantage, thereby further enhancing the appeal of this trade. Former legislators produce influence more efficiently than others who are less experienced in politics. The lower production costs they incur in influencing congressional outcomes ensure ex-legislators a comparative advantage in the market for lobbyists. This may explain why a large number (about 37 percent) of former members of Congress end up, one way or another, associated with lobbying during the course of their postelective employment.

Former legislators become lobbyists not solely to exploit their comparative advantage over other favor buyers; in addition, the skills associated with politics do not provide a wide assortment of occupational opportunities. That is, the human capital acquired in politics tends to be specialized to the practice of politics. The demand for the skills accumulated by legislators is sizable, since everyone needs assistance with government. Ironically, however, these skills lead to a limited set of vocations. And one of the few vocations that seem to necessitate training in politics is that of the repugnant lobbyist. Although not a particularly esteemed profession, lobbying pays well and makes good use of political skills and experiences, a transferability of human capital not found in many other occupations. For a large number of legislators, therefore, transferability of talent, a comparative advantage in political skills, the potential financial returns, and the limited market for their services lead to employment as lobbyists.

Equally troublesome is the fact that former legislators regularly find their way into lobbying at some point during the course of their postelective careers—again, a consequence of their on-the-job training in congressional politics which narrows the occupations that match their acquired skills. Legislators have considerable career mobility but little occupational variety. That is, a large number of legislators abandon their precongressional occupations, but occupational change often leads to lobbying.

It may be hard to believe, but there is an even uglier side to legislator lobbying: legislator-lobbyists, savvy about the political process, use their congressional know-how to aid groups seeking government transfers of some sort. The result is an economic loss to society. As in rent seeking, potentially productive individual effort is diverted to rent seeking and to acquiring lobbying-relevant skills because these investments yield the most profitable returns. Although legislators receive a good return on their investments, lobbying, with its emphasis on wealth transfers, contributes little to society. Paradoxically, then, lobbying-legislators augment their skills through congressional training, thereby enhancing the value of their human capital and their worth in the marketplace, but society suffers in the process because of their adeptness at extracting rents. So individual gain is society's loss.

A more positive spin can be put on this sour outcome: the losses to society conceivably would be considerably greater if less expert and knowledgeable individuals were involved in lobbying, thereby driving up the costs of rent seeking passed on to consumers. With savvy legislator-lobbyists, fewer resources are consumed in rent seeking; therefore, we are all better off as a result. The losses to society as a consequence of the efforts of well-trained legislator-lobbyists are less than would be incurred if careless, lazy lobbyists were involved in clumsily extracting rents for the special interests they serve. In short, lobbying costs society, but with well-trained legislator-lobbyists, the costs are arguably less. From our perspective, then, well-trained political practitioners reduce the costs of rent seeking because they minimize excessive expenditures of resources on the activity. This is small comfort, but in a rational, rent-seeking world, it may be the best for which we can hope.

In sum, when legislators enhance their human capital through congressional training, they engage in an entirely rational enterprise that unfortunately results in such externalities for society as legislators' adeptness as lobbyists. These externalities constitute one of the inescapable costs of political institutions behaving like firms and of coupling training with production: trained employees can always take their acquired skills elsewhere. Scholars have repeatedly bemoaned the difficult external costs democracies must tolerate; this one, however, appears to have escaped notice.

Summary and Discussion

Our inquiry began with the question of whether the study of human capital could contribute to our understanding of Congress. We believe that we have shed light on some important but heretofore ignored aspects of Congress. For instance, we have identified a rationale behind certain investment decisions in the acquisition of broad or specialized skill sets: preferences for salary maximization, employment versatility, or future career transitions. We have also demonstrated how congressional training can ensnare legislators into the lobbying trade, though a number of additional incentives also are present. Nonetheless, training in Congress provides skills that are easily transferred to lobbying, easing the transition from legislator to lobbyist, matters of conscience aside.

This human capital treatment of lobbying provides a theoretical alternative to the normal buying-and-selling-of-favors explanations for why ex-legislators turn to lobbying. While much of our analysis has been based on responses to questionnaire items as a result of the richness of these data, survey responses may be subject to personal distortion. Even so, we uncovered less obtrusive evidence relating to the investments of legislators (that is, years spent on committees) that revealed the same expected theoretical relationships: general training (prestige committee service) enhanced postelective salaries, while specialization (interest group committee service) promoted career mobility.

The application of human capital to legislative politics unmistakably has infused new life into the concepts of generalists and specialists, concepts historically designed merely to describe legislator trade-offs between scope and depth of knowledge. We have demonstrated the relevance of these concepts in accounting for postelective salaries and career mobility. Our analysis also points to a logic for some rather enduring features of Congress, such as decentralization and specialization and institutional changes in those directions, that emphasize the demand for training and the acquisition of human capital. Simply put, our findings and inferences reinforce the simple observation that began this study—that is, the study of the investments in and the accumulation of human capital can enrich our understanding of politicians' behavior by generating fresh insights into politics. In this vein, our study adds appreciably to an understanding of politicians by expanding the purview of analysis to include officeholders' future or prospective interests. We have demonstrated that legislator actions can be viewed, at least in part, as investment strategies designed to yield postelective returns.

In the conclusion to the introduction for the second edition of *Human Capital,* Becker (1993, 10) observed that "the prospects for the analysis of human capital look almost as bright to me today as they did during its salad days." We also feel that the study of human capital in politics will be a worthwhile investment, yielding the same level of profitable returns so evident in economics over the years. We might say that the study of human capital is only entering its salad days in political science; much remains to be done.

Appendix

Descriptive Statistics for Important Variables in the Analysis

Variable	N	Minimum	Maximum	Mean	S.D.
Precongressional salary	218	$17,437	$1,659,257	$275,107.49	$260,141.815
Year entered Congress	229	1947	1999	1974	10.894
Postcongressional salary	204	$34,016	$1,338,256	$247,062.19	$165,154.876
Year left Congress	229	1959	2003	1986	10.338
Broad skill set[a]	229	−3.65	2.61	.0000	1.000
Elite committee (years)	229	.00	38.00	3.8603	7.360
Interest committee (years)	229	.00	52.00	7.5983	7.758
Training capital[a]	229	−2.36	1.92	.0000	1.000
Nontraining capital[a]	229	−2.79	2.57	.0000	1.000
Life cycle investments[b]	229	−36.85	184.22	5.5116	19.195
General training[b]	229	−1.61	7.02	.4378	1.115
Reputational capital[a]	229	−3.68	8.47	.0000	1.000
Tenure (years)	229	1.00	40	11.62	8.255
Time in job 1 (months)	196	3.00	717	90.70	116.380
Time in job 2 (months)	121	3.00	408	74.49	76.276
Time in job 3 (months)	88	4.00	683	88.17	100.428
Senator[c]	229	0	1	.07	.248
Career change[c]	209	0	1	.43	.496
Lobbyist—first job[c]	229	0	1	.23	.420
Lobbyist—first 3 jobs[c]	229	0	1	.37	.484
Prior political office[c]	229	0	1	.22	.414
Party (1 = Democrat)[c]	229	0	1	.54	.533
PAC subsidies	114	0	.8374	.24	.225
Days until finding postcongressional job	162	0	4560	192.04	539.549

Source: Authors' survey of former members of Congress, 2004.

Note: S.D. = standard deviation.

[a]Variables are derived from factors scores.

[b]Variables represent interaction terms.

[c]Variables are dummy variables, coded 1 and 0.

Years of Tenure among Former Congressmen Born since 1929

Years of Congressional Service	Population (%)	Sample (%)
Less than 10 years	72.7	74.7
11–20 years	25.3	24.0
21+ years	2.0	1.3
Statistics		
Mean	8.14	8.11
S.D.	5.30	5.13
Number of cases	403	75

Source: Inter-University Consortium and McKibbin 1997; authors' survey of former members of Congress, 2004.
Note: S.D. = standard deviation.

Reason for Leaving Office among Former Congressmen Born since 1929

Reason for Departure	Population (%)	Sample (%)
Lost general election	37.3	41.1
Lost in the primary	8.7	5.5
Retired	22.1	19.2
Sought another office	25.5	31.5
Accepted federal office	3.1	
Resignation	3.4	2.7
Number of cases	357	73

Source: Inter-University Consortium and McKibbin 1997; authors' survey of former members of Congress, 2004.

References

Abraham, Katherine G., and Harry S. Farber. 1987. "Job Duration, Seniority, and Earnings." *American Economic Review* 77:278–97.

Acemoglu, Daron, and Jorn-Steffen Pischke. 1999. "The Structure of Wages and Investments in General Training." *Journal of Political Economy* 107:539–72.

"Advisory Opinion No.1: The Role of a Member of the House of Representatives in Communicating with Executive and Independent Agencies." 1970. *Congressional Record,* January 26, 116:1077.

Ainsworth, Scott. 1993. "Regulating Lobbyists and Interest Group Influence." *Journal of Politics* 55:41–56.

Akerlof, George. 1970. "The Market for 'Lemons': Quality Uncertainty and the Market Mechanism." *Quarterly Journal of Economics* 84:593–616.

Alchian, Armen A., and Harold Demsetz. 1972. "Production, Information Costs, and Economic Organization." *American Economic Review* 62:777–95.

Altonji, Joseph G., and Robert A. Shakotko. 1987. "Do Wages Rise with Job Seniority?" *Review of Economic Studies* 54:437–59.

Asher, Herbert B. 1973. "The Learning of Legislative Norms." *American Political Science Review* 67:499–513.

Asher, Herbert B. 1975. "The Changing Status of the Freshman Representative." In *Congress in Change: Evolution and Reform,* edited by Norman J. Ornstein, 216–39. New York: Praeger.

Austen-Smith, David. 1993. "Information and Influence: Lobbying for Agendas and Votes." *American Journal of Political Science* 37:799–833.

Austen-Smith, David, and John R. Wright. 1992. "Competitive Lobbying for a Legislator's Vote." *Social Choice and Welfare* 9:229–57.

Austen-Smith, David, and John R. Wright. 1994. "Counteractive Lobbying." *American Journal of Political Science* 38:25–44.

Bach, Stanley, and Steven S. Smith. 1988. *Managing Uncertainty in the House of Representatives.* Washington, D.C.: Brookings Institution.

Barber, James D. 1965. *The Lawmakers.* New Haven: Yale University Press.

Bauer, Raymond, Ithiel de Sola Pool, and Lewis Anthony Dexter. 1963. *American Business and Public Policy: The Politics of Foreign Trade.* New York: Atherton.

Baumgartner, Frank, and Bryan Jones. 1993. *Agendas and Instability in American Politics.* Chicago: University of Chicago Press.

Baumgartner, Frank, and Beth Leech. 1996. "The Multiple Ambiguities of 'Counteractive Lobbying.'" *American Journal of Political Science* 40:521–42.

Becker, Gary S. 1968. "Crime and Punishment: An Economic Approach." *Journal of Political Economy* 76:169–217.

Becker, Gary S. 1983. "A Theory of Competition among Pressure Groups for Political Influence." *Quarterly Journal of Economics* 98:371–400.

Becker, Gary S. 1993. *Human Capital: A Theoretical and Empirical Analysis, with Special Reference to Education.* 3d ed. Chicago: University of Chicago Press.

Ben-Porath, Yoram. 1967. "The Production of Human Capital and the Life Cycle of Earnings." *Journal of Political Economy* 75:352–65.

Bernstein, Jeffrey L., and Jennifer Wolak. 2002. "A Bicameral Perspective on Legislative Retirement: The Case of the Senate." *Political Research Quarterly* 55:375–90.

Birnbaum, Jeffrey H. 2007. "For Gephardt, a New Career in Lobbying—and a Lot More." *Washington Post*, July 31, 1–3.

Blaug, Mark. 1976. "The Empirical Status of Human Capital Theory: A Slightly Jaundiced Survey." *Journal of Economic Literature* 14:827–55.

Blinder, Alan S., and Yoram Weiss. 1976. "Human Capital and Labor Supply: A Synthesis." *Journal of Political Economy* 84:449–72.

Bloch, Farrell E., and Sharon P. Smith. 1977. "Human Capital and Labor Market Employment." *Journal of Human Resources* 12:550–60.

Borders, Rebecca, and C. C. Dockery. 1995. *Beyond the Hill: A Directory of Congress from 1984 to 1993.* Lanham, Md.: University Press of America.

Broder, John M. 2006. "Amid Scandals, States Overhaul Lobbying Laws." *New York Times*, January 24, A1, A19.

Bronars, Stephen G., and John R. Lott. 1997. "Do Campaign Donations Alter How a Politician Votes? Or Do Donors Support Candidates Who Value the Same Things That They Do?" *Journal of Law and Economics* 40:317–50.

Buchanan, James M., Robert D. Tollison, and Gordon Tullock, eds. 1980. *Toward a Theory of the Rent-Seeking Society.* College Station: Texas A&M University Press.

Cain, Bruce, John Ferejohn, and Morris P. Fiorina. 1987. *The Personal Vote: Constituency Service and Electoral Independence.* Cambridge: Harvard University Press.

Chappell, Henry. 1982. "Campaign Contributions and Congressional Voting: A Simultaneous Probit-Tobit Model." *Review of Economics and Statistics* 64:77–83.

Coase, Ronald H. 1990. *The Firm, the Market, and the Law.* Chicago: University of Chicago Press.

Coase, Ronald H. 2000. "The Acquisition of Fisher Body by General Motors." *Journal of Law and Economics* 43:15–31.

Coates, Dennis, and Michael C. Munger. 1995. "Win, Lose, or Withdraw: A Categorical Analysis of Career Patterns in the House of Representatives, 1948–1978." *Public Choice* 83:91–115.

Cohen, Mark A. 1991. "Explaining Judicial Behavior; or, What's 'Unconstitutional' about the Sentencing Commission?" *Journal of Law, Economics, and Organization* 7:183–99.

Cook, Thomas D., and Donald T. Campbell. 1979. *Quasi-Experimentation: Design and Analysis Issues for Field Settings.* Chicago: Rand McNally.

Cox, Gary W., and Mathew D. McCubbins. 1993. *Legislative Leviathan: Party Government in the House.* Berkeley: University of California Press.

Crain, W. Mark, Donald R. Leavens, and Robert D. Tollison. 1986. "Final Voting in Legislatures." *American Economic Review* 76:833–41.

Dahl, Robert A. 1956. *A Preface to Democratic Theory.* Chicago: University of Chicago Press.

Davidson, Roger H., and Walter J. Oleszek. 1977. *Congress against Itself.* Bloomington: Indiana University Press.

Davidson, Roger H., and Walter J. Oleszek. 2002. *Congress and Its Members.* 8th ed. Washington, D.C.: CQ Press.

Deering, Christopher J., and Steven S. Smith. 1997. *Committees in Congress.* 3d ed. Washington, D.C.: CQ Press.

Denzau, Arthur T., and Michael C. Munger. 1986. "Legislators and Interest Groups: How Unorganized Interests Get Represented." *American Political Science Review* 80:89–106.

Diermeier, Daniel, Michael Keane, and Anthony Merlo. 2004. "A Political Economy Model of Congressional Careers: Supplementary Material." http://pier.econ.upenn.edu/Archive/04-038.pdf.

Diermeier, Daniel, Michael Keane, and Antonio Merlo. 2005. "A Political Economy Model of Congressional Careers." *American Economic Review* 96:347–73.

Dodd, Lawrence C., and Richard L. Schott. 1979. *Congress and the Administrative State.* New York: Wiley.

Dougan, William R., and Michael C. Munger. 1989. "The Rationality of Ideology." *Journal of Law and Economics* 32:119–42.

Downs, Anthony. 1957. *An Economic Theory of Democracy.* New York: Harper and Row.

Downs, Anthony. 1967. *Inside Bureaucracy.* Boston: Little, Brown.

Eckert, Ross. 1981. "The Life Cycle of Regulatory Commissioners." *Journal of Law and Economics* 24:113–20.

Erikson, Robert S. 1976. "Is There Such a Thing as a Safe Seat?" *Polity* 8:623–32.

Evans, Diana M. 1986. "PAC Contributions and Roll-Call Voting: Conditional Power." In *Interest Group Politics,* 2d ed., edited by Allan J. Cigler and Burdett A. Loomis, 114–29. Washington, D.C.: CQ Press.

Faith, Roger L., Donald R. Leavens, and Robert D. Tollison. 1982. "Antitrust Pork Barrel." *Journal of Law and Economics* 25:329–42.

Federal Elections Commission. 1980–2004. "Detailed Files about Candidates, Parties, and Other Committees: Files by Election Cycle." http://www.fec.gov/finance/disclosure/ftpdet.shtml.

Fenno, Richard F., Jr. 1973. *Congressmen in Committees.* Boston: Little, Brown.

Fenno, Richard F., Jr. 1978. *Home Style: House Members in Their Districts.* Boston: Little, Brown.

Ferejohn, John A. 1974. *Pork Barrel Politics: Rivers and Harbors Legislation, 1947–1968.* Stanford University Press.

Fiorina, Morris P. 1989. *Congress: Keystone of the Washington Establishment.* 2d ed. New Haven: Yale University Press.

Frisch, Scott A., and Sean Q. Kelly. 2006. *Committee Assignment Politics in the U.S. House of Representatives.* Norman: University of Oklahoma Press.

Gibson, Betty B. 1980. "Estimating Demand Elasticities for Public Goods from Survey Data." *American Economic Review* 70:1069–76.

Goodwin, George, Jr. 1970. *The Little Legislatures: Committees of Congress.* Amherst: University of Massachusetts Press.

Graham, John W. 1981. "An Explanation for the Correlation of Stocks of Nonhuman Capital with Investments in Human Capital." *American Economic Review* 71:248–55.

Grenzke, Janet M. 1989. "Shopping in the Congressional Supermarket: The Currency Is Complex." *American Journal of Political Science* 33:1–24.

Grier, Kevin, and Michael C. Munger. 1991. "Committee Assignments, Constituent Preferences, and Campaign Contributions." *Economic Inquiry* 29:29–43.

Grier, Kevin, Michael C. Munger, and Brian Roberts. 1991. "The Industrial Organization of Corporate Political Participation." *Southern Economic Journal* 57:727–38.

Groseclose, Timothy, and Keith Krehbiel. 1994. "Golden Parachutes, Rubber Checks, and Strategic Retirements from the 102nd House." *American Journal of Political Science* 38:75–99.

Grossman, Gene M., and Carl Shapiro. 1982. "A Theory of Factor Mobility." *Journal of Political Economy* 90:1054–69.

Hall, Richard, and Alan V. Deardorff. 2006. "Lobbying as Legislative Subsidy." *American Political Science Review* 100:69–84.

Hall, Richard, and Robert Van Houweling. 1995. "Avarice and Ambition: Representatives' Decisions to Run or Retire from the U.S. House." *American Political Science Review* 89:121–36.

Hall, Richard, and Frank Wayman. 1990. "Buying Time: Moneyed Interests and the Mobilization of Bias in Congressional Committees." *American Political Science Review* 84:797–820.

Harris, Milton, and Yoram Weiss. 1984. "Job Matching with Finite Horizon and Risk Aversion." *Journal of Political Economy* 92:758–79.

Heinz, John P., Edward Laumann, Robert Nelson, and Robert H. Salisbury. 1993. *The Hollow Core: Private Interests in National Policy Making.* Cambridge: Harvard University Press.

Hennart, Jean-François, and Erin Anderson. 1993. "Countertrade and the Minimization of Transaction Costs: An Empirical Examination." *Journal of Law, Economics, and Organization* 9:290–313.

Hibbing, John. 1982a. "Voluntary Retirement from the House: The Costs of Congressional Service." *Legislative Studies Quarterly* 7:57–74.

Hibbing, John. 1982b. "Voluntary Retirement from the U.S. House of Representatives: Who Quits?" *American Journal of Political Science* 26:467–84.

Hibbing, John. 1991. "Contours of the Modern Congressional Career." *American Political Science Review* 85:405–28.

Huntington, Samuel P. 1965. "Congressional Responses to the Twentieth Century." In *The Congress and America's Future*, edited by David B. Truman, 5–31. Englewood Cliffs, N.J.: Prentice-Hall.

Inter-University Consortium for Political and Social Research and Carroll McKibbin. 1997. *Roster of United States Congressional Officeholders and Biographical Characteristics of Members of the United States Congress, 1789–1996.* ICPSR Study 7803. Ann Arbor: Inter-University Consortium for Political and Social Research.

Jewell, Malcolm E., and Chu Chi-Hung. 1974. "Membership Movement and Committee Attractiveness in the U.S. House of Representatives, 1963–1971." *American Journal of Political Science* 18:433–41.

Kalt, Joseph P., and Mark A. Zupan. 1984. "Capture and Ideology in the Economic Theory of Politics." *American Economic Review* 74:279–300.

Kau, James B., and Paul H. Rubin. 1982. *Congressmen, Constituents, and Contributors: Determinants of Roll-Call Voting in the House of Representatives.* Boston: Nijhoff.

Kelley, Matt, and Peter Eisler. 2006. "Relatives Have 'Inside Track' in Lobbying for Tax Dollars." *USA Today,* October 17, 1–7.

Killingsworth, Mark R. 1982. "'Learning by Doing' and 'Investments in Training': A Synthesis of Two 'Rival' Models of the Life Cycle." *Review of Economic Studies* 49:263–71.

Kingdon, John W. 1981. *Congressmen's Voting Decisions.* 2d ed. New York: Harper and Row.

Kingdon, John W. 1984. *Agendas, Alternatives, and Public Policies.* Boston: Little, Brown.

Kirkpatrick, David D. 2006a. "Lucrative Life in Revolving Door for Capitol Hill Staff Member and Lobbyist." *New York Times,* June 9, A10.

Kirkpatrick, David D. 2006b. "When Lobbyists Say 'I Do,' Should They Add 'I Won't,?'" *New York Times,* February 19, A17.

Klein, Benjamin. 2000. "Fisher–General Motors and the Nature of the Firm." *Journal of Law and Economics* 43:105–41.

Klein, Benjamin, and Keith Laffler. 1981. "The Role of Market Forces in Assuring Contractual Performance." *Journal of Political Economy* 89:615–41.

Kollman, Ken. 1997. "Inviting Friends to Lobby: Interest Groups, Ideological Bias, and Congressional Committees." *American Journal of Political Science* 41:519–44.

Kornblut, Anne E. 2006a. "Once Just an Aide, Now a King of K Street." *New York Times,* February 5, A11, A14.

Kornblut, Anne E. 2006b. "Scramble to Back Port Deal: Making of Political Disaster." *New York Times,* February 25, A10.

Krehbiel, Keith. 1991. *Information and Legislative Organization.* Ann Arbor: University of Michigan Press.

Krueger, Anne O. 1974. "The Political Economy of the Rent-Seeking Society." *American Economic Review* 64:291–303.

Kuhn, Thomas S. 1996. *The Structure of Scientific Revolutions.* 3d ed. Chicago: University of Chicago Press.

Lengel, Allan, and Jonathan Weisman. 2006. "For Deals, Jefferson Built Web of Firms." *Washington Post,* June 5, 1–3.

Lindblom, Charles E. 1965. *The Intelligence of Democracy: Decision Making through Mutual Adjustment.* New York: Free Press.

Lindsay, C. M. 1971. "Measuring Human Capital Returns." *Journal of Political Economy* 79:1195–1215.

Lott, John R. 1987. "Political Cheating." *Public Choice* 52:169–87.

Lott, John R. 1990. "Attendance Rates, Political Shirking, and the Effects of Post-Elective Office Employment." *Economic Inquiry* 28:133–50.

Lott, John R., and Robert W. Reed. 1989. "Shirking and Sorting in a Political Market with Finite-Lived Politicians." *Public Choice* 61:75–96.

Lowi, Theodore J. 1969. *The End of Liberalism: Ideology, Policy, and the Crisis of Public Authority.* New York: Norton.

Macdonald, Glenn M. 1980. "Person-Specific Information in the Labor Market." *Journal of Political Economy* 88:578–97.

Macdonald, Glenn M. 1982. "A Market Equilibrium Theory of Job Assignment and Sequential Accumulation of Information." *American Economic Review* 72:1038–55.

Mann, Thomas E. 1978. *Unsafe at Any Margin: Interpreting Congressional Elections.* Washington, D.C.: American Enterprise Institute.

Marshall, Robert C., and Gary A. Zarkin. 1987. "The Effect of Job Tenure on Wage Offers." *Journal of Labor Economics* 5:301–24.

Matthews, Donald R. 1960. *U.S. Senators and Their World.* New York: Random House.

Matthews, Donald R., and James A. Stimson. 1975. *Yeas and Nays: Normal Decision-Making in the U.S. House of Representatives.* New York: Wiley.

Mayers, David, and Clifford Smith Jr. 1988. "Ownership across Lines of Property-Casualty Insurance." *Journal of Law and Economics* 31:351–78.

Mayhew, David R. 1974. *Congress: The Electoral Connection.* New Haven: Yale University Press.

McChesney, Fred S. 1987. "Rent Extraction and Rent Creation in the Economic Theory of Regulation." *Journal of Legal Studies* 16:101–18.

McCormick, Robert E., and Robert D. Tollison. 1981. *Politicians, Legislation, and the Economy.* Boston: Nijhoff.

Milbrath, Lester. 1963. *The Washington Lobbyists.* Chicago: Rand McNally.

Mincer, Jacob. 1962. "On-the-Job Training: Costs, Returns, and Some Implications." *Journal of Political Economy* 70:50–79.

Mincer, Jacob. 1997. "The Production of Human Capital and the Life Cycle of Earnings: Variations on a Theme." *Journal of Labor Economics* 15:S26–S47.

Moore, Michael K., and John R. Hibbing. 1998. "Situational Dissatisfaction in Congress: Explaining Voluntary Departures." *Journal of Politics* 60:1088–1107.

Nelson, Philip. 1970. "Information and Consumer Behavior." *Journal of Political Economy* 78:311–29.

Niskanen, William. 1975. "Bureaucrats and Politicians." *Journal of Law and Economics* 18:617–44.

Oleszek, Walter J. 2001. *Congressional Procedures and the Policy Process.* 5th ed. Washington, D.C.: CQ Press.

Olson, Mancur, Jr. 1968. *The Logic of Collective Action: Public Goods and the Theory of Groups.* New York: Schocken.

Olson, Mancur, Jr. 1982. *The Rise and Decline of Nations: Economic Growth, Stagflation, and Social Rigidities.* New Haven: Yale University Press.

Ornstein, Norman J., Thomas E. Mann, and Michael J. Malbin. 1996. *Vital Statistics on Congress, 1995–1996.* Washington, D.C.: Congressional Quarterly.

Palank, Jacqueline. 2007. "Top Democrat Plans Advanced List of Earmarks." *New York Times,* June 12, A21.

Parker, Glenn R. 1986. *Homeward Bound: Explaining Changes in Congressional Behavior.* Pittsburgh: University of Pittsburgh Press.

Parker, Glenn R. 1992. *Institutional Change, Discretion, and the Making of Modern Congress: An Economic Interpretation.* Ann Arbor: University of Michigan Press.

Parker, Glenn R. 1996. *Congress and the Rent-Seeking Society.* Ann Arbor: University of Michigan Press.

Parker, Glenn R. 2004. *Self-Policing in Politics: The Political Economy of Reputational Controls on Politicians.* Princeton: Princeton University Press.

Parker, Glenn R., and Roger H. Davidson. 1979. "Why Do Americans Love Our Congressmen So Much More Than Their Congress?" *Legislative Studies Quarterly* 4:53–61.

Peltzman, Sam. 1984. "Constituent Interest and Congressional Voting." *Journal of Law and Economics* 27:181–210.

Polsby, Nelson W. 1968. "The Institutionalization of the House of Representatives." *American Political Science Review* 62:144–68.

Polsby, Nelson W., Miriam Gallagher, and Barry S. Rundquist. 1969. "The Growth of the Seniority System in the U.S. House of Representatives." *American Political Science Review* 63:787–807.

Prewitt, Kenneth. 1970. *The Recruitment of Political Leaders: A Study of Citizen-Politicians.* New York: Bobbs-Merrill.

Price, H. Douglas. 1975. "Congress and the Evolution of Legislative 'Professionalism.'" In *Congress in Change: Evolution and Reform,* edited by Norman J. Ornstein, 2–23. New York: Praeger.

Riley, John G. 1976. "Information, Screening and Human Capital." *American Economic Review* 66:254–60.

Rohde, David W. 1991. *Parties and Leaders in the Post-Reform House.* Chicago: University of Chicago Press.

Rose-Ackerman, Susan. 1978. *Corruption: A Study in Political Economy.* New York: Academic Press.

Rose-Ackerman, Susan. 1999. *Corruption and Government: Causes, Consequences, and Reform.* New York: Cambridge University Press.

Rudoren, Jodi, and Aron Pilhofer. 2006. "Hiring Lobbyists for Federal Aid, Towns Learn That Money Talks." *New York Times,* July 2, 13.

Rummel, R. J. 1970. *Applied Factor Analysis.* Evanston, Ill.: Northwestern University Press.

Salisbury, Robert H., and Kenneth A. Shepsle. 1981. "U.S. Congressmen as Enterprise." *Legislative Studies Quarterly* 6:559–76.

Schelling, Thomas C. 1960. *The Strategy of Conflict.* New York: Oxford University Press.

Schlesinger, Joseph A. 1966. *Ambition and Politics: Political Careers in the United States.* Chicago: Rand McNally.

Schlozman, Kay L., and John T. Tierney. 1986. *Organized Interests and American Democracy.* New York: Harper and Row.

Schultz, Theodore W. 1961. "Investments in Human Capital." *American Economic Review* 51:1–17.

Shaw, Katherine L. 1984. "A Formulation of the Earnings Function Using the Concept of Occupational Investment." *Journal of Human Resources* 19:319–40.

Shenon, Philip. 2006a. "Businessman Pleads Guilty to Bribing a Representative." *New York Times,* May 4, A14.

Shenon, Philip. 2006b. "Lobbying Cases Shine Spotlight on Family Ties." *New York Times,* April 9, 1, 20.

Shepsle, Kenneth A. 1978. *The Giant Jigsaw Puzzle: Democratic Committee Assignments in the Modern House.* Chicago: University of Chicago Press.

Shepsle, Kenneth A., and Barry R. Weingast. 1987. "The Institutional Foundations of Committee Power." *American Political Science Review* 81:85–104.

Sicherman, Nachum, and Oded Galor. 1990. "A Theory of Career Mobility." *Journal of Political Economy* 98:169–92.

Silberman, Jonathan, and Gary C. Durden. 1976. "Determining Legislative Preferences on the Minimum Wage: An Economic Approach." *Journal of Political Economy* 84:317–29.

Sinclair, Barbara. 1997. *Unorthodox Lawmaking: New Legislative Processes in the U.S. Congress.* Washington, D.C.: CQ Press.

Snyder, James. 1992. "Long-Term Investing in Politicians; or, Give Early, Give Often." *Journal of Law and Economics* 35:15–43.

Stigler, George J. 1971. "The Theory of Economic Regulation." *Bell Journal of Economics and Management Science* 2:3–21.

Stolberg, Sheryl Gay. 2006. "Ethics Issue at Capitol: Career Paths in Reverse." *New York Times,* February 26, A1, A15.

Stratmann, Thomas. 1998. "The Market for Congressional Votes: Is Timing of Contributions Everything?" *Journal of Law and Economics* 41:85–113.

Theriault, Sean M. 1998. "Moving up or Moving Out: Career Ceilings and Congressional Retirement." *Legislative Studies Quarterly* 23:419–33.

Tollison, Robert D. 1982. "Rent-Seeking: A Survey." *Kyklos* 35:575–602.

Topel, Robert. 1991. "Specific Capital, Mobility, and Wages: Wages Rise with Job Seniority." *Journal of Political Economy* 99:145–76.

Truman, David B. 1965. *The Congress and America's Future.* Englewood Cliffs, N.J.: Prentice-Hall.

Tullock, Gordon. 1967. "The Welfare Costs of Tariffs, Monopolies, and Theft." *Western Economic Journal* 5:224–32.

Tullock, Gordon. 1975. "The Transitional Gains Trap." *Bell Journal of Economics* 6:671–78.

Utt, Ronald D. 2006. "A Primer on Lobbyists, Earmarks, and Congressional Reform." *The Heritage Foundation, Backgrounder #1924,* April 27, 1–29. Available at http://www.heritage.org/research/budget/bg1924.cfm.

Weingast, Barry R. 1979. "A Rational Choice Perspective on Congressional Norms." *American Journal of Political Science* 23:245–62.

Weingast, Barry R., and William J. Marshall. 1988. "The Industrial Organization of Congress; or, Why Legislatures, Like Firms, Are Not Organized as Markets." *Journal of Political Economy* 96:132–63.

Weisman, Jonathan. 2006. "Lawmakers' Profits Are Scrutinized." *Washington Post,* June 22.

Welch, William P. 1980. "The Allocation of Political Monies: Economic Interest Groups." *Public Choice* 35:97–120.

Welch, William P. 1982. "Campaign Contributions and Legislative Voting: Milk Money and Dairy Price Supports." *Western Political Quarterly* 35:478–95.

Williams, Nicholas. 1991. "Reexamining the Wage, Tenure, and Experience Relationship." *Review of Economics and Statistics* 73:512–17.

Wilson, Rick K. 1986. "An Empirical Test of Preferences for the Political Pork Barrel: District Level Appropriations for River and Harbor Legislation, 1889–1913." *American Journal of Political Science* 30:729–54.

Wright, John R. 1985. "PACs, Contributions, and Roll Calls: An Organizational Perspective." *American Political Science Review* 79:400–414.

Ziobrowski, Alan. 2002. "Real Estate Holdings of United States Senators." *Appraisal Journal* 70:76–85.

Ziobrowski, Alan, and Alan McAlum. 2002. "The Real Estate Portfolio of the United States House of Representatives." *Journal of Real Estate Research* 24:97–116.

Ziobrowski, Alan, Ping Cheng, James W. Boyd, and Brigitte J. Ziobrowski. 2004. "Abnormal Returns from the Common Stock Investments of the U.S. Senate." *Journal of Financial and Quantitative Analysis* 39:661–76.

Name Index

Subject Index